THE F WORD

A Modern Guide to Finance, Freedom and Female Power

ISABEL KNIGHT

The F Word
A Modern Guide to Finance, Freedom and Female Power

ISBN: 978-1-9193954-1-8 (paperback)
ISBN: 978-1-9193954-2-5 (hardcover)
ISBN: 978-1-9193954-0-1 (kindle)

For enquiries regarding permissions, please contact: Isabel Knight

TABLE OF CONTENTS

BE BRAVE, NOT PERFECT

A Preface on Money, Meaning and Messiness

Nobody expected me to write a book about finance, least of all my father.

An English teacher with a pipe perpetually in hand, he would have raised an eyebrow at this news. "Really, Isabel? You've written a book?" English was my worst subject at school.

Business and finance simply weren't part of the conversation in our house. Money only came up as a reminder: "It doesn't grow on trees, Isabel!" Both my parents were teachers, devoted to their work but exhausted by it, and very clear about one thing: "Don't become a teacher; the pay is awful."

The irony, of course, is that here I am decades later, teaching. Not Shakespeare like my father or PE like my mum, but money; how to live with it, grow it, and free yourself through it. Life has a way of circling back on itself.

Driven, impatient, fast-moving, I was that competitive, sport mad girl swimming lengths after school, sprinting at the athletics club, dancing whenever I could. To this day, I talk at a million miles an hour. My friends would say I've never quite lost that sprinter's pace.

Money fascinated me early. Even now, I can picture that small blue bank passbook, the careful recording of each deposit, the quiet thrill of watching the numbers grow. The independence mattered more than the amount, whether from cleaning my parents' house or stacking shelves at Waitrose, having my own pay packet meant freedom.

What I didn't realise then was that those early savings habits were my first lessons in building wealth; the understanding that freedom comes from learning how money can work for you, not against you.

At sixteen, I wandered into my sixth-form careers department, well, "department" might be generous; it was really just a dusty shelf of leaflets pretending to be a resource. One leaflet caught my eye: men in colourful jackets shouting across a crowded floor of screens at the London Stock Exchange, the jobbers. Something about that picture of chaos fascinated me, planting a seed that would later draw me towards the City.

Back then, though, I didn't see a career in finance. My first love was science. I thought I'd end up in the drug industry, wearing a lab coat. I started in medicinal chemistry at university, but eventually realised it wasn't my path. So I changed my degree to economics. That willingness to about-turn has been one of the most important life skills I've learned: the ability to say, "This isn't working; what's next?"

Economics it was, having never studied it before and blagging my way onto the course. The summer after my first year, I went to live with a boyfriend's family in Los Angeles. Needing a job, I walked into UCLA's careers office with my UCL student card, thumb strategically covering the last letters. One cold call later, I'd landed my first finance role. The woman on the other end of the line said, "You've got a beautiful English accent; you're hired."

I didn't have a clue what stocks and bonds were, but I had a phone, a list of names, and the determination to make something happen. That summer taught me something I've never forgotten: opportunity doesn't always arrive dressed as certainty. Sometimes it begins with saying yes before you feel ready. Confidence compounds faster than capital. And I wanted to understand how the world and finance really worked.

Setbacks came too. Bain & Co. rejected me in my final year at university, despite getting down to the last three candidates. The letter said I was an excellent candidate but lacked business experience. Business experience? I'd been studying and living—I had no idea what that even meant. I nearly pursued a PhD studying global warming under Professor David Pearce, the field's grandfather. Eerily relevant today. But I chose differently.

Perhaps the boldest leap came after attending the Landmark Forum, when I began to believe that anything was possible. My boyfriend and I created a project to end the war in Ethiopia. We gathered 65,000 letters from children around the world, secured a donated private plane, and found ourselves in the Kremlin, handing those letters to Mrs Gorbachev. Twenty-two years old, standing in Moscow, asking the First Lady of the Soviet Union to help us stop a war. Absurd. Unlikely. And yet we did it.

That project wasn't about money, yet it taught me one of finance's greatest lessons: capital, like courage, is only powerful when it's in motion. Action creates flow. Extraordinary things happen when you're willing to act boldly.

When I returned from that adventure, I was broke in pounds but rich in perspective, something that later would prove more valuable than any bonus. My PhD was abandoned, my plan unclear, but I had an eclectic CV, a restless curiosity, and a quiet belief that anything was possible. I walked into the City, not even knowing what a fund manager was, and somehow landed the job. That began a career spanning fund management, property investment, business coaching, and private equity. As you'll read in this book, my path has zig-zagged more than most.

The reinventions continued. From a four-bedroom house in Putney to a tiny studio in Chamonix, knowing no one and starting from scratch. Property developer in France, despite barely speaking French and not knowing a hammer from a hacksaw. Surviving the financial crisis. Training as a coach when I felt washed up and useless. Packing up two small children and moving to a part of the UK where I knew only my mum, determined to rebuild a life. Saying yes to industries I knew nothing about, waste, recycling, technology, trusting I could figure it out.

I need to pause here, because motherhood changed everything. I didn't think I wanted children. Didn't think I'd be suited to it. (My best friend Mary definitely didn't think I was suited to it - champagne drinking, yes; nappy changing, no!) Right up until the birth of my son, I would have cancelled the contract if I could. And yet becoming a mother was the greatest, most unexpected gift of my life. My children became my why, the reason to keep going when life was challenging, the reason to be brave when it would have been easier to shrink back. Many of you reading this are mothers too, juggling kids, careers, businesses, or navigating divorce. I see you.

Motherhood shifted everything. What mattered wasn't numbers in a bank account, but the quieter, enduring gifts: love, purpose, and resilience.

Through all of these shifts, one truth emerged: bravery, not perfection, is what moves us forward. I don't stand here as a guru with the perfect playbook. My life has been anything but neat. It has been messy, diverse, a smorgasbord of trials, experiments, mistakes, and reinventions. If anything, I've created a diversified portfolio of life experiences, which is probably the best financial metaphor I could offer.

Yet, through it all, the themes repeat: initiative, resilience, the willingness to be uncomfortable, the love of business, the drive to keep contributing. That's why I wrote this book. Not to brag about success, not to stand on a pedestal, but to sit beside you, share what I've learned, and help you see that you can do it too.

There is no playbook for life. You make it up as you go. You laugh, you swear, you look up at the sky and say, "Really? Another lesson?" and then you move on. You keep moving.

Every chapter of my life has taught me something about what wealth really means and what it makes possible.

This book is about bringing the two together.

Let me offer you an invitation first.

INTRODUCTION

An Invitation to Reclaim the F Word

I've always loved money; there, I've said it.

Not for the status or the stuff, but for what it represents: choice, freedom, and flow.

The F word, *Finance,* has been my fascination, my nemesis, my teacher, and ultimately, my path to freedom. And I'm no longer apologising for it.

I remember walking into the lecture theatre at London Business School for my Master's in Finance; a sea of suits and testosterone. Only five women among sixty-five students. The professor, a former City executive with a booming voice, announced, "Finance isn't for the faint-hearted," his eyes lingering on us.

Little did he know I'd been preparing for that moment since childhood.

My fascination with money began long before that lecture theatre. What mattered now was how this world would treat me, and whether I could succeed in it without losing myself.

The financial world would try to reshape me, moulding me into something sharper, harder, less intuitive. The message was clear: leave your feminine energy at the door if you want to succeed.

Decades of experience have taught me this: we don't need more women in finance. We need more finance in women.

The Quietest Taboo

We can discuss our sex lives over brunch, debate politics at dinner parties, and share our relationship struggles with strangers, yet the moment someone asks, "So, how much do you make?", we freeze.

Money has become the conversation we never have; the quietest taboo of all.

I've watched brilliant, capable women who run households, teams, and businesses with grace suddenly shrink when money comes up. Women who wouldn't hesitate to negotiate a house price often hesitate to negotiate their own salaries. Women who plan holidays months in advance admit they've barely glanced at their pensions.

This isn't about blame or shame. Heaven knows I've made enough financial blunders to fill a few volumes. It's about understanding why we've been culturally conditioned to avoid finance, and how we can rewrite that story together.

True wealth is built on two F-words that belong together: finance and freedom. When a woman builds true wealth, she expresses her female power.

A New Kind of Mastery

For too long, finance has leaned on *masculine energy:* competitive, analytical, individualistic. But mastery needs its counterpart, the *feminine:* collaborative, intuitive, holistic. When one dominates, something vital is lost.

I know this imbalance because I lived it. My career began in one of the most masculine environments imaginable: the City, where sharp suits and sharper elbows were the norm. I learned to play that game well. By thirty, on paper, I had it all. But inside, I felt hollow; wealthy by society's standards, yet poor in spirit.

I was playing by someone else's rules, chasing success while ignoring the quieter, intuitive part of me whispering something was missing.

That realisation cracked everything open. It pushed me to begin a different kind of education; one that bridges finance with consciousness, money with meaning, material success with authenticity.

When you bring your whole self into your financial life, something shifts. Money stops being just a source of stress or status. It becomes a tool for freedom, choice, and transformation.

My path with money has been anything but straight. There have been shifts, detours, and more than a few hard-won lessons. But that's the point, you don't need perfection to walk this path. You just need the courage to begin.

This book is my invitation to cross that bridge with me, from ambition to authenticity, from finance as the F-word to finance as freedom.

Why This Book and Why Now

We stand at a pivotal moment.

Women control more wealth than ever before, and by some estimates will hold nearly two-thirds of the nation's wealth by 2030. Yet despite this growing economic power, the financial world still speaks a language written by men, for men.

Meanwhile, our world is shifting at an unprecedented pace. Technology, decentralised finance, and the redefinition of work are transforming the way wealth is created and held. The gap between those who understand money and those who don't is widening. For women, that gap is both a risk and an opportunity.

When women grow capital, studies show they reinvest around 90% of what they make back into their families and communities, compared to roughly 45% for men. That's not just an economic fact; it's a social revolution waiting to happen. When a woman builds wealth, it changes her life. When women build wealth, it changes the world.

This book isn't about getting rich quickly. It's about something far more meaningful. It's an invitation to reclaim your financial power, not through competition, but through conscious participation. To bring both wisdom and wealth to the table. To build not just financial independence, but financial influence. When women thrive financially, everyone rises with them.

Your Roadmap to Fearless Finance

This book is designed as a journey, mirroring how real change unfolds:

Awareness → Alignment → Activation.

Each part builds on the last so that by the end, you're not just *thinking* differently about money, you're *doing* it differently.

Part One: Awareness — Begin with You

We start by exploring your inner landscape: the stories, beliefs, and taboos that have shaped how you think and feel about money. You'll discover the link between money and energy, we'll reframe risk, and introduce *Energetic Alpha,* a benchmark for living authentically. You'll also look at your numbers clearly and without judgement. This is about raising your awareness so you're ready for what comes next.

Part Two: Alignment — Marry Money with Meaning

Here, inner work meets outer action. You'll clarify your values, define your *Financial Freedom Number*, and learn the foundations of investing: compounding, diversification, asset classes, and economic context. Then you'll build your *Investment Values Compass*, aligning your money with what matters most to you.

Part Three: Activation — Make It Real

Knowledge only matters when it's in motion. You'll use the *Wheel of Wealth* to design your own wealth strategy, from ETFs and Bitcoin to property, pensions, legacy, and protection. You'll learn to take brave financial action, master your inner game, and build the structures that sustain momentum.

It all culminates in the *AAA Cycle,* Authority, Accountability, and Acknowledgement, the framework that turns insight into action and keeps you growing long after you close the final page.

How to Use This Book

Start at the beginning and go chapter by chapter; it all builds.

Do the exercises. They're short, practical, and designed to get you taking action, because action, however small, compounds into confidence.

If a financial term feels murky, check the Glossary at the back; it's written in plain English to keep you moving, not stuck in jargon. You'll also find a quick-reference section bringing together the key frameworks from the book - including the Wheel of Authenticity, the Wheel of Wealth, and the AAA Cycle - so you can return to them easily as your understanding deepens and your strategy evolves.

This book was never meant to be a standalone experience.

Alongside it sits the **Fearless Wealth Playbook**, a companion guide designed to help you turn insight into action. It contains the worksheets, prompts, templates, and practical tools that bring this journey to life.

Think of this book as the *why* and the *what*, and the Playbook as the *how*.

You don't need to use them together perfectly or all at once. Some women read first and return later. Others work alongside it chapter by chapter. Trust what feels right for you.

You can access the **Fearless Wealth Playbook** at any time via the QR code here.

https://fearlessfemaleinvestor.com/playbook

This journey doesn't end with understanding. It begins with application.

Take it one step at a time. Momentum comes from small, consistent moves.

Finally, I encourage you to engage with this book fully. Let it challenge what you've believed about money and invite you to see yourself as the investor you already are.

A Note on Financial Education

I'm an educator and an experienced investor, not a regulated financial adviser. Everything on these pages is designed to help you understand how wealth-building works, blending solid financial education with my own lived experience.

When I write about how to open a brokerage account, read a chart, or make your first investment, I'm teaching you the *how,* not telling you *what* to buy. When I mention platforms, funds, or strategies, they're simply examples to illustrate the principles we're exploring together.

Your financial life is uniquely yours. All investments carry risk, including the potential loss of capital, and tax outcomes depend on your individual circumstances. For more complex areas - inheritance, trusts, or international assets, this is where an FCA-regulated adviser can provide tailored professional guidance.

My perspective is simple: women are not "bad with money." Most simply haven't been given the education, language, or permission to engage. You don't need permission here. You need understanding, confidence, and the courage to begin.

That is what this book offers.. What you choose to do with it is yours.

A New Relationship with Wealth

Many women tell me they feel as though they never got the memo about money. Capable women who've built careers, raised families, run businesses, and managed everything for everyone else, yet somehow missed the class on wealth.

If that's you, you're not alone, and you're certainly not late. You're part of a growing movement of women reclaiming money as a source of strength, freedom, and legacy.

Ambition is not a dirty word. Wealth can be a force for good. And your financial power is not separate from your feminine power; they're expressions of the same authentic self. When we integrate both our inner masculine and feminine, our strategy and our intuition, our action and our receptivity, we begin to access what I call Sovereign Feminine Power: the grounded, self-led authority from which women make their most aligned financial decisions.

This book is your invitation to speak freely, fearlessly, and in your own voice about finance. To build wealth on your own terms and for your highest purpose. To cross the bridge to true wealth, with confidence, integrity, and authenticity.

The world doesn't need more women shrinking to fit old systems. It needs women standing in their full power, financial and otherwise, to create new ones that work for everyone.

That's what this book ultimately calls for: a new paradigm of wealth creation that includes *everyone:* women, men, and anyone ready to live and invest as their whole, authentic self. Although I've written it through the female lens, the truths inside are universal. They're for anyone who wants to reclaim their power, invest boldly, and live authentically.

True wealth isn't gendered. It's human, grounded, present, and free.

This is where it begins.

PART 1

AWARENESS

Chapter 1

THE F WORD

Breaking the Silence Around Women and Finance

Fluency in finance is fluency in freedom

If we want to build true wealth, we must first name what holds us back. Breaking that silence is where our journey begins.

The Day My Life Cracked Open

A fine drizzle streaked the windows of a Putney pub, blurring the movement of hurried commuters outside. It was the turn of the millennium, a time when markets were soaring, and ambition felt like currency. I sat at a small wooden table, a large glass of white wine cool in my hand. It was the end of the day, and I was meant to be celebrating or at least moving into a new chapter of my career.

Instead, my ears still rang with the words from that morning: *It's political.*

The promotion I'd been promised, the one I'd worked sixty-hour weeks for, sacrificed weekends for, missed birthdays and anniversaries for, had been given to someone else. A man from another department who knew far less about our markets than I did. Perhaps it was about assets under management. Perhaps I'd been too honest in a feedback session. Perhaps I hadn't played the game. I'll never know the full reason.

On paper, I had everything. Managing over £500 million - the equivalent of around £1 billion today, in emerging European markets for a large global asset management company, one of the largest portfolios of its kind. I had a team spanning Russia, Poland, the Czech Republic, and Hungary. My salary placed me among the top earners in London.

And yet, in that pub, I felt bankrupt.

Not the kind you can see in a bank statement. My accounts were full, but my spirit was empty. I had become fluent in the language of money but lost fluency in the language of my own soul.

My world had shattered into a thousand pieces of glass. Everything I'd been working towards, the dream of joining the C-suite, the seat at the table I'd been climbing towards for years, lay in jagged shards around me. I stared at the rain on the window, unable to picture what came next. I'd built my entire life around this career. Now the foundation had crumbled.

My "wealth" was a home I rarely saw in daylight, clothes chosen to impress clients, holidays interrupted by calls, and restaurant meals eaten too tired to taste.

Somewhere between chasing the next bonus and the next promotion, I had lost the plot.

That rainy evening in Putney cracked something wide open in me. I had built a life focused almost entirely on money—income, bonuses, balance sheets—without ever questioning what any of it was for. I knew how to make money, but I didn't know how to make meaning. Financial wealth without inner wealth isn't wealth at all. It's just a more comfortable form of poverty.

My story wasn't unique; it was part of a much bigger narrative about the way women have been positioned, and too often excluded, in the world of finance. While my personal crisis that day was about inner bankruptcy, the challenges women face around money have roots that reach much further back. For most of history, finance wasn't just "a man's world"; it was literally a man's legal right.

In the UK until 1975, a woman couldn't open her own bank account without her husband's or father's signature. In the US, it took the Equal Credit Opportunity Act of 1974 to change the same rule. If you were running a business, you often needed a man to co-sign loans or sign cheques.

Whilst the laws have shifted, the conditioning they left behind runs deep, shaping how we see money, how we talk about it, and, crucially, whether we feel it's even *ours* to master.

Many of our mothers and grandmothers lived through these laws. They've shaped how women think about and behave with money.

The rules have changed. The conditioning lingers. Girls are taught to be careful with money, to save it, but not to grow it. We're encouraged to manage household budgets, not investment portfolios. Finance has been painted as technical, abstract, intimidating, best left to "the experts," who are still mostly men.

When I worked in the City, fewer than 10% of directors in my company were women. I wore sharp trouser suits and learned to play the game. I still remember walking into meetings with my male assistant and having brokers speak to him as if he were in charge. I would smile and say, "Excuse me, I'm the fund manager. I make the decisions."

When I was studying for my Master's in Finance, I was taught complex formulas and theories, but nothing about the emotional relationship we have with money. I learned about market efficiency, but not emotional intelligence. I studied risk assessment models, but not how to assess whether my financial decisions aligned with my deepest values.

What I came to understand later, after several spectacular failures, is that true financial mastery requires both: the analytical precision to understand the markets and the intuitive wisdom to understand yourself.

The data shows my story isn't unique. Globally, women hold just over 21% of senior leadership roles in financial services. In the UK, only 26% of women invest in the stock market compared to 43% of men. Women retire with 35% less in their pensions.

This isn't about blame. Many men champion women in finance. But centuries of exclusion have left us with inherited beliefs:

- Finance is *for them*, not for *us*.
- Talking about money is somehow unfeminine or greedy.
- Investing is risky and complicated.

Every time we avoid the conversation about finance or hand over financial decisions to others, we give away our power. The cost isn't just personal; it's societal. By playing small with our money, we limit our capacity to create positive change.

Money, Finance, and Wealth: The Distinction

Before we can reclaim the F Word, we need to know what we're really talking about.

Here's how I see it:

> **Money** is the flow: the current that moves through your life.
>
> **Finance** is how you direct that flow.
>
> **Wealth** is the life you create as a result.

Money is the raw material, the pounds and pence that flow into and out of your life. It's a medium of exchange, a way to store value, a means to meet needs and create opportunities.

Finance is the navigation system: the set of skills and strategies that decide where that money goes, how it works for you, and how it grows. Without navigation, money drifts aimlessly. With it, you can direct that flow towards the future you want.

Wealth is the outcome: the expanded capacity to live life on your own terms. True wealth isn't just money in the bank; it's security, freedom, choice, and the ability to shape your future. Alongside the investments you can count on a spreadsheet, there's another kind of wealth, the inner kind, built through health, relationships, purpose, and peace of mind. The two are inseparable: material wealth gives you options, and inner wealth gives those options meaning. Together, they create what I call *True Wealth.*

We live in a culture that celebrates visible displays of wealth, the car, the holiday, the designer brands, but true wealth is usually quiet. It lives in assets, freedom, and choice.

You Are Already an Investor

To build both material and inner wealth, you have to invest. To invest means putting resources, time, money, and energy into something with the expectation of a greater return in the future.

You are already doing that in other parts of your life. If you've nurtured relationships, raised children, improved your health, grown a career, or built a business, you've invested. You've researched before making big decisions, weighed risks and rewards, stayed committed when things got hard, and thought about the long-term impact of your choices. Those are the same skills you need to be a successful financial investor.

So if you've ever thought, "I'm not an investor", it's time to put that belief aside. You already are one, you just haven't been applying those skills to your money in the markets. The gap isn't in your ability; it's in recognising that finance is for you, and in learning how to use the navigation tools of finance to turn the flow of your money into lasting wealth.

That's what this book is about: teaching you how to move from investing in your life to investing in your financial future. So you're not just managing money, you're directing it. Not just earning an income, but building assets. Not just "being careful," but being confident, intentional, and in control.

When you combine the skills you already have with the knowledge of how to navigate the financial system, you stop drifting and start steering towards a future that is both financially secure and deeply fulfilling.

The Wake-Up Call: Why Now Matters

The world is changing faster than most of us realise, and the financial landscape is shifting beneath our feet.

Over the next decade, women will inherit more than £1 trillion in the UK alone, the largest transfer of wealth in modern history. But here's the risk: unless we learn to invest that wealth wisely, much of it will vanish, eroded by inflation, fees, or poor decisions.

Meanwhile, cash isn't the safe harbour it once was. A recent Deutsche Bank report, analysing more than 200 years of asset performance, shows that cash has historically been the riskiest asset of all. It quietly melts away, eaten by inflation and the expansion of the money supply. Playing it safe isn't safe anymore.

Add to this the rise of AI, decentralised finance, and digital currencies, and it's clear: the rules of the game are being rewritten. Women who understand how to invest, both their capital and their knowledge will have choices. Those who don't will be at the mercy of forces they can't control.

For generations, women have been taught to play it safe with money: to save, to budget, to protect. Those skills are valuable, but they're not enough in a world moving this fast. Safety without growth is slow erosion.

This book is about learning the new rules, building both material and inner wealth, and investing in ways that protect and grow what matters most.

Dismantling the Myths

Before we go any further, let's name some of the myths that hold so many women back from stepping into their power as investors.

These are the stories we've inherited, the whispers that sit at the back of our minds when we think about money. They sound so familiar that we mistake them for truth. But they're not true: they're conditioning.

Myth 1: Saving is safe.

We've been told cash in the bank is security. In reality, inflation and money printing eat away at your savings daily. What looks safe is actually slow erosion, and the hidden cost is opportunity. Every year you delay investing, you miss out on compounding growth that could have been working for you.

Myth 2: Investing is gambling.

We imagine flashing screens, frantic traders, and fortunes lost in minutes. Yet gambling is chance, while investing is ownership: of companies, ideas, and innovation that create real value in the world.

Myth 3: You have to be rich to invest.

This is one of the most powerful lies. You don't need a lump sum, a City salary, or a private banker. Today, you can start with as little as £25 a month. Wealth isn't built by waiting until you're rich; it's built by starting where you are and letting compounding do the heavy lifting.

Myth 4: Volatility Doesn't Equal Risk.

Volatility is movement. Risk is permanent loss. Markets go up and down, headlines scream, balances change colour, but volatility is not the end of the story. The real risk is being unprepared, undiversified, or paralysed by fear.

Myth 5: Investing is too complicated.

We're told we need to be experts, picking stocks across countries and sectors, watching endless charts and ratios. The reality is far simpler: diversification just means not putting all your eggs in one basket. One global fund can spread your money across thousands of companies, simple protection, not complexity.

These myths aren't harmless; they're walls that keep women out of the markets, away from building wealth, and cut off from their own power. The moment you see them for what they are, those walls begin to crumble.

When they do, something else becomes clear: women are already far better investors than they've been told.

Women's Natural Advantages

Here's something the industry rarely admits: women aren't more *risk-averse,* they're more *risk-aware.* Fidelity research shows women outperform men by an average of 0.4% a year, a small margin that compounds into a major difference over time.

The reason isn't taking fewer risks; it's taking smarter ones. Women tend to research thoroughly, stay committed during volatility, diversify naturally, and avoid impulsive trades.

These traits, patience, emotional intelligence, preparation, and perspective, are exactly what the markets reward over time. For too long, women have been labelled "cautious" or "risk averse." In truth, they are signs of mastery: the ability to balance confidence with discernment.

When women pair that discernment with education and ownership, they don't avoid risk; they manage it wisely, and the results speak for themselves. What the industry once interpreted as hesitation was often simply exclusion, not lack of ability

It's time to reclaim the F Word, now.

This isn't only about learning how to manage your money. It's about reclaiming something far bigger: your power to choose, to create, and to shape the life you want, on your terms.

In this chapter, we've pulled back the curtain on the cultural taboos and systemic barriers that have kept women from stepping fully into the world of finance. We've looked at why money, finance, and wealth are not the same thing, and why building wealth means taking what you already know about investing in your life and applying it to your money.

But knowing about something isn't the same as living it.

The world is shifting (technology, markets, currencies, and the way wealth itself moves). You can watch from the sidelines, or you can decide that from this moment on, you're no longer handing over the steering wheel to someone else.

You don't have to wait until you "feel ready." You can begin today with one choice, one action, one shift in perspective.

This isn't just about numbers on a spreadsheet or ticking off financial goals. It's about what those numbers make possible: designing a life that is truly yours, built with intention, meaning, and courage.

Key Takeaways

- **Finance is a universal skillset** - it's not a private club; you can learn this
- **Cultural taboos can be broken** - the silence around money has deep historical roots, but you have the power to break it
- **True wealth integrates both** - material and inner, money and meaning together
- **Investing builds power** - it's not gambling; it's a way to build influence, freedom, and impact
- **The time is now** - women stepping into financial power starts today

Practical Actions

1. **Name your fears** - Write down three worries or myths you hold about investing.
2. **Challenge one** - Spend ten minutes replacing it with truth, look up a term you don't understand, read one short article, or ask someone how they got started.
3. **Define your kind of wealth** - In your own words, what would a wealthy life feel like for you, beyond money?
4. **Notice your investments** - Where are you already investing your time, energy, or attention? Are those investments moving you toward the life you want?

Chapter 2

THE MOUNTAIN'S GIFT

Redefining Financial Freedom from the Inside Out

Freedom isn't just the absence of limits; it's the presence of choice. The powder snow flew up around my face like champagne bubbles, each crystal catching the alpine sunlight as I carved my first turn down the untouched slope. I had never skied powder before, never even imagined this feeling of floating, of flying, of pure, unfiltered joy coursing through every fibre of my being.

The mountain guide ahead of me had simply said, "Follow me, copy what I do, and let go."

Let go.

As the snow danced around my goggles and the mountain fell away beneath my skis, I felt something I hadn't experienced in years, perhaps ever. This was freedom. This was what it meant to be truly alive.

From the Cage to the Peaks

If Chapter 1 was the moment I realised the game was rigged, this was the moment I stopped playing it.

Just twelve months earlier, I'd stood in a football-pitch-sized office in the heart of the City, my world crumbling around me as I learned I'd been passed over for promotion. People paused briefly before carrying on, while my carefully constructed career plans lay in ruins at my feet.

I was materially wealthy, the house, the marriage, the six-figure salary, yet energetically bankrupt. I didn't know it then, but I was living in what I now call a beautifully decorated cage.

What I couldn't have foreseen in that devastating moment was that being overlooked would become the greatest gift the universe ever gave me.

For months afterwards, I drifted through my London life like a ghost haunting her own existence. The city felt suffocating, the golden handcuffs of the financial world tightening with every passing day. Something deep inside had shifted, and moving to another bank, the obvious solution, felt like trying to fix a broken compass by changing direction. The problem wasn't where I was pointing; it was that I'd lost my true north entirely.

The Question That Split My Life in Two

Then came the conversation that changed everything. Over dinner with a girlfriend, nothing more than casual chat over wine and pasta, she asked: "What are the dreams you put on the shelf? The ones you've forgotten about?"

Almost without thinking, I heard myself reply, "I've always wanted to ski like a pro. And I've always wished I could speak French fluently."

Such simple dreams. What impossible dreams. Or so I'd told myself.

Dreams have a way of resurfacing when you're ready to hear them. A few months later, I did something that would have terrified the old me, the me who followed the prescribed path, equated financial security with safety, and wanted to tick all the "successful" boxes.

I gave up everything.

Within weeks, I walked away from my marriage, rented out my house, and bought a one-way ferry ticket to the French Alps. I traded my smart suit and Gucci handbag for ski boots and an avalanche probe, my four-bed London house for a small studio in Chamonix, my carefully plotted future for the delicious uncertainty of following my heart.

A Letter from a Different Life

My parents thought I'd lost my mind. So a month after arriving in Chamonix, I wrote them a letter:

"For the first time ever, I feel that my soul is free. Free to do what I want, to follow long-held dreams, to feel truly liberated from the constraints that I felt society put on me, that I put on myself. I live for each day as it comes, and in doing so, I feel a huge sense of freedom."

The letter went on to describe the stark contrast between my old life, driven by promotions, pay rises, and the unspoken expectations of my Thatcher-era upbringing, and my new one, where my biggest decisions were when to ski, who to meet for tea, and what to cook for dinner.

I compared my old job to running endlessly on a hamster wheel, always chasing an undefined goal of "making it." Being passed over for promotion had pushed me off the wheel. At first, I panicked. Then I realised I didn't have to climb back on.

"My goodness, there is a huge and amazing world out here, and I'm just enjoying being in it for a bit. I don't know what's next, but I'm alive again."

Redefining Freedom

My time in the mountains taught me something that has shaped my life ever since: true wealth isn't about the size of your house or the numbers in your bank account. It's about the presence of choice. The choice to decide how you spend your time, who you spend it with, and where you place your energy.

Money can't buy happiness, but it can buy you options. And options give you more control over your time, focus and your energy.

For most of my life, I had believed wealth was about accumulation: the house, the marriage, the six-figure salary, the invitations to the right dinners with the right people. I'd ticked those boxes. But in having them, I'd learned they weren't meaningless, but they'd never been the point.

Life in Chamonix was stripped to its essence.

"Life is simple here. It's about what the weather is doing today, what the snow conditions are like, and who to ski with. People here don't stress about catching a train or earning enough to own a bigger house. Life is about appreciating what the Universe created and simply being alive and present now."

I wasn't chasing promotions or bonuses. I was skiing every day, speaking French, meeting people who'd chosen passion over pay cheques. And I began to understand something that's stayed with me ever since: you can have all the money and still feel trapped, or you can have very little and feel truly wealthy.

That winter, as I closed the letter to my parents, I wrote:

"I feel good, alive, and content."

I had no idea that those words would become the foundation of a philosophy I'd later teach to others. What looked like simplicity to the outside world wasn't 'settling' It was redefining wealth in a way that finally made sense to me.

Looking back, I can see that what I was really exploring that winter wasn't financial freedom at all; it was inner freedom. The kind that comes when you stop chasing approval, control, or certainty and start listening to your own truth. It was the freedom to wake up without expectation, to move at the pace of my own energy, and to live by what felt right rather than what looked right.

In hindsight, I realise that I was already financially free then, I just didn't recognise it. Financial freedom isn't about never working again; it's about having the flexibility and security to shape your life on your terms. It's the point where your money supports your life, not the other way around. It's when income from your assets, rather than your labour, supports your life, giving you the choice to decide how, where, and with whom you spend your time. It isn't a single number; it's a relationship with money that gives you agency.

Over time, I came to realise that inner freedom and financial freedom are not separate, but deeply connected. One gives you peace; the other gives you possibility. Together, they create a life that feels both grounded and secure.

One way to represent this, and a model I've found deeply useful in my own life and work, is to imagine two ladders that climb side by side: the inner experience of expansion and the outer structure that supports it. One is material; the other energetic. Together, they form what I call the Two Ladders of Freedom, a way to represent true wealth.

The Two Ladders of Freedom

Freedom rests on two ladders: the outer ladder of material wealth and the inner, energetic ladder of alignment and vitality:

- The outer ladder of **financial wealth** – income, savings, assets, and the structures that create choice.
- The inner ladder of **energetic wealth** – self-awareness, authenticity, purpose, and peace of mind.

These ladders aren't destinations; they're frameworks. Over the years, in my own life and in coaching others, I've seen both sides of this play out. Some people are financially secure but energetically adrift. Others are deeply centred but financially stretched.

Real freedom grows when both wealth and wisdom, money and meaning, climb side by side. Climb only one and you'll always feel unbalanced. Climb both, and you'll discover genuine freedom.

The Rungs of Each Ladder

Both ladders begin in scarcity and build toward abundance. The journey isn't about skipping steps, it's about climbing steadily, building resilience, balance, and choice as you go. Let's look at the rungs of each ladder.

The Financial Freedom Ladder

1. **Scarcity** – Living payday to payday. Constant financial stress.

2. **Survival** – Covering the basics with one or two months of security.
3. **Security** – Debt managed or cleared; an emergency fund cushions shocks.
4. **Growth** – Actively building assets, investing, and creating stability.
5. **Flexibility** – Options open up: sabbatical, retraining, relocation.
6. **Freedom** – Financial independence. Work becomes optional.
7. **Abundance / Legacy** – More than enough for your lifetime. Giving back flows naturally.

When I moved to Chamonix, I was somewhere between flexibility and freedom. My London house brought in rental income, and I had savings. I had the means to choose, and that choice, even without extravagance, was worth more than any bonus I'd ever earned.

Financial freedom gave me options, but inner freedom gave me peace. One builds flexibility; the other builds resilience. Together, they create the foundation for a life that feels both secure and alive.

The Energetic Freedom Ladder

1. **Fear / Scarcity** – Life lived in survival mode, guided by fear or approval.
2. **Awareness** – Seeing your patterns and beliefs clearly.
3. **Inner Stability** – Cultivating emotional strength and self-trust.
4. **Resilience** – Developing your inner cushion; fear no longer rules.
5. **Flow** – Trusting life's cycles and detours.
6. **Inner Freedom** – Choices guided from within, not external validation.
7. **Abundant Inner Wealth** – Living with joy, gratitude, and connection.

Energetically, when I first arrived in Chamonix, I was between inner stability and resilience.

"Opportunity presents itself at any moment, and if one is brave enough, one can step off the path one is on and follow another. There is no right or wrong path. There is, however, a truth in the heart, and that is what one should follow."

I hadn't realised it then, but I was climbing both ladders at once, not in perfect sync, but in balance. I was financially free enough to choose my path, and energetically free enough to trust it. True wealth is the intersection where material security meets energetic alignment. That's where freedom lives.

Defining Enough

Before we can start climbing, it helps to know what we're climbing towards. One of the biggest imbalances I see, and one I've lived myself, is when we focus on the outer ladder of financial success at the expense of the inner one. We chase the next promotion, the bigger house, the higher return, but lose sight of what all that striving is for.

That's why the idea of *enough* matters so much. It's not about limitation; it's about clarity. Your version of financial freedom will never look exactly like anyone else's, because it depends on what you truly want your life to feel like. When you define what "enough" means for you, not for your peers, your parents, or the world around you, you create your own measure of freedom.

One of the most liberating shifts you can make is defining what "enough" means for you. When you strip away the job titles, the status symbols, and the pressure to keep up with anyone else's definition of success, you discover something profound: you don't need as much as you think to live your version of the good life.

Enough isn't a fixed number. It's both a threshold and a feeling. It's the point at which your needs and values are met without sacrificing your health, relationships, or joy. It's the moment you can exhale and say, *I have what I need*

When I first moved to Chamonix, I lived on a fraction of my London salary, yet I'd never felt richer. Some of my friends in finance earned ten times more but felt trapped, unable to step away. They were high on the financial ladder but low on the freedom ladder.

True freedom isn't simply "working for yourself." It's creating a life that can thrive without your constant presence, so you can step away without everything collapsing around you.

We'll return to this idea of "enough" later, when you design your own Freedom Number in Chapter 10. For now, simply notice what freedom feels like to you, not what it costs.

Where You Stand, Where You Can Grow

So much of freedom is about awareness, noticing where you are and where you long to be. The ladders aren't there to measure success, they're there to give you language for what you already sense.

Perhaps you're financially secure but running on empty energetically. Maybe you're deeply aligned inside but uncertain about money. You might even be near the bottom of both ladders, finally ready to take the first step.

Wherever you find yourself, don't judge it. Just notice it. Awareness is the first step to balance.

You can use the Two Ladders as a compass, not a checklist. Look at where you are now and where you'd like to be in a year. Choose one small, real step that would move you up a rung, a financial action that builds security, or an energetic one that restores your peace. Over time, these small, conscious movements create momentum.

These ladders don't measure your worth, they simply show where you stand and where you can grow. That's the essence of freedom: the clarity to see where you are, the balance to honour both dimensions, and the choice to move consciously toward what matters most

As I wrote to my parents years ago:"I live for each day as it comes, and in choosing to do so, I feel a huge sense of freedom."

That integration of outer wealth and inner alignment, the ability to choose where you spend your time, energy, and resources, is what creates a life that reflects who you truly are.

In the chapters ahead, we'll explore how to expand this freedom, first through energy, then through the practical design of your financial life. When you reach Chapter 10, you'll translate these insights into your own Freedom Number and roadmap.

When you shift your inner energy, your outer financial reality shifts too. That's where we're heading next.

Key Takeaways

- **Freedom is choice, not luxury** - it begins with having options, not expensive things
- **Financial freedom means money serves you** - not the other way round
- **True wealth requires both ladders** - the outer ladder of financial wealth (income, assets, choice) and the inner ladder of energetic wealth (alignment, authenticity, vitality)
- **Defining "enough" creates clarity** - this is where your journey truly begins
- **Small steps build momentum** - and restore balance along the way
- **Freedom equals choice plus clarity plus balance** - all three working together

Practical Actions

1. Identify which rung of the financial ladder you're on.
2. Identify which rung of the energetic ladder you're on.
3. Define your personal version of "enough."
4. Choose one small action this month to move up a rung - financial or energetic.
5. Journal on where you feel most out of balance.

Chapter 3

THE FREQUENCY OF MONEY

Consciousness Creates Cash Flow

The UCL Student Counsellor's office felt suffocating. I stared at the ceiling, as tears dried on my cheeks, feeling like I was drowning in a world that suddenly made no sense. A week earlier, everything had changed.

I had just attended the Landmark Forum, a personal transformation programme that was intense, polarising, and utterly life-altering. In four days locked in a hotel room, I watched my reality crumble. Every story I'd told myself about being powerless, about life happening *to* me, dissolved.

The breakthrough was simple but seismic: I was the author of my own life. Even when I couldn't control events, I could always choose my response. That realisation was intoxicating.

Walking out, I was electric with possibility. The world looked sharper, complaints trivial, people blind to how they created their own misery. I had discovered the extraordinary power to choose.

Then the crash came. Back in the "real" world, I realised with crushing clarity, almost nobody lived like this. When I talked of being conscious, friends rolled their eyes, and my parents called it a phase. I felt like an alien who had glimpsed the truth yet had to live among those who preferred their complaints.

That loneliness took me to the counsellor's couch. But lying there, I whispered: "It isn't me. It's everybody else." I wasn't going back to sleep.

That choice changed everything. I stopped waiting for permission and started creating change, in my community, in my career choices, and ultimately in how I understood money itself. A year later, with nothing but determination and unshakable belief, I walked into the City of London determined to get my first finance job. Every rejection only strengthened me. "No" was someone else's limitation, not mine.

That shift in consciousness became the foundation of everything: my career, my maverick life choices, my understanding of money as energy, and ultimately, this book.

Consciousness is the Decision. Emotions are the Practice.

That Landmark breakthrough at 21 changed everything. In four days, I went from feeling like life was happening to me, to realising I was the author of my own story. It was a single decision: I take full responsibility for my life.

Consciousness, I learned, is surprisingly simple. You just decide. Victim or agent? Reactive or responsive? Asleep or awake? It's a choice you make in a moment.

What took me decades to understand, though, is that consciousness is the decision; emotions are the practice.

You can decide you're the author of your life, but if you don't learn to navigate your emotions, the fear, the anxiety, the FOMO, the scarcity, you'll keep sabotaging yourself. Emotions drive your actions. Actions create your results.

We'll explore consciousness, its levels, the ladders, and how awareness shapes everything. First, though, we need to go deeper. Emotional frequency matters. Emotions aren't just feelings you experience; they're signals you broadcast. Those signals shape what flows into your life, including money.

Emotions: Your Inner GPS for Financial Flow

If consciousness is the architecture of your financial life, then emotions are the signals showing you where you stand at any given moment. They are your inner GPS, subtle, powerful, and always guiding.

I learned this truth the hard way the first year I was back in the UK.

I was extracting myself from a property project in Plymouth with a delinquent business partner. Every week, I'd sit down with a calculator and spreadsheets, running the numbers, only to discover that at best we'd break even. The £350,000 profit we'd anticipated, gone. Delays in selling the flats meant my capital was completely tied up, and meanwhile, I'd been so focused on the property drama that I'd let my coaching business fall away entirely.

There I was: a single parent with no income, all my money locked in a failing project, trying to make ends meet.

The anxiety was crushing. I'd lie awake at night, wake up in the morning in a panic, with that familiar tightness in my chest. *How am I going to make ends meet?* I'd obsessively crunch numbers in my head, scribbling calculations on scraps of paper, desperately trying to make the maths work out differently. It never did.

Then one day, my very close friend Ella asked me a simple question: "Why don't you go back to coaching?"

I immediately listed my objections. "I haven't got any marketing. I don't know what to do. I've been out of it for a few years."

She said calmly, "Just trust. Put it out there. You're really good at it. Just intend that's what you want to do."

Something shifted in that moment.

It wasn't that the property situation changed; it didn't. The numbers were still terrible. However, Ella's question reminded me of something I'd forgotten: how much I *loved* coaching. How much impact I'd had on clients. The difference it made in their lives.

In that instant, I moved from a state of scarcity and anxiety to a state of possibility. Not love, exactly, but remembrance. Purpose. Flow.

Within *days*, I received a LinkedIn inquiry from a property company and estate agency. Someone had recommended me months earlier, and they'd finally reached out. That conversation turned into an 18-month contract with their team.

Shortly after, an ex-boyfriend from Pfizer found my website quite by chance and asked if I could offer coaching to his female staff. Another contract.

Same skills. Same experience. Same market. But a completely different frequency, and a completely different reality.

I'd moved from financial desperation to financial flow. The shift didn't come from changing my strategy, updating my marketing, or fixing the property deal. It came from changing my *emotional state.*

This is what I mean when I say emotions are your GPS. They don't just reflect your inner world, they shape your outer one.

Emotions as Frequency

Every emotion carries a frequency. Fear, guilt, anxiety, and desperation create contraction. Optimism, confidence, trust, and joy create expansion. Like tuning into a radio station, you can only receive opportunities that match the signal you're broadcasting.

This is why emotional regulation isn't just a wellness practice. It's a financial skill.

I saw this clearly during one of the most anxious periods of my life. Lying awake at night, running the numbers over and over, I was broadcasting scarcity. Everything felt stuck. Money dried up. Opportunities disappeared.

Then something shifted. Ella's question reminded me of possibility, of purpose, of a wider horizon. I stopped chasing. I stopped grasping. I simply became open again. And in that openness, money flowed.

This isn't mystical thinking. It's pattern recognition. I've seen it play out time and again. In anxiety, opportunities vanish. In trust, they appear.

Your financial portfolio will always reflect your emotional portfolio.

Your Wealth Emotional Ladder

We all move through different emotional states, especially when it comes to money. None of these states is wrong; they're simply points of awareness. The key is noticing where you are and understanding that even a small upward shift can radically change the quality of your decisions and the opportunities that appear.

Here's what the emotional spectrum looks like when it comes to wealth:

Emotional State	How It Feels	What Shows Up Financially
Abundant	Joyful, generous, grateful, "there's more where this came from"	Wealth compounds naturally, making it easy
Trust/Flow	Relaxed, expansive, "it will work out"	Money flows, opportunities appear "out of nowhere," synchronicities
Confidence	Grounded, clear, "I've done my homework"	Better investment decisions, steady action, calm through volatility
Curiosity	Open, exploratory, "I wonder what's possible..."	New ideas emerge, research feels expansive
Neutral/ Boredom	Going through the motions, flat, disconnected	Slow progress, inconsistent results
Resignation	Heavy, defeated, "why bother trying"	Minimal action, waiting for rescue, stagnation

Fear/Anxiety	Caught in your head, spinning, "it's not enough," constant calculation	Energy blocked, barrier goes up, clients/work don't flow
Desperation/ Scarcity	Chest tight, scrambling, obsessing over numbers, lying awake at night	Money dries up, opportunities vanish, and poor decisions are made from panic

When my emotional portfolio was 70% anxiety and 30% fear, my financial reality looked like: cash flow drying up, opportunities disappearing, and sleepless nights. When I shifted my emotional portfolio to 60% trust and 40% possibility, suddenly, LinkedIn inquiries, old connections resurfacing, and 18-month contracts materialised.

Why Emotional Mastery Matters

This is why emotional mastery matters so much, not just for investing, but for life itself. When you can navigate the full spectrum of human emotions, joy, fear, excitement, grief, confidence, and anxiety, without being hijacked by any of them, you develop something invaluable: inner security.

Not the kind of security that comes from a fat bank account (though that helps). The kind that comes from knowing, deep in your bones, that you can handle whatever comes. Any market crash. Any unexpected expense. Any moment of uncertainty.

Emotional mastery doesn't mean diminishing the emotions you feel. For any men reading this, it's not about reducing emotions to a handful of acceptable states. And for women, it's certainly not about becoming "less emotional." We're often told that our depth of feeling is a liability. It isn't.

Emotional range is more like market volatility: movement, not risk. Within a single day, we might feel joy, reflection, fierce determination, and deep tenderness. That isn't instability. It's aliveness. It's responsiveness. It's being fully human.

The mastery lies in regulation: experiencing the full, beautiful array of human emotions while not being controlled by them.

I've had money stolen from me in Paris. I've lost significant sums in what were effectively property scams. I've had difficult, challenging things happen. And in all of that, I know that I'm grounded enough to say: "It's OK. I wish it were otherwise, but I'm not going to fall into despair and anxiety anymore, because I can pull myself up to higher levels of emotional states. Because that's where magic happens."

That security creates confidence. And confidence is what allows you to take the brave actions that build wealth, the calculated risks, the bold moves, the leaps that others are too afraid to take.

We'll explore risk and courage in the next chapter. But it all starts here: with your ability to regulate your emotional state and trust yourself to navigate whatever arises.

Money as Energy

So why do emotions have this power? Why does your inner state determine what shows up in your outer world?

Money, at its core, is energy. Not in a mystical sense, but in a practical one: the flow of human attention, trust, and exchange. That flow responds to the presence you bring.

If "energy" feels too abstract, think of it this way: your emotional state affects everything—your body language, decision-making, the risks you take, the opportunities you notice, how others experience you, and whether you show up at all.

What if money isn't scarce, finite, or something that simply happens to you, but rather a responsive force that flows toward or away from you depending on your state of being?

When you operate from fear, scarcity, or desperation, everything contracts. You make worse decisions. You notice problems but miss opportunities. People sense your desperation and pull back. You withdraw from the very networks and relationships that could help you.

When you embody confidence, gratitude, and openness, everything expands. You think more clearly. You notice possibilities. People want to work with you. You show up in conversations, reach out to contacts, take the meeting, make the ask.

This is why your relationship with money is really a mirror of your relationship with yourself. If you doubt your worth, money will feel elusive. If you secretly believe that struggle is the only way to deserve success, your financial life will always be uphill. But when you recognize your inherent value and trust your ability to create, money responds accordingly.

This is why some people with advanced degrees and good financial knowledge still struggle with money, while others with far less education but a strong sense of self-worth generate wealth almost effortlessly. It isn't about what you know; it's about who you are being.

The Four Levels of Consciousness

Consciousness and emotions work together. The decision I made at twenty-one, to live as an agent rather than a victim, wasn't a single moment. It marked the beginning of a progression through deeper levels of awareness.

With each shift in consciousness, emotional regulation becomes easier. Fear loses its grip. What once hijacked you can be observed. Reaction gives way to response. Choice returns.

That moment in the Landmark Forum was my first taste of what I now teach: consciousness shapes everything, including our financial lives. Over the years, I've come to see that we move through four main levels of consciousness. None of us lives permanently in just one state; it's a dance. The key is noticing where you are and learning how to shift upward.

Level 1: Victim Consciousness – *"Money happens to me"*

This is the lowest rung of awareness. Life and money feel as if they are out of your hands. Circumstances dictate everything, and you feel powerless to change them. Financially, it sounds like: "Investing is too complicated. I'll never get ahead. Every time I try, something goes wrong."

Here, fear and resentment dominate. Money decisions tend to be ultra-conservative or paralysed by inaction.

Level 2: Agency / By Me – *"I can make things happen"*

This was my Landmark breakthrough: realising I could set goals, take responsibility, and steer my own life. I wasn't a passenger anymore. In money terms, this is when you start taking control, opening accounts, building savings, and beginning to invest. You stop waiting for someone else to fix things and begin orchestrating your own financial freedom.

The trap here is relying too heavily on external "rules" without yet questioning whether they truly align with your values.

Level 3: Flow / Through Me – *"I live in flow"*

Once you've built agency, something softer emerges. You trust intuition. You notice synchronicities. You loosen your grip on the steering wheel and find that life often supports you when you let it.

Financially, this looks like spotting opportunities almost effortlessly. being in the right conversation at the right time, or feeling guided in your choices. You're willing to take risks because you trust yourself to recover and learn.

I experienced this most vividly when I lost a six-figure sum on a failed property development. It hurt, but I didn't let it define me. Flow meant trusting that new opportunities would arise, and they did.

Level 4: Abundant / As Me – *"I am abundance"*

This is the highest state, though not one that most of us live in daily. Here, there's no separation between you and abundance. Money, purpose, relationships, all feel like expressions of the same whole.

Financially, this is where money becomes a tool for contribution and alignment with values. You might design a portfolio around impact investments, ESG funds, or legacy planning. Giving feels as natural as receiving.

I've seen it embodied by people like Chuck Feeney, the father of my friend Lesley in Chamonix, who gave away over $8 billion during his lifetime, keeping only what he and his wife defined as *"enough."* He called it *"giving while living."* That, to me, is abundance in action: money flowing through you, not just to you.

The Three Ladders: Consciousness, Inner, and Financial

These emotional states and consciousness levels aren't random; they correspond directly to where you are on the ladders of freedom we explored in Chapter 2. Over time, I've come to see that three ladders run parallel in our lives, and they're intimately connected.

> The **Consciousness Ladder** we've just explored
>
> *(Victim → By Me → Through Me → As Me)*
>
> maps directly onto the **Inner Freedom Ladder**:
>
> *Fear / Scarcity → Self-Reliance → Flow → Abundant Spirit.*
>
> These stages also correspond to the **Financial Freedom Ladder**:
>
> *Scarcity → Survival → Security → Growth → Flexibility → Freedom → Legacy Wealth.*

Consciousness Level	Inner Freedom Ladder	Financial Ladder	Emotional GPS
As Me (Abundance)	Abundant Spirit	Legacy / Generational Wealth	Joy, gratitude, contribution
Through Me (Flow)	Flow	Flexibility / Freedom	Trust, curiosity, openness
By Me (Agency)	Self-Reliance	Security / Growth	Determination, focus, confidence
To Me (Victim)	Fear / Scarcity	Scarcity	Fear, resentment, anxiety, desperation

As we discussed in Chapter 2, you cannot climb one ladder without the other, or life becomes lopsided. Consciousness helps to bridge your climb up both ladders, and your emotions help you to see where you are on all of them.

You can't skip rungs. I see this constantly in coaching: someone tries to jump from fear-based scarcity straight to freedom consciousness without building self-reliance. It doesn't stick. You have to walk each rung. Someone operating from victim consciousness, fear-based, reactive, will struggle to create lasting wealth because their emotional frequency keeps pulling them back to scarcity. But as you elevate your inner state, from fear to self-reliance to flow, your outer financial reality shifts too.

It isn't about the mechanics of money. It's about your frequency, who you are *being* as you engage with money.

The Foundation of Fearless Wealth

This isn't about perfection. You'll move between these states; we all do. The goal is simply greater awareness, more choice, and more time spent in the frequencies that attract both wealth and peace in equal measure.

Once you begin to see money as energy, and emotions as the frequency you broadcast, the next step becomes clear: how that energy grows. Growth always involves movement, and movement always involves risk.

For too long, women have been conditioned to play safe: to save diligently, stay within the lines, and avoid climbing too high. The truth is that avoiding risk is often the riskiest thing you can do with your money, and with your life.

When you learn to master your emotions - to experience the full, beautiful array of human emotion and regulate it, something fundamental shifts. You develop an unshakeable sense of security. Not financial security, though that often follows, but inner security. The deep knowing that you can handle any situation. Any market crash. Any unexpected loss. Any moment of uncertainty.

From that security, quiet, grounded confidence emerges.

Confidence is what allows you to take brave action.

Key Takeaways

- **Consciousness is a decision** - Victim or agent? You choose in a moment
- **Emotions are the practice** - Lifelong regulation is where transformation lives
- **Money is energy** - It flows toward or away from you based on your energetic state, not just your actions
- **Emotional mastery creates inner security** - The foundation for confident, brave action
- **The three ladders are connected** - As you climb the consciousness ladder, you simultaneously ascend both inner and financial freedom
- **Your emotional range is power, not weakness** - Volatility is movement, not risk

- **Small shifts create big changes** - You don't need to transform overnight; consistent micro-elevations compound into major results

Practical Actions

1. **Do a money check-in** - Next time you log into your accounts, pause first and notice how you feel. Write down the emotion before you act.
2. **Name your current rung** - Looking at the Wealth Emotional Ladder, where are you most often? Anxiety? Curiosity? Trust?
3. **Shift up one rung** - Choose one current money worry. Ask yourself: *"What's one step I can take to move up just one rung on the emotional ladder?"*
4. **Notice your patterns** - For one week, track: When does money flow easily? When does it feel stuck? What emotional state were you in each time?
5. **Practice the pause** - Before any financial decision, ask: *"Am I making this choice from fear... or from clarity?"* If the answer is fear, wait.

Chapter 4

BECOMING RISK ON

Reclaiming Your Power From Playing It Safe to Building Real Wealth

What if the thing you're most afraid of is actually the bridge to everything you want?

That thing is risk. And to understand why risk is a bridge rather than a barrier, we first need to understand what it actually is.

In the last chapter, we explored a radical idea: money is energy. Not metaphorically, literally. Everything in the universe, including money, vibrates at different frequencies and follows the same immutable laws.

The first law: Energy cannot be created or destroyed, only transformed and transferred. Your wealth isn't limited by what exists, but by how effectively you move energy from one form to another. A stagnant bank account isn't "safe money," it's trapped energy, slowly losing power while the world around it vibrates and grows.

The second law: Energy requires movement to be useful. Water behind a dam does not generate electricity until it flows through turbines. Likewise, money must move to multiply, not recklessly, but consciously and with direction.

The third law: Energy transfers most efficiently between systems vibrating at similar frequencies. This is the resonance principle from

Chapter 3: when two tuning forks vibrate at the same frequency, energy flows between them effortlessly. Your emotional frequency determines what financial opportunities resonate with you.

Risk is how you direct that energy flow.

In physics, a vector describes not just how much energy exists but *where it's going*, both the force and the direction. Risk is your wealth's vector. It's you choosing to move your money from the savings account (safe, static, slowly eroding) into investments (moving, growing, compounding), even when the outcome isn't guaranteed. *Risk is the conscious decision to direct your wealth's energy towards expansion.*

Risk isn't gambling. It's conscious movement.

What feels risky depends entirely on your frequency. From fear or scarcity, everything feels dangerous. From trust or curiosity, the same opportunity feels aligned. The risk hasn't changed; your frequency has.

Two people can look at the same investment: one sees disaster, the other possibility. They're vibrating at different frequencies, so their resonance and results differ.

When you take aligned risk from trust rather than fear, you generate momentum. That momentum attracts more flow, expanding your capacity. The energy moves, multiplies, and returns amplified.

First, it has to move.

Part 1: Reframing Risk - From Danger to Opportunity

I stood in the original dining room of a run-down, century-old building in the heart of Sallanches, France. Dust particles danced in the afternoon light streaming through grimy windows, and I could hear the echo of my footsteps on the bare floorboards. Through those windows, the majestic Mont Blanc chain stretched across the horizon, a view that should have been breathtaking.

All I could think was: *What on earth have I done?*

A few months earlier, over lunch, a new friend had pitched a property development opportunity. He needed capital; I needed direction.

Truth be told, I'd been a bit lost. I'd left the City, moved to Chamonix, had children, all wonderful, but I hadn't yet found what came next. This partnership felt like a door opening. We shook hands.

Now I'd committed a meaningful slice of my wealth to gutting this building and creating fourteen apartments, in the town's most visible spot, with a partner I barely knew, in a country whose building regulations I didn't understand, and in a language I could still only mangle.

I'd always been someone who took risks; I'd jumped out of helicopters to ski down crevasse-strewn mountains, dangled off ropes into couloirs where one mistake meant death. But this felt different. This wasn't adrenaline; I was stepping into a completely unknown world where my ignorance could cost me everything I'd worked for.

As I stood there, dust settling around me and the weight of the decision pressing down, I also felt something else: excitement. Yes, I knew very little about construction. Yes, my French was ropey at best. But I'd done my homework on the numbers. My intuition said this person was solid, trustworthy. And most importantly, I'd backed myself before, and it had worked out. Even when I didn't know all the steps forward, even when the path seemed impossibly complex, I'd found a way through. This was a manageable risk, even if it felt overwhelming at that moment.

That distinction between feeling scared and being reckless is everything.

Risk Isn't Reckless. It's Conscious.

From an early age, most of us were taught the same messages about risk: Be careful. Play it safe. Stay within the lines. Don't climb too high. Don't reach too far.

Safety nets are praised; risk-taking is frowned upon, especially for women.

We're handed money scripts that equate risk with danger:

- Better to save than to invest.
- Stick with what you know.
- If you lose, you'll never recover.

What are we really learning? Safety equals survival. Risk equals recklessness.

But here's the paradox: playing it too safe is itself a risk.

Leaving money parked in 'safe' accounts may feel secure, but inflation quietly erodes its power. Whilst it sits still, opportunities move on without you: compound growth, appreciation, new ventures. The world doesn't wait.

You cannot build wealth without risk. Not reckless, blind, throw-it-all-on-red risk, but conscious, aligned, thoughtful risk. The kind that stretches you, grows you, and rewards you. This is the risk you already take everywhere else in your life. Now we're bringing it to your money.

Fearless investing, in markets and in yourself, means:

- Assessing risk with clarity, not fear. Markets dip, but over time, well-researched risks pay off.
- Trusting your resilience. You've survived 100% of your worst days.
- Recognising that avoiding risk has its own cost: inflation erodes savings, opportunities pass you by, and confidence shrinks.

Risk avoidance is often fear in disguise. And fear loves to dress up as practicality.

Risk as the Price of Admission

Let me offer you a different frame: *risk is the price you pay for growth.*

Think about other areas of life where you've already accepted this trade-off:

Learning to walk: as babies, we fell hard and often, but we kept going. Freedom was worth a few bruises. No baby ever decided, "Walking's too risky. I'll crawl forever."

Getting an education: years of study, loans, delayed income, betting the payoff would come later.

Saying "I love you" first: that moment when you don't know if they'll say it back, the emotional version of putting capital at risk. We do it because a real connection is worth it.

Career moves: stepping up for a project, taking on a promotion, leading a team. There's always a chance of failure, criticism, or stress. But that's how growth happens. Those who rise fastest are usually the ones willing to pay that emotional price.

You've paid those kinds of fees before, just in different currencies. So when it comes to investing, the same principle applies.

Higher returns come with discomfort. You will see your portfolio drop temporarily. You won't always know the outcome. You'll have to be patient when every part of you wants results *now*. And you'll need to trust yourself when others doubt.

These aren't flaws in the system; they're features. They're the price of admission to wealth creation.

Somewhere along the way, many of us lost that bravery with money. We traded curiosity for caution, growth for comfort, possibility for predictability.

That is a terrible exchange rate.

Part 2: Understanding Risk - The Tools & Truth

So if risk isn't the enemy, if it's actually the price of admission to wealth, then what is it really?

What Risk Actually Is (And Isn't)

Remember from Chapter 1: volatility doesn't equal risk. This bears repeating because most people confuse the two. They see their portfolio drop 10% and think, "This is too risky, I need to get out." But they're misreading the signal.

Volatility is just movement. Think of it like the weather: some days are calm, some stormy. Neither is wrong. It's the natural rhythm of how systems behave. Markets breathe, up and down. If they never moved, no one would make money. Volatility is the heartbeat, not the hazard.

Real risk is something different. Risk is the gap between what you expect and what actually happens, and that gap can work both ways. Outcomes can exceed expectations or fall short.

The biggest risk isn't volatility. It's ignorance.

When you don't understand what you're investing in, when you're making decisions from fear or FOMO rather than strategy, that's risk. Avoid investing altogether and let inflation erode your savings? That's risk too.

Not taking a risk is itself the riskiest choice you can make.

Risk Tolerance Isn't Fixed. It's Expandable

Here's where I'll challenge something you've probably heard: "Match your investments to your risk tolerance."

Not wrong, but incomplete.

Traditional advice treats risk tolerance as fixed: take a questionnaire, get scored "conservative" or "aggressive," and invest accordingly for life. The problem? It assumes you can't change, that your current comfort level with financial uncertainty is permanent.

But your risk tolerance isn't who you are. It's where you are right now, with your current knowledge, confidence, and experience around money.

Here's what those questionnaires are really measuring: how confident you *feel* about investing, not your actual capacity for risk.

Consider a woman who scores as "risk-averse" on a financial questionnaire, yet manages a team at work, dates men she meets online, or starts a business from scratch. She's clearly comfortable taking risks, just not when it involves money.

Why? Because of conditioning. Women inherit beliefs that equate financial risk with danger. We've been taught to be cautious with money in ways men haven't.

So what those questionnaires really reveal is your current confidence level, and confidence grows through practice.

Risk tolerance expands through conscious work: education about how markets operate, community support during volatility, tools to manage emotions, and small wins that build belief.

The same person, different frequency.

They shift from fear (everything feels dangerous) to trust (calculated risks feel aligned).

And that's the real secret: financial education doesn't just teach you what to invest in, it builds the confidence to take aligned risk.

Once you understand that, the real question becomes not *how much* risk you can take, but *how* you take it.

Educated Risk vs. Reckless Risk

This chapter isn't an argument for recklessness or speculation. It isn't about throwing everything into high-risk assets or chasing returns without understanding the downside. It's an invitation to pause before accepting "I'm just risk-averse" as a fixed identity, and to question whether what feels like caution is actually fear, avoidance, or a lack of information.

Ask yourself:

- Is this truly who I am, or is it fear I've been taught?
- Have I genuinely educated myself, or am I avoiding learning?
- Am I risk-averse—or information-poor?

There's a profound difference between:

> **Reckless Risk:** investing in things you don't understand, chasing hot tips, making FOMO decisions.
>
> **Educated Risk:** understanding what you're investing in, diversifying strategically, deciding from clarity, not fear, and accepting short-term volatility for long-term growth.

In practice, two women each decide to invest £10,000 in cryptocurrency:

> **Woman A** hears about Bitcoin at a dinner party. Everyone's talking about it. She's afraid of missing out, so she puts all £10,000 into Bitcoin the next day without understanding blockchain, wallet security, or her own exit strategy. When it drops 30%, she panics and sells at a loss. This is reckless risk.
>
> **Woman B** spends three months learning about cryptocurrency: how it works, the technology behind it, the volatility patterns, the tax implications. She allocates £10,000 total, investing regularly over three months into a mix of established cryptocurrencies (pound-cost averaging to smooth out volatility), sets clear parameters for when she'd sell, and accepts that this portion might go to zero. When it drops 30%, she reviews her thesis, decides nothing fundamental has changed, and holds. This is educated risk.

Same asset class. Completely different approach. One is gambling. One is investing. Being risk on doesn't mean being reckless. It means being conscious, educated, and strategic.

How Risk Is Managed: The Skiing Analogy

I love skiing off-piste; it's objectively more dangerous than groomed runs, but that's also what makes it exhilarating. Here's what turns that danger into something manageable:

Training: I learned to ski in all conditions — powder, chopped snow, and breakable crust. Each demands a different skillset and judgment.

Education: I studied snowpack and weather patterns so I can make informed calls about when it's safe to go.

Equipment: I carry an avalanche probe and transceiver — precautions that dramatically improve outcomes if things go wrong.

Community: I never ski off-piste alone. My friends and I check conditions together, keep each other in sight, and know exactly what to do in an emergency.

I don't avoid the risk. I love off-piste skiing too much; the reward is too great. But I've built the *capacity* to take that risk consciously.

Investing follows the same principles:

- Education — understanding markets, asset classes, and your own psychology.
- Diversification — which we'll explore deeply in the next section.
- Tools — investment platforms, index funds, and professional advice.
- Community — learning from others and staying supported through volatility.
- Time horizon — giving your investments space to recover from dips.

Knowledge, tools and community turn risk from danger into adventure.

When Risk Doesn't Work Out: The Six-Figure Lesson

Even with education, tools, and preparation, some risks don't work out. And that's okay.

A few years ago, I invested a six-figure sum in a property development with someone I trusted. I'd done my research. My intuition said this person was solid. Everything looked good. Then 2020 happened. The project never recovered. I lost the entire investment.

It hurt. Of course it did.

What surprised me was what followed. I realised I could survive it. Financial losses feel catastrophic in the moment, yet most are recoverable. It didn't destroy me.

The experience also clarified something essential about my own parameters. I need to be directly involved in my investments. Not because others are untrustworthy, but because agency matters to me.

That loss didn't stop me from taking risks. It refined how I take them. I didn't retreat into fear. I adjusted my approach and kept going.

This is how growth actually works. Mistakes become data. Failures become tuition. Each one sharpens judgment and builds resilience.

You don't need a perfect track record. You need resilience, a willingness to learn, and the courage to continue.

Part 3: Taking Risk – Being Risk On in Investing & Life

Risk has already been reframed. It's no longer the enemy. You understand the difference between volatility and real risk, between gambling and educated investment. You know that risk capacity isn't fixed; it can grow.

The next step is simple, and not always easy: becoming more risk on. This isn't about recklessness. It's about expanding your capacity to take aligned, conscious action with your money, and with your life.

Risk aversion rarely stays confined to investing. It tends to shape how you live.

What Risk On Really Means

In financial markets, *risk on* describes the moment investors lean in, allocating capital to opportunities with higher potential returns, and accepting short-term volatility as the price of long-term growth.

Beyond markets, risk on is a mindset. It's a way of being. Choosing growth over comfort. Trusting yourself enough to try something new. Accepting that uncertainty is part of the journey, and recognising that the cost of playing small is often higher than the cost of stretching.

Being risk on doesn't mean saying yes to everything. It means saying yes to what's right - the opportunities that genuinely align with who you are, even when they make your stomach flip a little.

How to Start: The Practical Path to Risk On

If you've spent years playing it safe, becoming risk on can feel daunting. So let's break it down into manageable steps.

1. Start Small and Build Confidence

You don't need to overhaul your finances overnight. Start with a risk you can afford, emotionally and financially.

Open an investment account. Move a small amount into a low-cost index fund. Then watch what happens, not just to the money, but to you. Notice the emotions that surface. Every time you take a risk and come out stronger, your capacity expands.

2. Educate Yourself Relentlessly

The more you understand, the less fear controls you. Learn how markets work, how compounding quietly builds wealth, how diversification protects it.

Knowledge closes the gap between expectation and reality. It shifts your frequency from *I don't know what I'm doing* to *I can handle this.*

You don't need to know everything before you start. You just need enough to take the next step. Progress beats perfection, every time.

Every expert investor started by opening their first account. Every confident risk-taker started with one small step.

3. Find Your Community

One of the most powerful ways to become risk on is to be around people who already are. Find women who invest. Join an investment club or an online community. Work with an adviser who empowers rather than patronises.

When everyone around you plays it safe, that becomes normal. When you're surrounded by women taking conscious aligned risks, building wealth, growing together, that becomes normal too.

You were never meant to do this alone.

4. Manage Your Emotions (Not Eliminate Them)

Your emotions are your GPS. Fear isn't the enemy, unmanaged fear is. When it shows up, pause and ask yourself:

- Is this fear based on real risk or old conditioning?
- What do I need to learn to feel more confident?
- Am I in a low-frequency state that's amplifying the fear?

You don't have to wait until fear disappears to take action. Feel it. Name it. Then take one small step anyway.

Fearless investing isn't about feeling no fear. It's about refusing to let fear make all the decisions.

5. Accept Volatility as Normal

Markets rise and fall. Your portfolio will fluctuate. That's not failure, it's how it works.

The investors who build wealth aren't the ones who never lose money. They're the ones who don't panic when it happens.

Volatility is movement, not danger. Stay the course. Trust your strategy. Keep your frequency high.

Risk On in Life: Beyond Money

Once you start practising risk on with money, it spills into everything else.

It means:

- Taking the career leap you've been contemplating.
- Leaving relationships that no longer serve you.
- Starting the business you've been dreaming about.
- Speaking up when you've been silent.
- Writing the book.

This book is my risk right now. I'm sharing beliefs that challenge conventional financial wisdom, blending finance with spirituality, knowing that some will disagree or dismiss it.

That can feel terrifying. There are days I wonder what I'm doing, when the possibility of failure feels very real and I imagine this being torn apart.

And still, even in the fear, I feel alive and on purpose. That's what aligned risk feels like. Not the certainty of success, but energy in motion.

Being risk on in life doesn't mean the absence of fear. It means choosing growth and authenticity over comfort and approval.

The same is true for you. The moment you begin to question what you've been taught about money, safety, and success, you're already taking a risk. You're opening yourself to transformation.

We're in this together.

Part 4: Courage Compounds - The Returns Beyond Money

Here's the final piece I want to share with you: when you take aligned risk, the returns multiply beyond money.

Think back to my French property story at the beginning of this chapter. Yes, it worked out well financially. But the real return wasn't the profit. It was the confidence I gained from backing myself, the expansion of what I believed was possible, and the proof that I could navigate unfamiliar territory and come out stronger.

That's what happens when you take aligned risks. The financial returns matter, of course they do. But the real wealth shows up in how you feel about yourself, what you believe is possible, and how you move through the world.

When you take aligned risk, you generate momentum. That momentum attracts more opportunities. The energy moves, multiplies, and flows back to you amplified, not just in money, but in confidence, connections, freedom, and joy.

This is how courage compounds. Each brave action builds your capacity for the next one. Each risk you take and survive expands what you believe possible. The returns multiply in ways no spreadsheet can capture.

This is why risk isn't the enemy. Risk is the bridge. It's how you get from where you are to where you want to be. It's how trapped energy becomes flowing abundance.

The Bridge Awaits

Remember standing in that dusty French room, wondering what on earth I'd done? I had a choice: retreat to safety, or lean into the discomfort and see what was possible.

I chose to lean in. The returns (financial, emotional, and spiritual) exceeded anything I could have imagined.

You're already braver than you think. You've taken risks before: learned to walk, got educated, built a career, maybe raised children, navigated heartbreak, and survived challenges you never imagined you could.

You already know how to take risks. You've just been told not to apply it to money.

Now you know differently. You understand that risk is energy with direction, that your frequency shapes what feels risky, that your risk tolerance can expand, that brave action fuels authentic living, and that the returns go far beyond your portfolio.

This is what it means to become risk on: not reckless, but conscious. Not playing it safe whilst opportunities pass you by, but reclaiming your power to build real wealth.

Your moment awaits. You don't need certainty to step into it. Risk is the lever. Authenticity is the engine. Your courage is what moves it all forward.

Take the first step, one conscious, aligned risk at a time.

Key Takeaways

- **Risk is strategic action** - not reckless gambling
- **Your frequency determines risk perception** - shift your state, shift what feels risky
- **Fear is information** - not disqualification
- **Risk tolerance expands** - through education, community, and practice; it's not fixed
- **Volatility is movement, not risk** - ignorance is the real danger
- **Being "risk on" in investing teaches life** - it transforms how you show up everywhere
- **Brave action compounds** - returns multiply far beyond money

Practical Actions:

1. **Name one risk you've been avoiding** - Write down one opportunity you've put off because it feels risky, whether financial, professional, or personal. Note what's holding you back.
2. **Start small** - Open an investment account and invest a comfortable amount in a low-cost index fund. Watch your emotions, not just the returns.

3. **Educate relentlessly** - Read one investing book, listen to one podcast episode, or take one course this month. Knowledge shifts frequency.
4. **Find your community** - Join an investment club, follow women investors online, or find one friend to share your wealth-building journey with.
5. **Practice the pause** - Before any investment decision, ask: "Am I deciding from fear or clarity?" If fear, wait.
6. **Accept volatility** - When markets dip, remind yourself: "Volatility is movement, not risk. I'm in this for the long term."
7. **Track your growth** - Keep a journal of your "risk on" moments, financial and otherwise. Celebrate every time you choose growth over comfort.

Chapter 5

LIVING YOUR ENERGETIC ALPHA

The Return on Living Authentically

I want to begin with a confession and an epiphany.

For months, I avoided writing this book. I made spreadsheets about the structure instead of writing words. I created colour-coded outlines, dazzling flowcharts, and a dozen "final" versions of the table of contents. My friends teased me about my Olympic-level avoidance tactics. I convinced myself that if I planned it perfectly enough, I could skip the discomfort of actually writing it.

However, this morning, something shifted. I realised what was really happening: when you're in deep alignment with who you are, terrifying opportunities will find you. This book found me. And the terror I felt wasn't a warning, it was confirmation. The spreadsheets were safe; sharing myself wasn't. Writing this book, sharing my stories and beliefs, required me to live what I'm about to teach you.

It required authenticity.

What I've learned: authenticity isn't comfortable. When you're truly aligned, you don't feel calm and collected; you feel stretched, exposed, alive. The moment I stopped resisting and leaned into the discomfort, everything changed. The words started flowing. The book started writing itself.

That's Energetic Alpha in action, the compound return on choosing authenticity despite fear. Markets mean-revert. Authenticity doesn't. Authenticity always stretches before it liberates.

This chapter isn't just another step in your financial education. It's the capstone, the essential foundation for building True Wealth. The reality most finance books won't tell you is this: you can have all the money in the world and still feel bankrupt. And you can have deep inner peace yet remain stuck, unable to fully share your gifts or create the impact you're meant to make.

True Wealth requires both. And you cannot build it without authenticity.

From Market Alpha to Energetic Alpha

I spent years chasing market alpha, the holy grail of fund management. Alpha is the excess return you generate above a benchmark. If the FTSE rises 5% and your portfolio delivers 7%, that extra 2% is your alpha. It's what separates good fund managers from average ones. It's what I was paid to produce.

My job was to outperform. Month after month, I'd check my numbers, compare myself to the index, and feel the pressure mounting. When I beat the benchmark, I felt relief, not joy, just temporary relief. When I lagged, I felt terrible. The irony is that chasing short-term alpha often meant taking fewer risks, playing it safe to protect my track record rather than backing my conviction.

The brutal reality about market alpha is that it's a zero-sum game. If one fund manager wins, another loses. Over the long term, alpha tends to revert. Very few managers sustain outperformance indefinitely. It's scarce, contested, and temporary.

There's another kind of alpha, one that doesn't follow those rules.

Energetic Alpha is your personal outperformance. The measurable uplift in freedom, flow, finance, and fulfilment that accrues as your life becomes more authentic. It is one expression of your sovereign power, the natural authority that emerges when you honour your whole self: your masculine drive and your feminine wisdom, your capacity for focused action and receptive awareness, your ability to achieve and to simply be. In a world built almost entirely on masculine structures and metrics, reclaiming the feminine as equally valuable is revolutionary. That integration is where true power lives.

Energetic Alpha is not about outperforming others; it's about outperforming yourself. Are you living according to your deepest values? Are you showing up as your truest self? Are you expanding your capacity for courage, meaningful relationships, and vitality?

Market alpha is temporary. Energetic Alpha compounds forever.

It's abundant, not scarce. When you grow in authenticity, everyone around you benefits. Your courage gives others permission. Your light creates warmth. Your growth magnifies others' growth. That's why the bravest benchmark you can beat is yourself.

Authenticity is the engine. As we explored in the last chapter, risk is the lever. Without authenticity, Energetic Alpha doesn't exist. You're just moving through life on someone else's scoreboard, optimising for metrics that don't matter, climbing ladders leaning against the wrong walls.

What follows is how that outperformance actually comes into being, first by balancing two kinds of wealth, then by embodying authenticity so it shows up in every choice.

Inner and Outer Wealth: The Two Circles

We've been building toward this moment since Chapter 1, where I told you that true wealth is both material and spiritual, money and meaning together.

In Chapter 2, we named the two ladders of freedom: the Financial Freedom Ladder (Outer Wealth) and the Spiritual Freedom Ladder (Inner Wealth). We saw that climbing only one leaf leaves you lopsided. The high-powered CEO on rung 6 financially but rung 2 spiritually, exhausted, disconnected, living for approval. The spiritually abundant artist is on rung 7 but financially dependent, unable to fully share their gifts.

In Chapter 3, we understood that consciousness creates cash flow. We mapped the Consciousness Ladder (Victim → By Me → Through Me → As Me) and saw how it corresponds to both the Spiritual Freedom Ladder and the Financial Freedom Ladder. You cannot climb one without the other, or life becomes unbalanced.

In Chapter 4, we learned that risk is the lever for growth, conscious risk, aligned with who you are.

Now we bring it all together.

True Wealth is where Inner Wealth and Outer Wealth intersect.

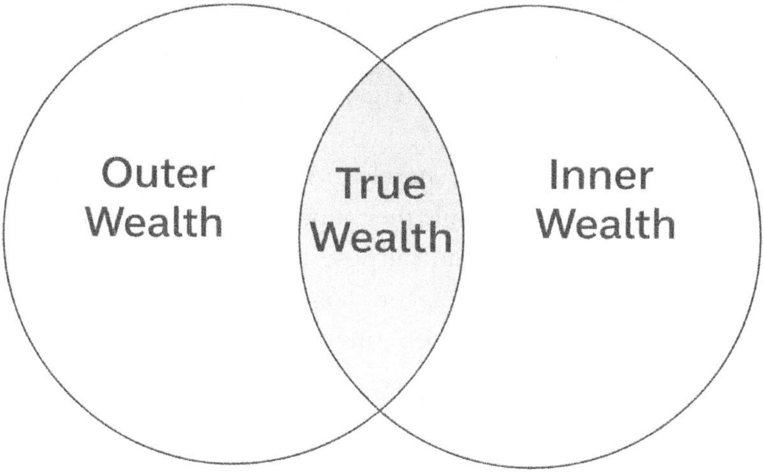

Where True Freedom Lives

Before we go any further, let's name what each circle represents:

- **Outer Wealth (Material Wealth):** Your tangible assets, money, investments, property, business, and income streams. These are the financial structures that create stability, security, and choice.
- **Inner Wealth (Spiritual Wealth):** Your intangible assets, awareness, authenticity, vitality, purpose, peace, resilience. This is the energetic foundation that sustains everything else.

Where those two circles overlap lies True Wealth, wealth that feels as good as it looks. It's sustainable, meaningful, and aligned with who you are.

What most financial education misses is that we've been taught to build Outer Wealth using almost exclusively masculine principles: accumulation, competition, individual achievement, linear growth. Even our language reveals it: "aggressive" investment strategies, "beating" the market, "conquering" fear. But Inner Wealth operates on different principles. It grows through receptivity, not force. Through connection, not competition. Through cycles and rhythms, not linear progress. Through being, not just doing. When you integrate both circles, you're not just balancing your portfolio. You're embodying both energies and that's where sustainable wealth lives.

Most people live almost entirely in one circle or the other. They maximise material wealth while their inner world quietly fractures. Or they cultivate deep peace and purpose but remain financially stuck, unable to turn their gifts into security or impact.

This chapter is about the circle most people skip, Inner Wealth.

It's the energetic capital that fuels every decision, every investment, every act of courage. Without it, even the smartest spreadsheet can't fix the leak.

Inner Wealth is the fuel. Energetic Alpha is the return. When your inner world strengthens, your outer world compounds.

How Authenticity Becomes Energetic Alpha

Energetic Alpha isn't theory; it's what happens when authenticity becomes embodied, when your inner alignment starts shaping every choice you make.

It's the moment awareness stops being an idea and becomes a way of living.

For years, I lived out of alignment. I stayed in jobs, relationships, and friendships that no longer reflected who I was. I performed rather than showed up. The cost was enormous, not just in energy and peace, but in the opportunities I couldn't see because I was too busy maintaining the façade.

Eventually, I walked away. I left the City career. I left the marriage. I left the beautifully decorated cage. At the time, the pain was sharp. I gave up prestige, financial certainty, and the approval of people whose opinions I'd been chasing for years.

But what I gained was infinitely greater: myself. Congruence. The freedom to live aligned with who I really am. And ultimately, that choice led to my greatest gifts, my children, my coaching work, and this book.

That's the truth of risk aligned with authenticity: it doesn't drain you, it compounds your energetic wealth. The returns show up not just in one area of life, but across all of them. This is how your Energetic Alpha grows.

To sustain that growth, you need a way to tend your Inner Wealth, to see where energy flows and where it leaks. That's what the **Wheel of Authenticity** is for: your framework for building Inner Wealth, the energetic portfolio that powers every decision, relationship, and investment.

The Wheel of Authenticity: Your Inner Wealth Framework

Inner Wealth can't be built through theory alone; it's lived through awareness and action. The Wheel of Authenticity helps you see both the energy that fuels you and the actions that express it.

It maps the core dimensions of authentic living, like a financial portfolio maps assets and risk.

The Wheel of Authenticity

The Wheel has eight spokes, and you'll notice something about them: they honour both masculine and feminine ways of knowing and being.

- Values-Driven and Clarity of Purpose give you direction: yang, outward, purposeful.
- Self-Awareness and Inner Peace ground you in receptivity: yin, inward, observant.
- Brave Action and Self-Congruence are expressions: the masculine energy of doing.
- Real Relationships and Energy & Vitality are foundations: the feminine energy of being.

This isn't accidental. True power, sovereign power, requires both. The integration is the breakthrough.

Authenticity isn't linear; it's rhythmic. Each spoke of the Wheel moves between being and doing, between awareness and action, reflection and expression. You might begin in stillness, reconnecting with your values and awareness, then move outward into purpose, brave action, and relationship. That movement then brings you home again, to congruence, vitality, and peace.

It's the same rhythm that runs through life itself: inhale and exhale, give and receive, masculine and feminine, doing and being. These qualities aren't opposites; they're partners in growth. When you honour both, when your inner alignment fuels outer action, and your outer action deepens inner alignment, you create a living circuit of authenticity. That's where Energetic Alpha compounds.

Although the Wheel has an order, it isn't rigid. You'll circle through these spokes many times as life expands and contracts. Some seasons call for more courage, others for more peace. The sequence I share reflects how most of us grow, yet it remains cyclical, fluid, and deeply human. You don't tick these off; you cycle through them, each turn deepening your alignment.

1. **Values-Driven**

   Living by what truly matters to you. Your internal compass keeps decisions clear even under pressure. When your choices reflect your values, you feel grounded and self-assured. Misalignment shows up as frustration, anxiety, or a sense that something is "off."

   We'll explore this in depth in the Alignment section. Values are the cornerstone of both Inner and Outer Wealth.

2. **Self-Awareness**

   The reflective capacity to see yourself clearly, your thoughts, emotions, motives, and impact. Awareness is the hinge that keeps the Wheel aligned. Without it, you're operating on autopilot, reacting rather than responding.

   Emotional regulation, a core part of Self-Awareness, gets its own deep dive later in the book, in the Money Mastery chapter in the Activation section, as your financial portfolio will always reflect your emotional portfolio.

3. **Clarity of Purpose**

   Knowing your why for this part of your life. Purpose gives money and action meaning. It turns movement into momentum. Without a clear why, wealth is just accumulation. With purpose, money becomes fuel for your mission.

4. **Brave Action**

   Courage in motion, taking values-aligned risks, setting boundaries, speaking truth. As we explored in Chapter 4, risk is the lever for growth. But risk without authenticity is recklessness. Brave Action happens when you take conscious risks rooted in who you are.

5. **Self-Congruence**

   Walking your talk. Integrity in action. Accountability for your choices. Do your actions match your words? Do you feel whole, not divided? This is where moral responsibility lives: owning your mistakes, keeping promises, and being the same person privately and publicly.

6. **Real Relationships**

   Depth over performance. Relationships built on honesty, empathy, and mutual respect. Authenticity thrives in connections that see and support the real you. When relationships are shallow or transactional, energy leaks.

7. **Energy & Vitality**

   The physical and emotional aliveness that arises when you stop leaking energy through misalignment. Alignment is somatic: jaw unclenches, breath deepens, sleep returns. Energy is the currency of authentic living. Without it, alignment collapses.

8. **Inner Peace**

   Calm acceptance of what is. The shift from blame to responsibility, where consciousness replaces the need for control. This is existential responsibility: accepting that you are the author of your life, no longer the victim of circumstance.

I know this might feel abstract, eight spokes, compounding returns. Let me make this real.

You often recognise authenticity first by its absence. Just as with values, it's often what drains you, frustrates you, or makes you quietly shrink that shows you where alignment is missing.

You're in a meeting and someone suggests something that goes against your gut. You feel it, the tightening in your chest, the quiet voice that says this isn't right, but you silence yourself because you don't want to make things awkward. Later, you replay that moment again and again, wishing you'd spoken up. That's the cost of self-censorship over truth.

Or, you know deep down your job no longer fits. Every Sunday night, your stomach knots, but you talk yourself out of changing direction because leaving feels too risky. You tell yourself you should be grateful, but your body knows the truth long before your mind admits it.

Maybe it's the friendship that's slowly turned toxic, the one that leaves you depleted instead of uplifted. You show up out of habit, perform instead of being seen, and leave a little smaller each time.

Perhaps it's subtler: the project you'd love to start but can't seem to make time for. The "yes" that should have been a "no." The promise you keep to others but break to yourself.

These moments aren't failures; they're feedback. They're invitations to realign, to choose honesty over habit, courage over comfort.

Your intuition, your energy, even your physical sensations are often the first to signal that something's off. The Wheel simply gives you a way to understand what those signals are trying to show you.

For me, it was finally choosing to write this book after months of avoidance. That was Brave Action, feeling the fear and doing it anyway.

It was walking away from a relationship when I knew staying would keep me small. That was Self-Congruence, choosing wholeness over pleasing.

It was setting boundaries with friendships that cost more energy than they gave. That was Real Relationships, depth over habit.

Each authentic choice creates space for the next one. That's how Energetic Alpha compounds, not in giant leaps, but in small, courageous adjustments that ripple outward.

The Four F-Words of Energetic Alpha

When your Wheel of Authenticity is turning, four unmistakable outcomes appear:

1. **Freedom** — Life expands rather than contracts around you. Freedom is choice, the ability to spend your time, energy, and resources according to your values.
2. **Flow** — Effortless momentum. Opportunities appear as if by design. Aligned, the uphill push becomes moving with the current.
3. **Finance** — The tangible stability and growth that follow from inner coherence. When your inner state is aligned, your financial decisions improve: you invest from clarity, take conscious risks, and build wealth that reflects your values.
4. **Fulfilment** — Purpose realised. Contribution aligned with joy. The deep satisfaction that comes not from achievement, but from integrity with who you are.

Freedom, Flow, Finance, Fulfilment. They are the outer evidence of Inner Wealth, and the inner signature of Outer Wealth done well. This is Energetic Alpha made visible.

Measuring Your Energetic Alpha

Frameworks are only useful if they help you move. Let's turn this from insight into something tangible that you can track and measure.

Don't aim for perfection; aim for honesty. This is a conversation with yourself.

Score yourself honestly on each of the eight spokes, from 0 to 10:

- 0 = completely out of alignment, neglected
- 10 = fully embodied, deeply aligned

Don't overthink it. Trust your instincts. There are no right or wrong answers. This is about where you feel you are today, not where you think you "should" be.

Examples:

1. **Values-Driven** — Do my daily choices match what I say I stand for?

   Score by: % of time I act in line with my values.

2. **Self-Awareness** — Do I see my patterns, emotions, and impact clearly?

   Score by: how often I pause to reflect rather than react.

3. **Clarity of Purpose** — Do I have clarity on where I'm headed and why?

   Score by: ability to articulate my "why" + how often it guides decisions.

4. **Brave Action** — Am I taking courageous, aligned steps despite fear?

   Score by: recent bold actions taken vs avoided.

5. **Self-Congruence** — Is my outer life consistent with my inner truth?

   Score by: how much mask-wearing vs true expression I notice.

6. **Real Relationships** — Am I building authentic connections?

   Score by: depth and quality of relationships, contribution felt.

7. **Energy & Vitality** — Do my choices fuel me or drain me?

   Score by: energy levels, health, rest, vitality practices.

8. **Inner Peace** — Can I rest easy with my choices, or am I restless and unsettled?

   Score by: ability to sleep at night / felt sense of calm.

Once you've scored all eight spokes, add your total.

Maximum total = 80 (8 spokes × 10).

Calculate your Energetic Alpha score: (Total ÷ 80) × 100 = your % alignment.

Example: Total = 48 → (48 ÷ 80) × 100 = 60% Energetic Alpha score.

Understanding Your Score

This isn't about judgement; it's about curiosity. You can't improve what you don't observe.

- 0–40% → A strong opportunity to realign.
- 40–60% → Partial alignment; some areas strong, others need attention.
- 60–80% → Solid authenticity; you're living much of your life in alignment.
- 80–100% → Deep congruence; authenticity is embodied across most domains.

Your aim isn't a perfect number; it's a rising trend. Revisit this every few months. Even small shifts make a difference. Awareness alone can move the needle, and consistent reflection compounds over time.

This is your personal performance metric, the benchmark that money alone can't capture.

The Real Returns of Living Authentically

Authentic living doesn't mean life stops throwing curveballs. Businesses falter. Relationships end. Health and financial challenges arise. The storms still come, but you meet them differently.

Not because life is easier, but because authenticity anchors you. Resilience grows. Clarity sharpens. Energy replenishes. The returns are emotional, spiritual, and deeply practical. They ripple outward into wiser choices, stronger connections, and better financial decisions, because you're investing from alignment, not fear.

That is the compounding power of Energetic Alpha: the return on being fully yourself.

What I've personally discovered is when you give yourself permission to lead from wholeness rather than just achievement, when you honour both your drive and your stillness, your doing and your being, you create a permission field around you. Other women see you being still and powerful, vulnerable and authoritative. They realise they don't have to perform to matter. Men see it too, that there's another way to be successful, to be worthy. Your integration gives everyone permission to reclaim their wholeness.

This is the handshake between Inner and Outer Wealth, your energetic and financial portfolios moving in harmony. Know who you are, and your investing follows: fewer fads, less fear, more alignment. That's what makes you a fearless investor.

The Journey Begins Here

Authenticity is the capstone for True Wealth, the foundation of Inner Wealth that makes Outer Wealth sustainable and meaningful.

Knowing this intellectually isn't enough. To actually live it, to walk this journey toward True Wealth, you need two things:

First, you need the right mindset, because how you think shapes who you are being and what you're doing. If you believe "this isn't possible for me," authenticity and wealth stay theoretical.

Second, you need to know where you are right now, your starting point. You can't navigate a journey without knowing where you're standing. We'll map that clearly so you can see the path forward.

Once you've unlocked your mindset and assessed your current reality, we move into Alignment, clarifying your values, creating your vision, and building the financial knowledge that turns awareness into strategy. From there, we activate through the Wheel of Wealth, building Material Wealth with intention and integrity.

This is a journey toward financial freedom, toward deeper authenticity, toward True Wealth. Every journey begins with clarity: what you think, and where you stand.

The greatest alpha you'll ever generate isn't in basis points.

It's in the distance between who you were… and who you've become.

Key Takeaways

- **Market alpha is temporary** - Energetic Alpha compounds forever
- **True Wealth integrates both** - Inner and Outer Wealth require honouring masculine energy (direction, action, building) and feminine energy (receptivity, cycles, connection); that integration is sovereign power
- **Authenticity is the engine, risk is the lever** - congruence fuels growth, and aligned risks compound
- **The Wheel of Authenticity is your inner portfolio** - measure and build the energetic assets that power everything else
- **The Four F-Words are evidence** - Freedom, Flow, Fulfilment, Finance show your Wheel is turning smoothly
- **Friction signals misalignment** - you often recognise authenticity by its absence
- **Track over time** - the delta shows your Energetic Alpha improving and compounding

Practical Actions

1. **Score Your Wheel of Authenticity** - Rate each spoke from 0–10 honestly. Calculate your Energetic Alpha score.
2. **Spot your lowest score** - That's your greatest opportunity. What one small step could you take this month to move it up by just one point?
3. **Notice the friction** - Where in your life do you feel the tightness, the drain, the misalignment? That's your inner compass showing you where to focus.
4. **Choose one authentic risk** - Pick one small area where you've been playing safe against your values. Take a step toward courage this week.
5. **Revisit in three months** - Track how your Wheel shifts. That's how you see your Energetic Alpha compounding.

Chapter 6

BREAKING THE MONEY MINDSET TRAP

If You Want Different Results, Think Differently

In the last chapter, we explored how authentic living compounds your returns - your Energetic Alpha. What I didn't tell you though is that I couldn't access that authentic state until I debugged my mental operating system. Authenticity without the right mindset is like having a Ferrari with faulty code; beautiful on the outside, going nowhere.

You can have the perfect investment strategy, the clearest financial goals, and the most detailed wealth-building plan, but if your unconscious beliefs about money are working against you, you'll sabotage your success every time.

After years of experiencing this in my own life and witnessing it in my clients, I know that our mindset is the most powerful tool that we have to create change and the life we want. Our thoughts drive our emotions, and our emotional state shapes how we take risks, attract opportunities, and relate to money.

This isn't separate from what we explored in earlier chapters about money as energy, risk, and emotions. It's all one system:

- **Scarcity mindset** → Low frequency (fear, lack) → Risk aversion *or* reckless gambling → Poor investment decisions → Reinforces scarcity

- **Abundance mindset** → High frequency (trust, possibility) → Calibrated risk-taking → Aligned investment decisions → Reinforces abundance

Think of your mindset as source code or the operating system running in the background of your financial life. Change the code, and everything downstream changes naturally: your emotions shift, your frequency rises, money flows differently, and risk looks completely different.

This chapter is about debugging your money operating system, seeing the faulty code clearly, rewriting it consciously, and installing practices that keep the new code running.

One Line of Code Can Crash the Entire System

I left the City with money in the bank and mountains of experience. I'd managed significant funds and understood markets.

However, I carried one invisible wound: being passed over for a promotion I'd earned. That rejection created a fault in my mental operating system.

Where I'd once thought, "I can do this, I'm good at this", I now carried a different script: "I'm not good enough. I don't know how anymore".

The impact of that tiny change in mindset was huge.

When I moved to Chamonix, choosing powder days and mountain freedom over the London commute, a friend suggested buying property there in the early 2000s. I said no: "I don't know how to do that." I turned down the opportunity because I didn't trust myself.

Instead, I grabbed at things, buying properties without a strategy, from panic, not a plan. A second home in the South of France while heavily pregnant. A studio in St Gervais. A rental in Turkey. Then the US. Each was bought with big dreams, poorly researched.

I outsourced decisions to people I shouldn't have trusted. I was clutching at straws, making desperate moves rather than conscious choices.

The irony is that I'd managed hundreds of millions for others but couldn't trust myself with my own money.

Here I was, making terrible decisions because fear had taken the wheel instead of consciousness.

The Honest Framing

Before we go further, I want to take a moment to highlight something. Throughout this book, you're going to hear stories about investments that went wrong, money lost to FOMO, bad property deals, dodgy developers, poor timing. All told, I've probably lost close to £400,000 across various investments.

You might wonder: should I be listening to someone who's lost that much?

The reality is that those losses weren't random bad luck. Every single one can be traced back to the mindset I had at the time: scarcity thinking, fear-based decisions, ego spending, and desperation investing.

I've since built a robust property portfolio and invested in companies that position me well for the future. However, the real wealth isn't in those assets; it's in the transformed mindset that now guides my decisions.

So when you read those loss stories in the chapters ahead, see them for what they are: lessons that revealed faulty code in my money mindset. Each one led me to the tools I now use daily and share with you in this book.

That transformation, from fear-based decisions to conscious, aligned investing, is what this chapter is about, because once you change the operating system, everything else follows.

The Trap: How Faulty Code Manifests

When faulty code is running, it shows up in three predictable patterns. I've lived all three.

Pattern 1: Ego Spending (Retail Therapy)

When I was working in the City with money flowing in, I spent freely, Gucci handbags, designer clothes, jewellery, the works. It was ego spending. A way of proving (to myself and others) that I was successful. The handbags sat in my wardrobe for years, completely impractical for life in the Alps, but they symbolised the emptiness I was trying to fill.

It gives a quick hit, but fades fast, often leaving guilt in its place.

The danger is that what feels like therapy in the moment quietly undermines your longer-term financial freedom.

Pattern 2: Fear Paralysis

For others, the trap looks like the opposite: they freeze. Not opening bank statements. Not reviewing pensions. (I avoided this for years.) Avoiding any conversation about investments because "I don't understand" or "it's too risky."

This isn't wisdom, it's fear masquerading as caution. It's the faulty code saying, "I can't handle this," or "I'm not capable."

Pattern 3: Desperation Investing

This is where I landed after the City. Not handbags this time, desperation investing. Jumping on property deals without due diligence, fuelled by FOMO and the same old scarcity conditioning.

Different behaviour, same root cause:

- Ego says: spend to prove your worth
- Fear says: grab the opportunity or you'll miss out
- Scarcity says: you'll never have enough, so cling or gamble

That's the trap. It robs you of peace, drains your energy, and derails your wealth.

Until you recognise it for what it is, a pattern, a faulty operating system, you can break free.

Where Does the Faulty Code Come From?

My childhood gave me good training in scarcity thinking.

My parents were meticulous about writing down everything they spent and were always saying that money doesn't grow on trees. My mother would scour sales for yellow-label "bargains" at Waitrose, even if we didn't like the random items she bought. Frugality was the religion of my childhood.

And as children do, I rebelled.

On a rain-soaked US camping trip, ten-year-old me refused to stay at a drenched campsite. When I cheekily asked for a motel with a pool, my mum laughed: "Isabel, you have expensive tastes. You'll have to marry a millionaire." Without missing a beat, I replied: 'I don't need to marry a millionaire. I'm going to be one.

Even then, I knew I wanted something different, to create abundance for myself.

Those early scripts run deep, though. I did go on to earn a six-figure salary in the City; however, I wasn't overcoming the scarcity mindset. I was *compensating* for it. Earning to prove I'd made it. Spending to prove that money wasn't scarce. The original code was still running underneath; I'd just layered new behaviour on top.

That's what made the rejection so devastating. It cracked through my compensating behaviour and exposed the original scarcity thinking that had been running underneath all along. Suddenly, childhood scarcity plus adult rejection plus "I'm a fraud" all merged into one: "I'm not good enough, I don't know how, and there will never be enough."

Mindsets aren't simple. They're layered. Written in childhood, compensated for in adulthood, then reinforced or rewritten in the flash of a single moment. You can be running multiple layers of code, some lift you and others quietly sabotage you.

Looking back, I can see exactly how these early experiences helped create the pattern that would later trap me:

- **Scarcity conditioning** → the belief that money is always on the verge of running out
- **Ego spending** → using purchases to soothe, signal worth, or fill a space inside

- **Shame and guilt** → the story that wanting wealth makes you greedy, unfeminine, or "not a good person"

None of us is at fault for this.These beliefs are inherited, formed in childhood, mirrored by society.

How the faulty code got there matters less than learning to recognise it and and consciously rewrite it.

The Mechanism: How Source Code Creates Results

Here's how the system actually works, and why changing your mindset changes everything:

THOUGHT (unconscious operating system running in the background)

↓

EMOTION (the frequency/energy that gets emitted, this is what broadcasts into the field)

↓

ATTRACTION (that frequency pulls in matching experiences, money, people, opportunities)

↓

ACTION (what you do from that emotional state)

↓

RESULT (the wealth outcome)

↓

THOUGHT (reinforces thinking)

This is a continuous feedback loop. Your thoughts run in the background, mostly unconscious. Your emotions broadcast externally; that's your frequency. When you're thinking "I'm going to lose everything," even unconsciously, you feel anxious and from that state you're far more likely to avoid opportunities, second-guess decisions, or attract people who reinforce that fear.

Your emotions tell you, in real time, what your unconscious thoughts are broadcasting. The power is in noticing the emotion, tracing it back to the thought, and then choosing a different one.

Let me show you how this plays out in real investing situations.

How Your Inner Operating System Shapes Financial Outcomes

Scenario	Old Operating System	New Operating System
Market drop	**Thought:** "I'm losing everything." **Emotion:** Panic, fear **Action:** Sell at the bottom **Result:** Loss locked in	**Thought:** "Markets fluctuate, this is temporary." **Emotion:** Calm, curious **Action:** Hold or buy the dip **Result:** Wealth protected or increased
Investment opportunity	**Thought:** "I'll miss out." **Emotion:** Anxiety, urgency **Action:** Jump in without research **Result:** Poor investment, money lost	**Thought:** "I make aligned decisions." **Emotion:** Grounded, clear **Action:** Research thoroughly **Result:** Pass or invest wisely

Negotiation Opportunity

Job offer or client pricing discussion

> **Old OS:** "I should be grateful for what I'm offered" → Anxiety, unworthiness → Accept first offer → Underearning reinforced
>
> **New OS:** "I know my value" → Confident calm → Counter-offer professionally → Fair compensation, self-respect grows
>
> Same stimulus. Different source code. Different frequency. Different wealth outcome.

This is why mindset is the foundation. Change the source code, and everything else changes naturally.

The Beautiful Truth: One Moment Can Rewrite It

One faulty belief, "I'm not good enough, I don't know how", can sabotage your entire financial life. However, like a programme developer, you can rewrite it, through a simple, systematic process of recognition and choice. One moment of consciousness can begin to rewrite it.

I'm not saying this is magic or that if you change one belief, you'll make a million in three days. This isn't snake oil. What I *am* saying is: do this exercise. Uncover your faulty code. Rewrite it consciously. Measure your progress. Stay vigilant.

When you do that, life starts to change. You choose the thought. The thought creates the emotion. The emotion drives the action. The action creates the result. That's the power you have.

Someone once said that doing the same thing while expecting different results is insanity. I prefer to think of it differently: if you want different results, think differently.

Rewriting the Code: The Process That Works

Let's debug your money operating system.

This is the process I use with every client and the one that transformed my own financial life. It's simple and powerful, but it requires honesty.

This isn't about blame. It's not about your childhood, your parents or that boss who rejected you. It's about finding the faulty line of code and fixing it.

You can do this right now, in the next 20 minutes, if you choose to do the work.

Step 1: Expose the Operating System

Get two pieces of paper or open a document. Create two columns.

Left column: Actions I take (or avoid)

Write down every financial action you avoid or that sabotages you. Be ruthlessly honest.

Examples:

- I avoid looking at my bank statements
- I don't open pension statements
- I don't invest because it feels too risky
- I shy away from conversations about finance
- I spend money when I'm stressed
- I say yes to investments without research

Right column: "Because…"

For each action (or avoidance), write the reason or your justification. To dig deeper, keep asking yourself "why?" until you hit the feeling.

Examples:

- I avoid bank statements → Because I don't know how to fix it → I feel stupid

- I don't invest in private equity → Because I think it's too risky → I'm scared I'll fail
- I get frustrated with my broker platform → Because I might mess it up → I'm scared I'll lose everything
- I shy away from finance conversations → Because I don't understand → I feel inadequate

Keep going. Every action that doesn't serve you. Every sabotaging pattern. Write it down and trace it to the feeling.

Step 2: Find the Root Code

Now look at your right column, all those feelings, all those beliefs.

What's the one that's running the whole show?

Common root codes:

- "I'm scared I'm going to lose all my money"
- "I don't know how"
- "I've lost money before doing this"
- "I'm not smart enough for this"
- "Investing is for other people, not me"

Circle it. Highlight it. Say it out loud. Hearing it in your own voice makes it real. That's your money operating system, the faulty code running your financial life.

Step 3: Write New Code (That Your Brain Will Accept)

This is where many people get stuck. They try to flip the belief to a positive, and their brain immediately rejects it as false.

If your root code is "I'm not good enough," you can't just affirm "I am enough" if your brain doesn't believe it. That's a costume, not code that will run.

You need something that is:

- Present tense (happening now, not "I will...")
- Positive (what you *are*, not what you're not)
- Believable (your brain doesn't roll its eyes)
- Enabling (points toward possibility, not just away from fear)

You're not creating something from nothing - you're rediscovering a part of yourself that was always there, like finding a coat in your wardrobe you'd forgotten about.You put it on and think, *ah yes, this fits. I remember this feeling.*

Examples of new code:

Old: "I'm scared I'll lose everything"

Not this: "I'm not scared anymore" *(negative, brain rejects)*

Try this: "I'm learning to make wise financial decisions" or "My knowledge grows with every investment I study."

Old: "I don't know how"

Not this: "I know everything" *(brain: Rubbish!)*

Try this: "I am learning and growing financially every day" or "I have the capacity to figure this out."

Old: "I'm not good enough"

Try this: Borrow confidence from another area of your life. When I hit this, I couldn't authentically say "I'm enough." So I leaned into what *was* true: my capacity to learn, my resilience, my commitment to growth. I created a new mindset: "I am strong and resilient, and I can learn how to do this well."

Find *your* coat.

For money specifically, your new code might be:

- "I know my investments can help me generate wealth"
- "I'm capable of learning what I need to know"

- "Money flows when I'm aligned and conscious"
- "I'm a master manifestor" (if that genuinely resonates)

Write it down. Make it specific to your root code.

Step 4: Install and Measure

This is the piece that makes it stick.

Installation:

- Write your new code where you'll see it daily
- Set it as a phone wallpaper, sticky note on the mirror, or at the top of your journal
- Call it to mind *especially* in stressful or triggering moments

When old code resurfaces (and it will), don't spiral into shame. That's just more faulty code running. Instead: Notice it. Name it. Choose again. That's the practice. Consciousness, not perfection.

Measurement:

Without measurement, it's just an interesting exercise. Every month, ask yourself: "Out of 100, how much did I use my new mindset this month?" Month 1 might be 30%, Month 2, 45%, Month 6, 80%. Measurement keeps you conscious and shows you progress. Old code loves to creep back in when you're stressed, triggered, or tired. This is how you stay vigilant.

Track it. Measure it. Celebrate progress.

In my experience, meaningful shifts happen within 3-6 months of consistent practice, but this is ongoing work, not a one-time fix.

Real Applications

One of my clients, who is a coach, used to say, "I'm just not a numbers person." She avoided her finances completely. When she rewrote that script to, "I'm capable of learning my numbers. I deserve to feel confident about my money," she hired a bookkeeper, started reviewing monthly updates, and now runs a thriving business.

A lawyer friend used to say, "I don't have time to learn about investing." It wasn't really about time; it was a protective script: "It's safer not to know." Because knowing meant facing her unhappiness, her spending patterns, the need for change. Once she named that script, she rewrote it: "I'm strong enough to look. I'm allowed to build something better." She joined a women's investment club and made her first private equity investment.

Same women. New code. Very different results and lives.

Something to note is that people running old code often surround themselves with others running the same code. New code needs new inputs, e.g.books, communities, mentors who operate from abundance. When you rewrite your operating system, consciously add voices that normalise investing and celebrate financial growth rather than reinforce scarcity and fear.

Where Real Wealth Begins

Mindset is the foundation. Without it, even the best strategies crumble. With it, everything becomes possible.

Looking back, losing money was excruciating, but priceless. It forced me to see I couldn't build wealth with the same mindset that had lost it. I had to rewrite my money operating system.

You've just done what most people never will: you've seen your money operating system clearly and chosen to rewrite it. That's not small work; that's the foundation of everything that follows. With your mindset reset, you're ready for the next essential step: facing your numbers with courage. Because you can't navigate to financial freedom without knowing where you stand today. That's the work of Chapter 7. And now, with new code running, you're finally ready for it.

Key Takeaways

- **Mindset is your source code** - change it, and everything shifts
- **One belief can crash the system** - most are installed in childhood or moments of fear.
- **Your emotions are your GPS** - they reveal the thoughts driving your financial actions.
- **Rewriting begins with awareness** - spot the faulty code, replace it, and practise daily.
- **Progress is measurable** - track shifts in how you think, feel, and respond around money.

Practical Actions

1. **Create a money mindset journal** – Record your thoughts, triggers, and wins as you apply the new code.
2. **Weekly mindset check-in** – Note one moment each week where you caught yourself choosing differently.
3. **Anchor your new code** – Read your new belief daily or pair it with a simple habit like morning coffee.
4. **Do a monthly energy audit** – Review your money actions through how they *felt*, not just what they cost.
5. **Celebrate progress** – Acknowledge every time you act from calm, clarity, or courage.

Chapter 7

FINDING YOUR FINANCIAL BLUE DOT

You Can't Plan Your Future Until You Know Where You're Starting From

Part 1: The Journey Begins

A couple of years ago, when facing the reality of my son leaving home for university, I threw a few clothes into my van, packed a plug-in fridge for my gin and tonic, carrots and hummus (life's essentials), and set off on a solo road trip across Europe. I knew I had to be in Portugal for a lunch date two weeks later. That was the destination. Everything else was up for discovery.

Halfway across the channel, it occurred to me that I hadn't actually planned anything about this trip beyond the ferry ticket. No map, no itinerary, just a challenge I'd set myself to see if I could trust the journey on my own. I've always leaned into being risk on like that.

With the freedom to go anywhere, it could have been overwhelming to plot a course for the next few weeks. What grounded me was knowing that at any moment, I could look at my phone and see on my GPS where I was. From there, I could look at the map and choose the next stop on my journey. The blue dot on the map meant I always knew exactly where I was starting from.

That little dot gave me confidence to explore, detour, and keep moving south. I could get lost and still find my way again, because I always had a reference point.

Money works the same way.

Before you can design your future, you need to know exactly where you are today. Without that, you're driving blind. This chapter is about finding your financial blue dot, your true starting point.

Part 2: Why Now Matters

Knowing Where You Are Changes Everything

Here's the irony: I've always loved numbers. I'll happily calculate distances, margins, or time zones in my head for fun. But for years, I avoided looking at my own numbers.

Back in my City days, I could analyse company accounts in minutes; spot weaknesses, test assumptions, and see beyond the glossy surface. Yet I never applied the same scrutiny to my own financial life.

I told myself I was "too busy," but the truth was more subtle: I didn't want to see what I'd find. Facing my own numbers felt too personal. Too confronting. What was the impact of this avoidance? No clarity, fuzzy thinking, and combined with the poor mindset we explored in the last chapter, I was making poor financial decisions and not living authentically.

I know I am not alone in my fear of looking at financial reality. And for women, this avoidance carries consequences we simply cannot afford anymore.

The Uncomfortable Truth: Why This Matters More for Women

Right now, in 2026, there's a quiet financial time bomb ticking away for millions of women that could determine whether you spend your later years in comfort or in constant compromise.

The Gender Pension Gap

The numbers are stark. Women aged 55–59 face an average pension gap of almost 50% compared to men. While men in this age group have built pension pots of around £156,000, women have managed roughly £81,000. When converted to annual retirement income, that's £11,000 versus £6,000; the difference between modest comfort and choosing between heating your home or buying groceries.

The Perfect Storm

Decades of pay inequality, career breaks, and longer life spans all conspire against women's financial futures. We need retirement funds that stretch further, not shorter, yet we're building significantly less.

The gender pension gap isn't someone else's problem; it affects almost every woman. Yet the biggest gap isn't in our ability, it's in our confidence and in access to clear financial knowledge.

The good news? Unlike pay gaps or workplace discrimination, this is one area where we hold the power to change our own outcomes.

It all begins with knowing exactly where you stand today.

The Day I Found My Financial Blue Dot

Let me tell you about my own moment of truth, not to suggest my journey is yours, but to show you what becomes possible when you finally look. When I finally did face my numbers, the picture surprised me. It wasn't nearly as bad as I'd imagined, and that's usually the case. Numbers are rarely as frightening as the stories we tell about them.

By the time I sat down to map my own balance sheet of life, I was living in France and renting out my house in Putney. For years, I'd thought of that house as a source of pride, proof that I'd "made it." But I'd never questioned whether it was helping or hindering me financially.

When I looked properly, I realised something I'd missed all along: the moment that house began earning income instead of draining it, it had quietly transformed from a liability into an asset.

My Putney House: From Liability to Asset

Back in London, I genuinely believed my Putney house was an asset. After all, it was worth nearly £600,000. It was appreciating in value. It made me feel wealthy and secure.

But according to the real definition of wealth, my house was actually a massive liability. Every month, money flowed out of my pocket to pay for:

- Mortgage payments
- Council tax
- Insurance
- Maintenance and repairs
- Utilities

Let me show you the actual numbers that revealed this transformation:

On my balance sheet:

House = £600,000 asset

Mortgage = £400,000 liability

Net worth = £200,000

On my cash flow statement:

Monthly outgoings = £2,000+

Monthly income from house = £0

After I knew I was moving to France permanently, I realised I needed to rent my Putney house to cover these costs. This was the start of my education about real-world assets.

Suddenly, my house transformed:

On my balance sheet:

House = £600,000 asset

Mortgage = £400,000 liability

Net worth = £200,000

On my cash flow statement:

Rental income = £3,500

Costs = £2,000

Net monthly cash flow = £1,500 positive

Same house, completely different financial impact. It moved from draining my wealth to building it, showing up as both a balance sheet asset and generating positive monthly cash flow.

That was the penny drop moment. I finally understood that wealth isn't about what you own; it's about what adds value to your life.

If something earns for you, it's an asset. If it costs you, it's a liability. Simple, liberating, life-changing.

That single insight sparked my property journey. I could intentionally build more of these assets. I could make my money work for me.

You might be wondering: how did a fund manager, who analysed balance sheets for a living, not understand this about her own finances.

I grew up in a middle-class family with no business owners or property investors. The script was clear: get educated, get a well-paid job, save in your pension, buy a bigger house to live in. That was considered success.

In the City, everyone followed the same script, just with bigger numbers. Higher salaries, bigger houses in better postcodes, more expensive cars. We were all on the same treadmill, just running faster.

Building income-generating assets, creating multiple income streams; none of that was in my world. Not because I wasn't capable, but because I'd never been exposed to it. I literally didn't know what I didn't know.

If you're a lawyer, doctor, consultant, or corporate executive thinking "But I'm just a salaried person," that's exactly where I was. The shift from corporate thinking to asset-building isn't about being entrepreneurial. It's about unlearning the script and seeing possibilities that were always there.

You don't have to leave your job to build assets. You just have to start thinking differently about how you use the money you earn.

There was one more revelation to come. For years, I'd filed away pension statements unopened, too complicated, too remote, too 'future me's problem.' When I finally looked, I discovered far more than I'd imagined. We'll explore this in depth in Chapter 24, Pensions, Reimagined since it was a game-changer for me.

The things we avoid often hold our power. We have to be willing to look.

Part 3: Your Two Maps

The Map That Brings Clarity

Every solid business has a balance sheet, a snapshot of what it owns and owes, and a cash-flow statement that shows money moving in and out. Together, they tell the truth.

Your personal finances are no different.

Your Balance Sheet: A Snapshot of Your Wealth

Let me break this down simply, starting with your snapshot. Think of your balance sheet as the still photograph of your life: your assets and your liabilities in one clear frame.

Your net worth = Total Assets - Total Liabilities

Your Assets:

- Savings accounts and cash (earning interest)
- Investment accounts (ISAs, pensions, stocks, bonds, funds)
- Property you rent out (with positive cash flow)
- Businesses you own or have stakes in

Your Liabilities:

- Mortgage balances
- Car loans and hire purchase agreements
- Credit card debt
- Student loans
- Personal loans

Your Cash Flow Statement: The Money Movement

Then imagine your cash flow as the video, the movement of money in real time, month to month.

Cash flow tells you whether you're living within your means and whether your financial lifestyle is sustainable.

Monthly Income:

- Salary after tax
- Rental income
- Investment dividends or interest
- Any side business income

Monthly Expenses:

- Mortgage/rent payments
- Utilities, council tax, insurance
- Food, transport, and childcare
- Loan repayments
- Subscriptions, entertainment

Why Both Matter

Here's what separates wealthy people from everyone else: they focus obsessively on building assets that *generate positive cash flow.*

Most people focus on accumulating things that look valuable on their balance sheet: a big house, an expensive car, designer possessions.

But wealthy people ask a different question: "Does this put money in my pocket every month?"

They use their balance sheet to build their cash flow. They acquire assets specifically because those assets generate income. The two statements work together; one feeds the other.

Both matter. One shows your wealth position right now; the other shows whether you're building or draining it every single month.

Most people never create either. They have a vague sense of being "okay" or "a bit behind," but no clear data to back it up. Once you know your blue dot, your exact coordinates, you can make decisions based on facts, not feelings.

Part 4: Finding Your Blue Dot

Facing the Numbers With Kindness

I know for many women, this step can feel confronting. Even accomplished business owners sometimes shy away from their personal accounts. We're raised to believe that money management is dry, masculine, or intimidating.

But it doesn't have to be.

What's important to understand: you're not solving anything yet. You're not making investment decisions. You're not becoming a financial expert overnight. You're simply gathering information, looking at what is, without judgment, without needing to fix anything immediately.

This is purely about awareness. You're finding your blue dot, not plotting the entire route to Portugal.

It just takes some time and patience. When you finally sit down and face your numbers, when you see the whole picture in black and white, for many, it won't be as bad as you fear. In fact, it's often far better.

If the numbers are worse than you hoped, then now you know. Knowing means you can act. You can make a plan. You can seek advice. You can start making different choices today rather than discovering the problem at retirement when it's too late to fix.

The women I know who've faced difficult financial realities all say the same thing: the knowing was hard for a day or a week, but the not knowing had a low-grade anxiety every single day for years. Awareness might sting briefly, but ignorance is a chronic pain that never heals.

Your blue dot is your blue dot. No judgment, no shame, just your starting point. You realise you're not lost. You've just been travelling without a map.

There's something deeply satisfying about gathering those numbers, bank statements, investments, pensions, loans, and seeing them together for the first time. It's the financial equivalent of that blue dot appearing on your phone.

You're here. You know where you are. And from here, anything is possible.

This is clarity, and it's empowering. Awareness gives you a choice. You stop guessing. You stop hoping. You start planning.

The Invitation

Before you rush on, take a moment. This is where awareness turns into action.

Getting clear about your financial position is incredibly liberating. It stops the fuzzy thinking, the sleepless nights, wondering *"What if?"*, and the mental energy wasted on financial confusion. When you know exactly where you stand, you can make informed decisions instead of emotional ones.

If you're noticing resistance here, check your mindset. These are the stories that keep us stuck:

> "I'll do it when things settle down." *(They never do.)*
>
> "I'll wait until I earn more." *(The pattern follows you.)*
>
> "My partner handles the money." *(What if they leave or die?)*
>
> "I'm scared I'll find out something terrible." *(Not knowing is worse.)*

Whatever story you've been telling yourself, notice it, acknowledge it, and do it anyway. You've got this.

In the *Fearless Wealth Playbook*, you'll find a guided version of this exercise: *Map the Balance Sheet of Your Life*. It walks you through listing everything you own, everything you owe, and the movement of money through your life each month.

You don't have to do it perfectly. You just have to start.

It might take an hour, an afternoon, or a few weeks. I promise you this: when you've done it, you'll feel lighter, clearer, and more in control than you have in years.

So get yourself a coffee (or a gin and tonic) and make a date with your finances. Set aside dedicated time in your diary, an hour or two if you can, to gather what you need:

- Bank statements and savings accounts
- Pension statements and investment accounts
- Mortgage balances and property details
- Credit cards, loans, and any other debts

Use the downloadable spreadsheet in the Playbook to guide you step by step. You don't need perfection right now; rough estimates are fine; you can fill in more details later.

It might feel confronting, especially if you've avoided looking at the full picture until now. That's normal. But this step is essential.

This is the moment you reclaim authority over your financial story.

So when you're ready, open the Playbook and find your blue dot.

Part 5: What Comes Next

Understanding your numbers isn't about judgement or shame; it's about truth. I avoided doing this for many years, and it cost me years of potential wealth-building.

Once you know your coordinates, you can plot any course you choose. Without it, you can't build wealth intentionally, and you'll need these numbers in the next chapter, where we move from Awareness into Alignment, translating clarity into strategy, and designing your own version of financial freedom.

In Chapter 10, we'll use these numbers to calculate something powerful: your Freedom Number. This is the figure that tells you exactly how much you need to live life on your terms, whether that means early retirement, working part-time, or having the security to take bold risks.

You can't calculate your Freedom Number without first knowing your blue dot. You can't design where you're going until you know where you are.

Your current financial position, whether positive or negative, is simply your starting point. What matters is that you know it, you own it, and you're ready to work with it.

Once you know where you are, you can choose where to go next.

Key Takeaways

- **Your financial blue dot is your true starting point** - the moment you face your numbers with honesty and compassion
- **Clarity brings calm** - facts replace fear, and you regain control
- **Awareness isn't criticism, it's freedom** - knowing creates choice
- **Wealth is about cash flow** - it's not about what you own; it's about what puts money in your pocket
- **Assets versus liabilities matter** - an asset puts money in your pocket; a liability takes money out
- **You need two maps** - your balance sheet (what you own vs. owe) and your cash flow (money in vs. money out)
- **Every month matters** - the gender wealh gap means women can't afford to delay

Practical Actions

1. **Go to the Fearless Wealth Playbook** and complete the Balance Sheet of Life exercise.
2. **Set aside time**, a full hour or two, to gather your figures honestly.
3. **Review your cash flow** - what comes in, what goes out, and where small changes could make a big difference.
4. **Celebrate progress** - the simple act of knowing your numbers is a profound act of self-respect.

PART 2

ALIGNMENT

Chapter 8

ALIGN BEFORE YOU INVEST

The Values That Shape Your Life: Not Just Your Wealth

If you only read one chapter of this book, let it be this one.

Not because it has the cleverest framework or the neatest diagrams, but because this is the moment everything you've learned so far finds its home. This is where numbers become nourishment. Where strategy meets soul. Where wealth stops being something you chase and starts becoming something you live.

In the last section, we explored *Awareness*, how to raise your consciousness around finance and freedom, upgrade your mindset and what happens when you lead from authenticity. You saw how your Energetic Alpha grows as you live more truthfully, and how the Wheel of Authenticity helps you build Inner Wealth, the energetic foundation that powers everything else.

This section, Alignment, is where that inner work meets the outer world. Alignment is the living connection between who you are and how you create, earn, and invest to build wealth.

It starts here, with the first spoke on the Wheel of Authenticity: Values.

Understanding and living your values is the foundation of authentic wealth. Values aren't slogans for a wall or words to get "right." They're the personal drivers that have been moving through you your entire life, the unseen architecture of your choices. When you honour them, you feel grounded, energised, and quietly confident. When you violate them, you feel the drag: a tightness in your chest, the fog of indecision, the sense that you're working hard and still moving against the grain.

For years, I mistook success for alignment. I had the impressive job title, the big salary, the rhythm of deals and decisions. On paper, it looked perfect. Except it wasn't working. Not really.

Inside, I felt disconnected. I could optimise my strategy for the market's benchmark, yet I was underperforming my own. That wasn't a failure of strategy; it was a failure of congruence. I hadn't asked the simplest question: *Does this align with who I am?*

Living your values doesn't make life magically effortless, but it does become clearer. You simply know what fits and what doesn't. The same clarity flows into your finances: you stop chasing what sparkles and start choosing what sustains. Each time you make a values-aligned choice, you're compounding your Energetic Alpha.

This chapter isn't about "values-based investing" as a niche. It's about understanding who you are so deeply that every part of your life can rest on something true.

When I finally named my values, Learning, Connecting, and Achieving, so much of my life made sudden sense. Why I had done what I have, why some things lit me up and others drained me. Why certain conversations gave me energy for days. Why the most satisfying "wins" were not always the biggest. Once I could see what was important to me, I could choose differently.

That's what I want for you here, not a perfect list of words, but a felt recognition. The moment your body leans forward a little, because a word is true for you. The soft exhale when you stop trying to want what you're "supposed" to want. The relief of naming what already is.

We're going to keep this simple and spacious. You won't rush this in an evening; you'll live with it for a short while. You'll notice where your energy rises and where it drops. You'll try words on like a favourite jumper and see if they fit. And you'll let the noisy "shoulds" fall quiet enough for something real to surface.

As you do, remember: alignment isn't a test to pass. It's a way to live. You will wobble. I do. But each time you make a choice based on your values, you strengthen the structure. You reclaim a little more freedom, in your time, in your work, in your wealth.

Later, when we reach chapter 16 *The Investment Values Compass,* you'll translate these values into the way you invest and grow your money, not as rules, but as a filter that honours who you are. For now, we begin where all authentic lives begin: with the drivers that have been quietly guiding you all along.

The Day the City Went Woo-Woo

By the time this story begins, I was long gone from the City. I'd swapped the skyline for the mountains and spreadsheets for ski boots. But old worlds have a way of calling you back, and one day I was asked to help a fast-growing finance startup build a high-performance culture; to create a business that could sustainably scale without losing its soul.

It felt deliciously ironic: here I was, a coach with frost still in my hair from Chamonix, stepping back into pinstripe territory. My brief was to help them shape strategy, structure, and sustainability. Instead, I brought a deck of *values cards.*

The first meeting was priceless.

When I suggested we begin by exploring values, you could almost hear the collective eye-roll.

"Values? Isn't that HR fluff?" one said.

Another looked at me as if I'd just proposed a group hug.

The third just muttered, "Can we get back to the numbers?"

They were brilliant men, sharp, relentless, alpha in every sense. And precisely because they were so focused on outcomes, they couldn't see that their outcomes were faltering for a reason they couldn't quantify.

So I asked them to humour me for thirty minutes.

We stood around a whiteboard, a set of values cards on the table. At first, there was polite resistance, the corporate equivalent of crossed arms. But then something shifted. One of them paused at a card labelled "reliability." Another went straight for "results." The third hesitated, then picked "respect."

Within an hour, the energy had completely shifted. What began as an awkward exercise turned into a conversation about what really drove them, not their quarterly targets, but what kind of company they wanted to build and what kind of leaders they wanted to be. They realised that their best decisions, including letting someone go who didn't share their ethos, had already been driven by those values. They just hadn't named them.

Over the next few years, their shared values became their framework. They shaped hiring, client relationships, and growth decisions. The business didn't turn into a meditation retreat; it remained fiercely commercial. But it gained coherence, a shared backbone that anchored all that ambition.

That experience cemented something for me: values work isn't "soft." It's structural. It's what keeps high-performance cultures from tearing themselves apart.

Zappos in the U.S. gets this. They hire for values first. If they realise the fit isn't right, they'll literally pay you to leave. Because they know you can train skills, but you can't train alignment.

Knowing your values is the foundation for alignment, whether you're a company or a person. They create clarity and a framework to make values-based decisions that align with what feels right.

From the Boardroom to the Kitchen Table

I've seen this same shift everywhere, from leadership teams to families, from investors to teenagers figuring out who they are.

Once people name what truly matters, confusion dissolves. Decisions align. Relationships ease. It's like switching the lights on in a room you didn't realise was dim.

This isn't magic. It's consciousness. Values reconnect you to yourself, and once you're reconnected, the outer world starts to arrange itself around that clarity.

So What Are Core Values Really?

Think of a stick of seaside rock (for non-UK readers: candy with letters running all the way through). That's what values are like: they run through your life, visible in every slice if you look closely enough.

Values *are* your compass, the quiet drivers shaping how you spend your time, energy, and attention. They're personal and unique: two people can share the same word but live it completely differently. They are innate and unlikely to change. Your values describe how you are "being": the behaviours and how you act and show up daily. They are definitely felt more than explained; lived, not laminated.

Understanding what they are not is as important as knowing what they are. Values *are not* aspirations, strengths or "ought tos".

And they most definitely are not corporate slogans, remember Enron? Their stated values, "Integrity, Communication, Respect, and Excellence," sounded noble, but the company collapsed in one of the biggest corporate fraud scandals in history. Or Volkswagen, which spoke of environmental responsibility while quietly cheating emissions tests. Words don't build culture; behaviour does.

Knowing your core values changes everything. When you're living in alignment with your values, life feels like it flows. You feel fulfilled and energised. When your values aren't being met, whether in relationships, work, or investments, everything feels jarring and difficult, though you might struggle to put your finger on why.

Most of us walk around disconnected from our values. We make decisions based on what we think we should want, or what looks good on paper. But when you identify and honour your real drivers, everything clicks into place. The right opportunities find you. Relationships strengthen. You stop second-guessing because your internal compass finally works.

So how do you actually figure out what your values are when you've been operating on autopilot for years? Let me share my own journey because it wasn't as straightforward as I expected.

My Values Discovery Journey

I first learned about values during my coach training. That session stayed with me because it was so profound. I'd never heard of values before, and I realised how powerful they were. I sat with the exercise for weeks, grouping, testing, regrouping, until I landed on three words that felt true in my bones: Learning, Connecting, and Achieving. I realised that these values had been running throughout my entire life, even when I wasn't consciously aware of them. They were patterns I finally recognised, and it felt like I had a way to explain why I did what I did and why I felt "off" in certain situations.

Learning is my number one value. It's always been at the heart of who I am. I loved school, am endlessly curious and driven to know how things work. It's also why I've explored so many paths: finance, property, coaching, scaling companies. Growth and discovery light me up.

Connecting was like flipping a switch. I'd always assumed "family" was my driver, but when I dug deeper, I realised it was bigger than that. My energy comes from connecting with people, engaging in conversations, understanding their stories, building relationships. This is my engine.

Achieving came third. I've always been driven, high-energy, and goal-oriented. The shadow side of this value? Over-achievement. Naming it helped me channel it rather than let it run me. Even making a lovely family dinner became a way to honour this value: achievement doesn't have to be grand; it just has to feel intentional.

Understanding these three values changed everything. It made sense of every choice I'd made, every career pivot, every investment decision, even the moments of frustration or disconnection. Those values now act as filters for my investments: if a strategy starves learning or connection, I know why it feels off.

As a coach, I always begin by eliciting or verifying a client's values. And I experience such joy the moment the penny drops, the *aha* when someone finally sees the pattern that's been driving them all along. That clarity changes everything: how you see yourself, and everything you choose next.

Discovering Your Core Values

Now it's your turn to discover the values that will guide not only your investment journey, but your whole life.

This is not a quiz; it's a conversation with your life. There is no right or wrong core value; they are personal, unique and deserve respect. Take your time finding them.

What matters is that you discover what's actually true for you, not what you think should be true.

How to Use This Section

I'm going to walk you through the process I use with clients exactly as I would in person. You'll need some space, some honesty, and a willingness to surprise yourself.

If you'd like the full, step-by-step guided process (worksheets, prompts, and a printable values list), you'll find it in the **Fearless Wealth Playbook** companion resources. It's worth doing properly. If you only take one practice from this book, make it this.

Step 1 – Initial Reflection

Over the next few days, notice when you feel most alive, absorbed, or at peace. When are you in flow? What moments make time disappear? And when do you feel that inner scratch of frustration, the sense that something's off? Those contrasts are clues.

Step 2 – Choose What Resonates

Use the values list in the **Fearless Wealth Playbook** to find the words that fit when you're in flow. Circle fifteen or twenty words that *land.* Don't analyse, feel. If your body leans forward, it's probably yours.

Step 3 – Group and Simplify

Cluster similar words until themes emerge. This is where patterns reveal themselves: curiosity and growth might merge into *Learning*. Belonging and empathy might become *Connection*.

Step 4 – Test Each One

Say it aloud: "I am someone who values ____."

Does it feel expansive or tight? Live with it for a week. Notice when it shows up in your choices. Notice how you feel when it's ignored.

Step 5 – Rank Your Top Five

Order matters. Your highest-value driver often explains every major decision you've ever made, and every one you've avoided .The job you didn't take, the relationship you walked away from, the investment that never felt right

Step 6 – Sanity Check

Test each one by asking: where am I honouring these values, and where am I starving it? When one client realised her top value was 'freedom,' she suddenly understood why her high-paying legal job felt suffocating despite the prestige; she was trading her highest value for external validation.

Often patterns of frustration trace back to a value being violated.

Most importantly, remember that values are simply labels. What matters is what they mean *to you*. One client swore his top value was "Excellence" until he realised what he really meant was "discernment", the joy of being a connoisseur. Another hesitated to admit that "recognition" mattered to him until he saw it was really about stewardship and standards.

This deserves your attention and your time. Let this unfold. I know from experience that clarity isn't forced; it's revealed.

Avoiding Common Traps

Watch out for "should" values. If you picked it because you think you *should* value it, it's probably not yours. Values aren't moral statements; they're personal drivers.

Avoid aspirational values. "Wealth" isn't a value if you don't currently have much money. What would wealth *give* you? That's where your real value lies (security, freedom, recognition, etc.).

Question the obvious. Sometimes our real values hide behind the most obvious ones. "Family" might actually be "loyalty" or "connection" or "security."

Remember, there's no hierarchy of virtue here. "Recognition" isn't shallow; "freedom" isn't flaky. If it's yours, it's yours; own it.

Your values aren't goals to hit; they're ground to stand on.

From Knowing to Living

Discovering your values is not a nice-to-have; it's the foundation spoke of the Wheel of Authenticity, the ground everything stands on. It's the point where inner wealth meets outer wealth. When those two align, life doesn't just feel better, it works better. Choices get clearer. Energy returns. Opportunities fit.

It really can feel like magic, not because life stops being life, but because friction falls away. You stop forcing yourself through doors that were never yours, and the ones that are meant for you open more easily.

This isn't about perfection. It's about practice. When your wealth, in all its forms, rests on your values, every decision carries integrity. And when circumstances shift (they will), you have a way back to yourself.

Values are the silent structure of freedom.

Once you know them, you don't lose your way in life, in work, or in wealth.

You might be sitting with this right now feeling thoughtful, or uncertain, or maybe unexpectedly emotional. Good. That means you're touching something real. Live with what you've discovered. Notice it. Test it. Let it settle. We will return to values at the end of this section.

Next: we turn this clarity into everyday momentum. In "Wake Up - Becoming Conscious with Money," you'll install two simple, powerful practices: pay yourself first and spend consciously. Your money will start reflecting what matters most to you in real time.

Key Takeaways

- **Values are your invisible drivers** - they're already shaping every decision you make
- **True values describe natural operation** - how you actually work, not how you think you should
- **Alignment creates flow** - misalignment creates friction
- **Testing reveals truth faster** - reflection works better than analysis alone
- **Starting with values simplifies everything** - every choice that follows becomes lighter, simpler, and more powerful

Practical Actions:

- **Look at the values list** at the end of this book and circle 15-20 words that make you lean forward.
- **Notice your energy over the next week** - When do you feel most alive, and when does something feel "off"?
- **Test each value by saying aloud** - "I am someone who values ______." Does it feel expansive or tight?
- **Group similar words** until 3-5 core themes emerge, then rank them in order of importance.
- **Ask yourself** - "Where am I currently honouring these values, and where am I starving them?"
- **Live with your top values** for a week before finalising them - Notice when they show up in your daily choices.

Chapter 9

WAKE UP

Becoming Conscious with Money

The foundation practices that stop the drift

By now, you've looked at your numbers, the real ones, not the ones you hoped were there. You've identified what truly matters to you. You understand how money flows towards or away from you based on your level of consciousness. Once you know your numbers and what matters most, you can design the life and freedom you want.

That sounds so simple. So logical. Know where you are, know what you value, design your future.

Yet knowing isn't enough. You can understand consciousness intellectually. We explored this back in Chapter 3 when we looked at the four levels, the emotional ladder, and how money flows towards or away from you based on your energetic state. That was the map. The framework. The theory. But consciousness isn't something you learn about. It's something you become. You can't think your way to a higher level of consciousness.

Most of us don't consciously choose to wake up. Life wakes us up. Usually through pain. Through crisis. Through that moment when everything you've been avoiding suddenly becomes impossible to ignore. This is the story of how life woke me up and what I learned about becoming conscious with money, not just understanding it, but embodying it.

Let me take you back to France...

My Wake-Up Call

When I moved to France, I thought I was escaping. I left behind my comfortable life in the City, my marriage, my Putney home, my six-figure salary, and moved into a tiny studio in Chamonix. From high heels and boardrooms to ski boots and mountain air.

At first, it felt intoxicating. I had savings and rental income from my London house that covered my living costs. I could ski, hike, and live in the mountains without working. By any objective measure, I had financial freedom. But I didn't feel free. I felt anxious. Lacking. Not enough.

In the City, I'd been validated by external markers: my title, my salary, my business card. Director of a bank, don't you know. I mattered because the world told me I mattered. When I left that behind, I lost my compass. I had no internal sense of what I was building towards, only what I was running from.

Now I was comparing myself to my City friends with their six-figure salaries and bonuses, and to my new friends in Chamonix, their businesses, their chalets, their seemingly effortless Alpine lives. I was operating from scarcity consciousness, always looking at what others had, never seeing what I already possessed. I stuck my head in the sand when it came to my finances. I told myself I'd earned this freedom, that I deserved to just enjoy life. I was recovering from a difficult time.

But I wasn't building anything. I was drifting.

I had rental income. I had property. I had capital. If I'd been awake, truly conscious, I could have protected that freedom. I could have invested strategically, made different choices. I could have built real wealth. Instead, I let it slip through my fingers because I had no plan, no vision, no conscious direction. I was so unconscious about money that I couldn't recognise freedom when I was living it.

The truth was, I didn't have the tools. I didn't recognise I had a faulty mindset, we covered that in the previous chapter. I didn't know how to create a clear vision. I didn't believe I could. And without those tools, I was entirely focused on what I didn't want: the stress of City life, the corporate pressure, the marriage that hadn't worked. But I had no clarity about what I did want. Where was I going? What was I building? What kind of life did I actually want to create?

I had no answers. And without those answers, I just... drifted.

After my daughter's birth, I launched a property company in France. For a while, it worked. Until it didn't. After the financial crisis, everything unravelled. Years of projects that didn't turn out as I'd hoped, endless renovations, spiralling costs, all while raising two small children.

I remember one day sitting on my kitchen floor, with my two small children looking at me bewildered, while I sobbed my heart out. I felt lost, overwhelmed, exhausted, like I was failing at everything. I'd left the City believing I was building freedom. Instead, I was drowning. I had two wonderful children, but I felt like I was failing at motherhood. I felt like I had nothing to offer the world. All that promise, all that potential from my City career, where had it gone?

That was my nadir. And yet, rock bottom became a turning point.

The Pivot

That moment on the kitchen floor was my wake-up call. Something shifted. I stopped asking "Why is this happening to me?" and started asking "What am I creating here?"

I moved from victim consciousness to agency consciousness. From Level 1 to Level 2. From "money happens to me" to "I create my financial reality."

It wasn't comfortable. It wasn't pretty.

I got brutally honest about my money. I looked at the properties I'd bought unconsciously, the opportunities I'd missed, where I'd been operating from fear and FOMO. I raised my awareness about all of it.

That consciousness was what turned things around. Not a clever strategy. Not a budgeting trick. Just waking up and seeing clearly.

You've already begun this work. Back in Chapter 7, Your Financial Blue Dot you looked at where you are today, your balance sheet, your cash flow, your reality. That's consciousness work.

But consciousness without practice doesn't last. When life gets chaotic, when fear creeps in, when old patterns call, you need more than awareness. You need habits that keep you conscious.

Looking back, I'd actually been doing some things right: putting money aside, trying to invest, thinking about spending. But I was doing all of it unconsciously. Investing in properties bought from emotion. Making choices from comparison rather than values. I had the right instincts. I just didn't have consciousness behind them.

So while consciousness itself was what woke me up, stopping the drift requires two things. First, you need to wake up to where your money is actually going and install practices that keep you conscious. Second, you need to get crystal clear about where you want to go: your vision, your freedom number, the life you're designing.

This chapter covers the first part: the foundation practices that stop unconscious spending and keep you awake. The next chapter tackles the second: creating a clear, compelling vision of the wealthy life you want to build. Both are essential. You can't design your future if you're haemorrhaging money unconsciously. And you can't stay motivated to manage your spending if you don't know what you're building towards.

There are two fundamental habits that, when practised consciously rather than on autopilot, become the foundation for everything else. These aren't the habits that saved me; consciousness did that. These are the habits that kept me awake, that turned awareness into sustainable change.

Let me share them with you, not as revolutionary concepts, but as practices you might already be doing unconsciously that need to become conscious choices.

Habit 1: Pay Yourself First

The first habit sounds simple, but there's a world of difference between doing it unconsciously and doing it with awareness.

Growing up, my grandfather Ernie gave my brother Andrew and me 50p each for the slot machines at the seaside in Llandudno. Andrew would spend his entire 50p and enjoy every second of it. I always spent half and pocketed the rest. Less excitement but quiet security.

That instinct stayed with me. Like many women of her generation, my mother was taught to save, and she passed that lesson on to me. I loved earning money as a teenager and taking it to the Co-op, watching the numbers grow in my passbook. There was something deeply satisfying about seeing my money accumulate.

That instinct to put money aside. That's paying yourself first. Not spending everything and hoping there's something left over, but deliberately moving money into your future before you spend on anything else.

Many of you might be in a similar place. You're responsible. You're putting money into savings. You've probably accumulated quite a stash of cash. That's good, it's the foundation. But you cannot build wealth from saving alone.

There are actually two stages you need to master, and most people only ever complete the first.

Stage 1: Save

This is about where your money goes, and the order in which it goes there.

Most people operate like this: Earnings → Expenses → Maybe save what's left

Conscious wealth-builders flip the formula: Earnings → Pay Yourself First → Spend what's left

If you're already doing this, brilliant. You've mastered Stage 1. But there's a second stage that's equally crucial.

Stage 2: Invest

Saving protects your money. Investing grows it. If you want to build wealth and freedom, you need both.

Saving is important: security, protection, your safety net. But safety alone won't get you where you want to go.

This is the trap many women fall into. We've been taught to play it safe, to be responsible savers. And we are good at it. We put money aside diligently, build emergency funds, and watch accounts grow slowly. But we stop there. We save, but we don't invest. We protect, but we don't build.

I was doing exactly this. Money in savings accounts, yes. But not consciously investing to grow wealth. And when I did start investing, I was doing it from fear and comparison, not strategy.

When you truly pay yourself first, you're not just tucking money away for a rainy day. You're prioritising wealth-building, putting money to work consciously and strategically so it compounds and grows and buys you freedom.

How to Put This Into Practice, Consciously

1. Automate It

Choose a percentage, 5%, 10%, or £50 a month, and set up automatic transfers as soon as you get paid. Remove willpower. Make it effortless. Use a separate account. Later, we'll explore automating investments themselves: ETFs, index funds, and wealth-building vehicles. For now, just start the habit.

2. Prioritise Toxic Debt

Not all debt is bad. Mortgages that build equity, business loans, strategic leverage, debt can be a wealth-building tool when used consciously.

But toxic debt, high-interest credit cards, payday loans, double-digit rates, is wealth destruction. Negative compounding is working against you.

If your credit card APR exceeds your expected investment return, clearing that debt is your best investment. Not sexy, but essential.

3. Review and Adjust, Stay Conscious

This is crucial. Set up automation, then... forget about it for years? No. Consciousness requires attention.

Revisit every six months. Block it in your calendar: *"Money Consciousness Check-In."*

Ask:

- Has my income changed?
- Can I increase contributions?
- Am I still just saving, or consciously investing to grow?
- Is my money working as hard as I am?

This regular review keeps you awake. It prevents slipping back into unconsciousness. It ensures paying yourself first remains a conscious choice, not autopilot.

The Bottom Line

Paying yourself first isn't about depriving yourself today. It's about buying your future freedom. Every pound consciously invested buys you options. This is where financial freedom begins.

Habit 2: Spend Consciously

Once you've started paying yourself first, the next step is spending consciously, being intentional about where the rest goes.

This is about far more than trimming lattes. It's about deliberate choices: spend freely on things that genuinely add value, ruthlessly cut back on everything else.

My Story: Spending from Comparison

I thought I was thoughtful about my spending in France. I wasn't frivolous. I was considering purchases. But I was making choices based on comparison and scarcity, not consciousness and values.

I'd see my friends' beautifully renovated chalets and feel mine wasn't good enough. I'd compare what they had and make spending decisions to keep up, not because those things aligned with what mattered to me.

The difference isn't always *what* you buy, it's *why* you buy it. From values or comparison? Abundance or scarcity? Choice or autopilot?

Every Pound Has Opportunity Cost

Back in Chapter 7, we explored how retail therapy gives a quick high but erodes long-term freedom, and how "investment therapy" is the antidote.

Every pound spent today is a pound that could work for your future. Compound that across years, and the difference between unconscious and conscious spending can run into hundreds of thousands.

I'm not finger-wagging about the occasional coffee or meal out. I'm showing you the opportunity cost of unconscious spending. It's not about deprivation, it's about conscious choice.

Here are some examples:

Unconscious subscriptions: £75/month on magazines you don't read, streaming services you don't watch, apps you signed up for and forgot about. Over five years: £4,500 spent, or around £5,800 invested at 10% return. Over fifteen years: £13,500 spent, or around £31,000 invested. That's three years of university fees.

Unconscious treats: £160/month on the T-shirt here, the lipstick there, the home décor item you didn't need, purchases bought from habit or comparison rather than genuine desire. Over five years: £9,600 spent, or around £12,300 invested. Over fifteen years: £28,800 spent, or around £66,000 invested. A property deposit. A business investment.

I'm not saying never treat yourself. I'm saying: be conscious about it.

Putting It Into Action

Go back to your cashflow sheet from Chapter 7. Look with fresh eyes and ask yourself three questions about each expense:

1. Does this align with my core values? (The ones you identified in Chapter 7)
2. Does this bring lasting value or fleeting pleasure?
3. Am I buying this consciously or from comparison?

Now highlight two or three areas where you're spending unconsciously. Then choose one, just one, to redirect into your future freedom fund.

Pick the most unconscious, most misaligned. Then automate the change. Cancel the subscription. Set up an automatic transfer instead.

The Bottom Line

When you combine paying yourself first with spending consciously, you create a simple, powerful system that accelerates your journey to financial freedom.

You're not depriving yourself. You're not penny-pinching or living small. You're making conscious choices, spending freely on what matters, redirecting what doesn't, and building the freedom that gives you even more choices in the future.

This isn't about guilt. It's about consciousness. Every pound working for you instead of against you.

From Drift to Design

You've now installed two consciousness practices.

A habit is automatic, without thinking. A consciousness practice is done with awareness, intention, purpose.

Every time you pay yourself first, you choose future freedom over immediate gratification. Agency, not autopilot. Every time you spend consciously, you ask: "Does this align with my values? Or am I buying from comparison, from fear?" And every time you review, every six months, you stay awake. You ensure you haven't slipped back. These practices keep you conscious. They keep you choosing. They stop the drift.

Remember, stopping the drift requires two things. You've now mastered the first: waking up to where your money is going and installing practices that keep you conscious. Now it's time for the second part: getting crystal clear about where you're going.

What does financial freedom mean for you? Not your City friends, Chamonix neighbours, or Instagram influencers. For you. What's the life you're designing? The number that buys that freedom?

Most people never ask. They drift, hoping things work out, without getting specific about what that even means.

What follows is different. It's conscious, intentional visioning about the wealthy life you want to create, and it starts with permission.

Permission to prosper. Permission to build real wealth. Permission to want more than just "enough".

Key Takeaways

- **Consciousness requires practice** - it's something you become, not just understand
- **Stopping the drift has two parts** - wake up to where your money goes (this chapter) and get clear on where you're going (next chapter)
- **Paying yourself first has two stages** - putting money aside, then investing it to grow
- **Conscious spending aligns with values** - it's not about deprivation, it's about intention
- **Review every six months** - regular adjustment keeps you conscious

Practical Actions

1. **Set up your money consciousness check-in** - Block two dates in your calendar, six months apart. Label them: "Money Consciousness Check-In."
2. **Automate pay yourself first** - Set up an automatic transfer to a separate account on payday. Start with 5-10% of your income.
3. **Audit your unconscious spending** - Review your cashflow sheet. Circle three unconscious expenses. Choose one to change this week.
4. **Cancel one subscription** - Find one subscription you don't use. Cancel it today. Redirect that amount to your future freedom fund.
5. **Create your spending check** - Before purchases over £50, ask: Does this align with my values? Am I buying from comparison or choice?

Chapter 10

DREAM BIG

Designing Your Roadmap To Financial Freedom

This is where it gets exciting, where your heart might jump a little. This is where you start creating the life you actually want. Not the life you think you should want. Not the life that looks good on paper. The life that makes you come alive. The truly wealthy life you deserve to create.

In Chapter 7, you looked at where you are. You faced your numbers, perhaps for the first time. That took courage, and it may have been uncomfortable. This is where we move from consciousness to vision. From waking up to dreaming big. From knowing where you are to imagining where you're going.

As we explore this, we're going to navigate the creative tension between wanting more and appreciating what you have. This isn't stress, it's the kind of tension that creates momentum. Nature abhors a vacuum, and when you clarify what you want, you create a pull toward it. This is the dance I've learned to embrace over many years, and there are a few things I want to unpack first.

Part 1. Authentic Permission - Building Wealth from Your Truth

You can't give yourself permission to prosper while old conditioning is still running. You can't dream big while comparing yourself to others.

You can't envision your wealthy life while the conditioning whispers "wanting more is greedy."

So this is the next step: I'd like you to give yourself permission to build wealth. Permission from you. Not from me, not from society, your parents, your partner, or your peers. But from you to yourself.

Permission to want wealth. Real, substantial, generational wealth.

Permission to build it boldly, invest confidently, prosper unapologetically.

Permission to design a life that is abundant, free, and entirely yours.

But permission without perspective can become another trap.

I learned this during my City years. I found myself chasing ever-bigger numbers simply because the people around me were earning more. It bred jealousy, comparison, and a smaller, meaner life. The irony was I was wealthy by any objective measure, yet I felt poor because I was always looking sideways.

When I moved to the mountains, I thought I'd left that behind. But I hadn't. I still caught myself measuring my worth by other people's success: the bigger chalets, the newer cars, the lifestyle posts. It took time and humility to realise I was still trying to prove I was enough.

Today, I know I am enough without proving. I don't need a bigger house to feel worthy. I'm content in my smaller home because it's filled with love, laughter, and the people who matter. My wealth is in the quality of those friendships, the richness of my work, and the contribution I make. That's conscious wealth, the kind you don't need to show off.

I've watched friends earn millions, still comparing upwards, still chasing the next bonus or bigger house. They have extraordinary wealth, yet no peace. Andrew Wilkinson captures this perfectly in his book *Never Enough: From Barista to Billionaire.* He reveals a hard truth: even immense wealth can feel empty if it's only about keeping score. That mindset breeds scarcity, not freedom, no matter how many zeros are in your bank account.

Let's name the kind of permission that's needed here.

If you want the Ferrari because it makes you feel respected or "enough" in someone else's eyes, you'll always be chasing approval you can't buy.

Wanting it for the joy of driving, the beauty of the design, or the sense of celebration it represents is something different. That kind of desire doesn't need defending, it just needs owning.

Authentic wealth isn't about denial. It's about awareness.

This is where your Chapter 5 Wheel of Authenticity work becomes crucial. Giving yourself permission to build wealth isn't about guilt or greed; it's about honesty. And honesty eventually leads you to define what "enough" means for you.

Rather than chasing someone else's benchmark of success, ask yourself:

What is enough for me to live well and enjoy what I value?

What's enough to give back, contribute, and create impact in ways that matter to me?

What's big enough to inspire action, but not so big that I lose sight of why I'm doing it?

When you define your own enough, you stop the endless comparison. You stop looking sideways and start looking forward. You build from abundance, not scarcity. From purpose, not just accumulation.

One thing I know: when women build wealth from this place, their prosperity creates ripples far beyond themselves. Research shows that women reinvest up to 90% of their wealth back into families and communities, compared to just over 50% for men.

Your wealth isn't just for you. It's a catalyst for change. So before we go any further, I invite you to ask yourself: Have I given myself permission to be wealthy, in every way?

Notice what stirs inside you when you ask that. If there's resistance, that's just the old conditioning trying to keep you safe. Smile at it, thank it, and gently let it go. Permission isn't selfish. It's essential. Permission grounded in your authentic values is the foundation of everything we're about to build.

Part 2. The Power of Imagination - Why Vision Isn't Wishful Thinking

Now that you've given yourself authentic permission, grounded in your values, not comparison, let's translate that clarity into vision.

I love this quote from Einstein: *"Imagination is more important than knowledge."*

Knowledge is limited to what you already know, what's already been done. But imagination allows you to transcend those boundaries and envision what isn't real yet. This isn't wishful thinking, there's actual neuroscience behind this.

Our brains cannot distinguish between vividly imagined events and real ones. When you visualise something powerfully, when you see it, feel it, experience it in your mind, the same neural pathways fire as if you were actually living that reality right now.

This activates your Reticular Activating System (RAS), the part of your brain that filters information and focuses on what matters to you. When you imagine clearly, you're priming your mind and body to notice opportunities, to act, to create the circumstances that move you towards what you've envisioned.

This is why, after you decide you want a blue car, you suddenly see them everywhere. Your RAS is now tuned to that frequency.

The exercise we're about to do isn't about magical thinking or manifesting something out of thin air. It's about conscious design. It's giving your brain a clear target to move towards.

The Chalet Story

It was 2013. Richard and I were sitting in an architect's office in the Chamonix Valley. We had a vision for our dream chalet: big windows framing 360° mountain views, light flooding every room, an open-plan living space that felt spacious yet cozy, and of course, the perfect balcony for late-afternoon aperitifs with friends and family.

I poured it all out to him, every detail, every feeling, every element of what we wanted to create. Then we left him to turn our vision into something tangible.

A few weeks later, he called. "I have something to show you," he said.

This was 2013, long before VR headsets were a thing, but he'd created something extraordinary: a CAD walkthrough of the chalet. A 3D rendering we could move through.

And suddenly, there I was, standing in my future.

I was walking through rooms that didn't yet exist. Looking out of windows that hadn't been built. I could feel the sunlight that would one day flood the kitchen. I was standing on that staircase, turning to take in the view of Mont Blanc.

It was surreal. What had been just a dream in my head, just words I had spoken, was now something I could see and feel and almost touch.

That's when I understood: the moment you can see it clearly in your mind, you can create it in reality.

That chalet got built. It became real. Not because of magic, but because having a vivid vision pulls you into a compelling future. It keeps you taking action despite setbacks and obstacles. It creates that creative tension, the pull between where you are and where you're going, that generates momentum.

Part 3. The Visioning Exercise

I'm going to walk you through a visioning exercise I do every year and use with every coaching client. This is powerful work, and I want you to give yourself the space to do it properly.

Step One: Set Your Future Date

Grab a blank sheet of paper and write down a date, one year, two years, or three years from now. Your choice. Place that paper on the floor in front of you. That piece of paper represents your future.

Step Two: Walk Into Your Future

Stand where you are now; this is your present. When you're ready, physically walk forward and stand on that paper with your future date. Close your eyes. Take a few deep breaths. Arrive there fully.

Step Three: Immerse Yourself

You're now standing in this future. You've created the financial freedom you want. You're living the life you designed. Take a moment to just be present in this time. This is your future self.

Give yourself permission to feel pure joy, freedom, that feeling of possibility and expansion.

Then ask yourself these questions slowly, giving yourself time to feel into the answers:

- How do you feel in your body knowing you've created this?
- What emotions are you experiencing right now?
- What are you saying to yourself about your life?
- Who's with you in this moment?
- What sounds do you hear around you?
- What can you see? What's the view?
- What does financial freedom smell like to you?
- How do you feel when you check your financial statements now?

The greater the detail, the richer this vision becomes. Maybe it's having a leisurely coffee on a Tuesday morning because you don't need to be anywhere. Maybe it's the sea breeze from your dream holiday home. Maybe it's the snow flying past your face on a powder day in the Alps. Whatever it is for you, capture that sensation. Feel it fully.

Step Four: Capture It

If you're with someone, ask them to write down what you say as you speak. If you're alone, record it on your phone. Later, write it all down. This will become your personal wealth vision document.

If this exercise feels silly or impossible, that's completely normal. The resistance is showing you exactly where your growth edge is, where your old conditioning is still holding on.

Trust the process. Take the time to enjoy the experience, and then come back to the next part when you're ready.

Part 4. From Vision to Numbers

Welcome back. I hope after that exercise you're feeling a little glow of excitement, sitting in this beautifully expansive creative space. Now we need to move to the next part, and I'm going to ask you to look at some numbers.

For some of you, this may be the moment the energy drops. Those fears come flooding back. You might notice huge resistance rising up. If this is you, I get it completely.

The visioning you just did was heart space, expansive, emotional, and essential. Your brain now believes your future is possible because you've experienced it. Moving to numbers feels different. It's head space rather than heart space. It can feel like a letdown, like we're abandoning the magic.

But we're not. We're giving your dream structure. Numbers create specificity, and specificity creates momentum. Numbers take the wishy-washy and turn it into design. They give your vision shape and a target you can move toward.

This is how dreamers become designers. This is how your vision becomes reality. We're not betraying your dream by adding numbers to it. We're valuing it enough to make it real.

Your Freedom Number

I was on an options trading course last year, and the instructor asked me what seemed like a straightforward question: "How much additional income do you want each month?"

"£10,000," I said without hesitating.

"Why £10,000?"

I paused. And I realised I had absolutely no idea. It just sounded like a good number. It felt significant without being absurd.

That moment stopped me because I realised that numbers without reasons don't move us. They're just figures on a page, pulled out of thin air, with no meaning or motivation behind them.

So I went home and started putting numbers to the life I wanted. I priced the travel, the experiences I wanted to give my children, the ways I wanted to contribute, and the choices I wanted available to me. I put figures against my actual vision.

When I added it all up, my number wasn't an additional £10,000 a month. It was £7,200 a month. Less than my instinctive answer, but far more motivating because it was real. It was mine. It was based on the life I'd actually designed, not a number that sounded impressive.

That's what we're doing now. We're taking everything you just envisioned and putting actual figures against it.

Your Ideal Lifestyle Exercise

Here's how: look at all the things you want in your financially free life over a year. Work out the price or cost of each item. Then put them into the spreadsheet in the Fearless Wealth Playbook.

Rough numbers are completely fine. You're not creating a perfect budget; you're getting a sense of scale.

Some things to consider:

Where would you love to travel, and how often would you go?

Do you want a second home? Or to renovate the one you have?

What experiences do you want to give your children or the people you love?

How do you want to give back? What causes, what community work, what philanthropy lights you up?

Could you see yourself working less? Or retiring earlier? Or choosing different work because you're not dependent on the income?

Write it all down. The spreadsheet will add it up. This is your Freedom Number.

If you divide the number by 12, you'll get the monthly income from assets you would need to live the life you just designed.

Part 5. Your Freedom Gap - Creating the Pull Towards Your Future

Now comes the part that might feel uncomfortable.

Compare your Freedom Number to where you are today. Pull out those financial statements you created back in Chapter 7, your balance sheet, your cash flow. Look at them alongside the number you just wrote down.

Ask yourself:

- How much income am I already generating from assets? From rentals, dividends, interest, anything that comes in without me actively working?
- What savings, pensions, and investments are already working for me?
- Where are the shortfalls? Where are the gaps?

The difference between your Freedom Number and where you are today is your Freedom Gap.

For most people, this moment is sobering. The gap is often larger than expected. Thoughts arise: "This is impossible. I've left it too late. I'll never close the gap."

This isn't a problem. It's creative tension.

In physics, tension is the force that exists between two points. It's not inherently stressful; it's simply energy waiting to be directed. When you know exactly where you are and exactly where you want to be, you create a natural pull forward.

Nature abhors a vacuum. When you clarify what you want and acknowledge where you are, you create the conditions for movement. This gap isn't something to fix desperately or stress about. It's the space that generates momentum.

I know this feels uncomfortable. I was sitting on my kitchen floor in France, having lost hundreds of thousands of pounds through poor decisions and failed projects. The gap felt insurmountable. I thought I'd ruined everything.

But I didn't stay on that floor. I got up, became conscious, created a strategy, and put compounding to work. The gap closed not through force or panic, but through clarity and aligned action.

The gap you're looking at isn't a judgement. It's not a measure of failure or worth. It's just data. And data gives you power.

You're not drifting any more. You have a target. You have a starting position. You know the distance between here and there.

This isn't the finish line. This is your starting line.

For now, just acknowledge your Freedom Gap. Don't let it crush you. Let it inform you. Let it create that pull forward.

Part 6. Your New Starting Line - Standing in Your Designed Future

You started this chapter having raised your consciousness and installed new practices around money.

You're ending it with a vision of your future that is real and vivid. You have your Freedom Number and you understand your Freedom Gap. That's not just progress. That's transformation.

Hold your vision lightly but confidently. In the next section of this book, we're going to build the financial knowledge you need to make this real: compounding, assets, diversification, and strategic investing. You'll discover that small, consistent actions compound into extraordinary results.

Then in Part Three, we'll use the Wheel of Wealth to assess where you are across all dimensions of your financial life and create your strategic plan to work with that gap. Not through force, but through flow. Not through stress, but through aligned action.

Right now, just sit with what you've created. You're no longer drifting. You've designed your financial freedom.

Key Takeaways

- **Permission unlocks imagination** - you can't design what you haven't given yourself permission to want
- **Define your enough** - not someone else's benchmark or definition of success
- **Your brain responds to vivid envisioning** - this isn't wishful thinking, it's neuroscience
- **Specificity creates momentum** - your Freedom Number turns abstract dreams into concrete targets
- **Your Freedom Gap generates movement** - it's not a problem; it's creative tension that propels you forward

Practical Actions

1. **Say this out loud** - "I give myself permission to be wealthy, in every way." Notice what comes up for you.
2. **Write down your definition of *"enough"*** - What does prosperity actually mean to you?
3. **Do the future walkthrough exercise** - Write your vision down and keep it somewhere you'll see it as you're going to need this in Part Three.
4. **Price out your ideal lifestyle -** and calculate your Freedom Number.
5. **Compare your Freedom Number** to where you are today (your Chapter 7 financial statements) to find your Freedom Gap

Chapter 11

YOUR SECRET WEALTH WEAPON: TIME

How Small Steps Build Big Wealth

Your most powerful wealth-building tool isn't luck, a hot tip, or perfect timing, it's compounding.

If I'd truly grasped this at 20, many of my choices would have been different. I'd have started earlier, chosen better, and let time do the heavy lifting. But the wonderful thing is that it's never too late to start.

You've mapped your Freedom Number. Maybe the gap between where you are and where you want to be feels daunting. That's normal. Compounding is the bridge, the simple, reliable way to move from here to there.

Compounding is the quiet engine that turns small, repeatable actions into outsized results. It rewards two unfashionable virtues: patience and consistency. It rarely looks exciting at the start; in fact it often looks dull. Give it time though, and the results become extraordinary.

The only real question is whether it's already working for you or against you.

Albert Einstein called compounding "the eighth wonder of the world." And there's no doubt that compounding is one of the most powerful forces in finance and in life. It shows up in your health, your learning, your relationships, and your career. When small actions align with your values and are repeated over time, progress compounds.

In this chapter, we'll make that power tangible with stories, simple maths, and practical steps you can automate, so time becomes your greatest ally.

My £15 Wake-Up Call

Most of us understand compounding on some level, but we don't really *get* the concept. My entire career in the City actually launched on compounding. My very first interview began with the question: "If you had £100 at 10% interest, how much would you have after two years?"

I answered *"£121"* and the interviewer's eyes lit up. "You understand compounding." That one answer got me the job.

So yes, I understood the maths. However, what I *didn't* understand was that where you put your money matters just as much as putting it away in the first place.

When I was 18, a salesman convinced me to sign up for a life insurance policy. £15 a month felt manageable, even smart. I was being "responsible," planning ahead. Small, consistent contributions over time. I got the principle right.

What I didn't get was that I'd just handed my power over to someone else.

Thirty-five years later, I cashed it in. The total: barely £10,000.

If I'd put that same £15 into a low-cost fund tracking the stock market instead, I'd have had around £58,000. High fees and poor investment choices had quietly eaten away what should have been mine. My money *was* compounding, just not for me.

That one decision cost me £48,000.

Now, £48,000 over 35 years isn't a fortune. But it's real money; a year's salary for many women, a house deposit, breathing room.

If there's one lesson I'd share with every woman, especially young women, it's this: don't just save consistently; invest where compounding actually works in your favour. Low fees. Broad market exposure. Your control, not someone else's commission.

The Compound Effect in Life

Compounding isn't just about money. It's everywhere.

Five years ago, my daughter, Charlotte, picked up a rugby ball for the first time. Week after week, she trained, rising at 6 am for the past two years to get to Exeter Rugby Academy while her friends were still asleep. This year she walked onto the pitch at Twickenham and scored a try in the Under-18s final. Her team won.

That's compounding in action: discipline and focus, repeated over time, rewarded in the most extraordinary way.

I've seen the same principles everywhere in my life, building my coaching career from zero, in long-term friendships that later changed my life, and reading just a few pages a day to expand my knowledge. Skill, trust and wisdom all grow through small steps repeated consistently over time.

Compounding doesn't only build wealth, it builds you.

When Compounding Works Against You

Here's an uncomfortable truth: compounding is neutral. It doesn't care whether it's building wealth or destroying it. It simply multiplies whatever you feed it.

Living beyond your means every month quietly compounds into financial strain, anxiety and fragility. You don't notice it right away, but the spiral is always there in the background, affecting millions of people.

Think about the patterns in your own life:

- Overspending compounds into debt, stress, and constraint
- Neglecting your health compounds into decline and illness
- Negative self-talk compounds into stuckness and depression
- Procrastination compounds into missed opportunities and regret

However, the great thing is that the moment you flip the script, the moment you start living within your means and investing even a little, you reverse the spiral. You shift compounding from enemy to ally. That one choice can change everything.

The Power of Starting Now

If my 20-year-old son Thomas invested £100 today in a NASDAQ ETF and added £100 every month for 30 years at a 10% average return, he'd end up with around £230,000. Keep going another 10 years and the figure jumps to around £640,000.

At first, it doesn't look like much, just small deposits disappearing quietly each month. But behind the scenes, growth is gathering pace. That's the raw power of compounding.

Now imagine he waits just 10 years to begin. That delay would cost him hundreds of thousands in lost growth. Whilst this is illustrative and not a guarantee of returns, it clearly shows the principle.

You'll find a Compound Interest Calculator in your **Fearless Wealth Playbook.**

Use it to play with the numbers yourself. Try different starting sums, e.g. £100, £1000, £10,000 and add money each month, £25, £250, £2,000 and watch what happens when you add time. Do it for your children, too. Their faces will light up when they see how a small decision today can shape an entire future.

Let me show you what this actually looks like. These aren't theoretical numbers, this is what happens when you automate consistent investing into a low-cost ETF:

Years	£100/month @10%	£200/month @10%
10	£20,000	£40,000
20	£70,000	£138,000
30	£230,000	£460,000
40	£640,000	£1,300,000

Look at that 40-year line: £200 a month, less than £7 a day, becomes £1.3 million. This is totally passive investing, set up an automated monthly transfer into a low-cost ETF (you'll learn more about these later), then leave the rest to time.

Compounding is the quiet escalator beneath your feet; you just need to stay on it. Maybe you wish you'd started earlier, most of us do, but compounding doesn't vanish with time; it's available right now. *Every pound invested today works harder than one invested tomorrow.*

A Story That Captures It All

A few weeks ago, I had dinner with a friend and his 17-year-old daughter. Over dessert, she asked how my book was going. When I told her I'd been writing about compounding, she grinned and said,

"Mum told me about that, I've started putting £50 a month away from my allowance so I can retire early."

I nearly jumped out of my seat with joy. That conversation captured everything this chapter is about. Once you understand compounding, you can't *unsee* it. You just start, quietly, and the rest unfolds.

That's why I'm writing this chapter so more of us, and our children, can start early and let time become our greatest ally.

Making It Real

I hope you've seen the power of compounding. We've looked at the numbers together, and you understand the principle. Actually, you probably understood it before, to be fair.

The most important question now is: will you start? For yourself, for your children? Not next month. Not when you've figured everything out. Not when you have more money.

Today.

And all there is to do is this: open a brokerage account (we'll cover the details in Chapter 19 on investing in ETFs) and set up a standing order into a low-cost tracker fund. The same principle as

Chapter 9: pay yourself first. Invest whatever you can manage consistently every month.

You'll hear this called Pound-Cost Averaging in the UK, or Dollar-Cost Averaging elsewhere. Don't let the jargon put you off as it's a really simple concept. Some months you'll buy when the market's higher, some months when it's low. Over time, it averages out. More importantly, it removes the emotion from the equation. You're not trying to guess the market. You're not trying to be clever. You're just being consistent.

Then you leave it alone.

Set your dividends to reinvest automatically. Don't cash out. Let your earnings earn. This is where your compounding accelerates.

Now, you *could* spend hours doing technical analysis to pick the perfect moment. You *could* listen to market pundits telling you to wait because "the market's too high" or "there's going to be a crash."

With automatic investing, you simply ignore them.

There will always be an expert with an opinion. But I can tell you with absolute certainty: *time in the market beats timing the market.* Every single time.

It has become a cliché because it's irrefutably true. It's really hard to beat the market or outsmart it, very few can do that consistently. Wealth doesn't come from finding the perfect day to invest. It comes from staying invested long enough for compounding to do its work.

Your future self is already grateful. And if you have children, you've just changed their story too.

Reading the Financial Weather

Compounding is the engine behind your wealth, both material and inner wealth. But engines don't run in a vacuum.

The speed at which your money grows isn't just about what you invest, it's also shaped by the financial "weather" around you. Inflation, interest rates, economic cycles. These forces can either accelerate your growth or quietly erode it.

You don't need to react to every shift in the wind. But understanding what's happening around you makes you a more confident investor.

When the markets drop, and they will, you won't panic and sell. You'll recognise it as part of the cycle. When inflation rises, you'll understand why your returns look different. When interest rates change, you'll know what it means for your strategy.

In the next chapter, we'll learn to read these patterns. Not so you can time the market or constantly adjust your approach, but so you can stay calm, stay invested, and navigate whatever the economy throws at you.

Key Takeaways

- **Compounding is neutral** - it multiplies whatever you feed it, good or bad
- **Time is your greatest ally** - the earlier you start, the more powerful the effect
- **Consistency beats drama** - small, consistent actions deliver bigger results than dramatic one-offs
- **Time IN beats timing** - your greatest wealth-building edge isn't timing the market; it's time IN the market

Practical Actions

1. **Identify where compounding is already working for you** - career growth, health habits, relationships.
2. **Spot where compounding is working against you** - spending, negative self-talk, procrastination.
3. **Choose one small financial habit to start this week** - even £25 a month compounds meaningfully.
4. **Calculate what your monthly investment could become** in 20, 30, or 40 years using the calculator in your Playbook.

Chapter 12

NAVIGATING THE ECONOMIC WEATHER

How To Protect And Amplify Your Compounding Power

In the last chapter, we explored how compounding quietly builds wealth over time. But there's another side to the story: powerful external forces can accelerate your growth, or quietly erode it. To make compounding truly work for you, it helps to step back and see the bigger picture.

The Village That Forgot About Money

Once upon a time, nestled between two great valleys, there was a luminous little village called Solara. Its people were kind, curious, and spiritually awake. They meditated at dawn, traded smiles at the market, and gathered around the fire to talk about the soul.

But there was one thing they *never* talked about: money.

"Oh no," the elders would chuckle, "money is a dirty thing, a tool of ego and greed. Let the greedy cities beyond the ridge obsess over gold and numbers. We don't need that here. We are rich in spirit."

So, no one learned how money worked or what inflation meant. When merchants arrived with shiny tools and clever contracts, the villagers gave away their best land, their strongest crops, and their future, without ever asking why.

Over time, the soil thinned, the gardens shrank, and the stars seemed dimmer.

Until one day, a young woman named Alkemi stood in the square and said:

"We've mastered the language of the soul but ignored the language that shapes our lives. We meditate and pray, but we don't invest, plan, or defend our value.

The world runs on a system we've forgotten. We need to talk about economics."

A child raised her hand. "Is this going to be boring?"

Alkemi smiled. "Only if we ignore it. Economics is like the weather. You can't control it, but you can learn to read it. And when you do, you'll know where to live, what to plant, and when to seek shelter."

Why This Chapter Matters

I know a chapter on economics doesn't sound exciting. It might seem dry, dull, or even intimidating, and the temptation might be to skip this bit. The truth is, though, that economics quietly shapes every financial decision you'll ever make, whether you realise it or not.

You don't need to become an economist or wade through graphs and equations to understand it. What you *do* need is a simple grasp of the key financial "weather patterns," because they affect:

- how your savings hold value
- how investments behave
- when property makes sense
- how to build a portfolio that weathers storms.

This chapter provides *context.* When you understand the bigger forces: inflation, interest rates, growth and confidence, you stop feeling at the mercy of headlines or politicians. You start seeing how those forces ripple through your savings, pensions, and investments.

You'll learn to notice how changes in interest rates affect mortgage costs and property prices, how inflation erodes cash returns, and why some assets thrive when others stumble. The aim isn't to turn you into a market forecaster, it's to help you recognise patterns so you can make steady, well-timed decisions instead of reactive ones.

Most people never learn this stuff properly, and that's why even smart investors get caught off guard by "unexpected" shifts. Once you start to see how these patterns connect, it's like switching from black-and-white to colour; suddenly, the financial world makes sense and your choices start to feel calmer, clearer, and more deliberate.

How I Got Here - From Explosions to Economics

I didn't start in finance. I began studying medicinal chemistry, dreaming of a career in pharmaceuticals. Until one afternoon in a university lab, I accidentally blew up the fume cupboard. My professor took one look at the wreckage, sighed, and said, "Isabel, perhaps your talents lie elsewhere."

Turns out, he was right.

That summer, I landed a job in California, not in a lab, but in a stockbroking office. I sat among ringing phones and barking traders, having no idea what a "stock" even was. Every morning, I'd pick up the *Wall Street Journal* and try to decode a foreign language: P/E ratios, indices, bond yields. It was baffling, but fascinating.

That summer, I realised something big: to really understand the world, I needed to understand money.

Back in London, I promptly confused my parents by swapping my lab coat for graphs, growth curves, and a whole new kind of experiment, economics.

Almost immediately, the fog lifted. I discovered economics wasn't about dry numbers; it was about human behaviour, power, energy, and value. It was about the systems shaping our lives every day.

Economics Is Just the Weather Forecast

Over the years, I've realised that economic trends aren't mysterious forces; they're patterns we can learn to spot, just as we can with weather. Think of it like being a gardener: understanding the weather helps you know when to…

- plant seeds (invest)
- seek shelter (hold cash)
- notice where the sun is shining (spot growth opportunities)

Or like driving on a long road trip:

- If it's sunny, you take the scenic route with the top down.
- If rain is ahead, you slow down and turn your lights on.
- If a storm's brewing, you might delay the journey altogether.

Once you know how to read the signs, you stop feeling at the mercy of it all, and you start feeling prepared.

Your Economic Dashboard: The Numbers That Tell Your Story

Think of these indicators like the dashboard in a company. Every successful business tracks a handful of key metrics: revenue, cash flow, customer numbers, profit margins. One month's data means little, but six months of tracking reveals patterns. Twelve months tells a story.

A good CEO doesn't need to understand complex econometrics, they just need to watch their numbers and notice when something shifts. Your personal economy works exactly the same way.

The following seven indicators are your financial KPIs, the numbers that tell you what's happening in the economic weather around your money. Track them monthly, and within six months, you'll start seeing the story. You'll notice how inflation affects your portfolio differently than interest rates do. You'll spot when conditions favour growth versus safety. Numbers always tell a story, you just need to give them time to speak. Here's how to think about them:

The Big Three: Your Primary Metrics

Like revenue, profit, and cash flow, these drive everything else and interact constantly: central banks watch inflation, adjust interest rates to control it, and manage money supply to influence both.

Of the three, money supply is the least understood and the one most investors ignore. However, it's also the most powerful for understanding why assets rise or fall. To build wealth your assets need to grow, not just in absolute terms, but relative to the money printing press. Master this, and you'll understand why stock markets can surge even when the economy feels shaky.

1. Inflation – The Leaky Bucket

Inflation is the rate at which prices rise over time, slowly eroding the value of your money. Imagine your savings as a bucket of water. Every year, inflation pokes tiny holes in the bottom:

- At 2% inflation, £100 today buys about £82 worth of goods in 10 years.
- At 5% inflation, that same £100 shrinks to £55.

However, the official number doesn't always match your reality. Your personal inflation, what you actually spend on, may be higher.

If you're saving for school fees or travel, your costs may rise much faster than headline CPI.

Why it matters: Your wealth isn't what you have, it's what you can buy. If your savings grow 3% but inflation runs at 5%, you are getting poorer. This is why tracking your personal inflation rate is so important; it tells you whether you're really keeping pace.

What to watch: UK CPI (Consumer Price Index) and CPIH (includes housing costs). Published monthly by the ONS (Office for National Statistics).

2. Interest Rates – The Thermostat

If inflation is the "temperature" of the economy, interest rates are the thermostat. Central banks raise or cut rates to control heat:

- High rates → borrowing becomes expensive → spending slows → inflation cools.
- Low rates → borrowing gets cheaper → spending rises → growth accelerates.

For you, interest rates affect:

- Mortgages → higher rates mean higher payments and lower affordability.
- Savings → some return on your cash.
- Investments → high rates often hurt equities but boost bonds.

Why it matters: Interest rates ripple through everything you own. They determine whether property becomes more or less affordable, whether your pension grows or stalls, whether it makes sense to pay down debt or invest for growth.

What to watch: Bank of England Base Rate (announced at MPC meetings, usually eight times a year). Also watch the yield curve, (official interest rates for different time periods) when short-term rates exceed long-term rates, it often signals trouble ahead.

3. Money Supply (M2/M4) – The Tide Beneath the Surface

If inflation is the leak in your bucket, money supply is the water level rising around it. This is the concept that separates informed investors from confused ones.

Central banks control how much money exists in the economy. When they "print money" (technically, they create it electronically through quantitative easing and other mechanisms), the total supply of money increases. Economists track "broad money" to measure this:

- **UK: M4**
- **US: M2**
- **Euro area: M3**

When central banks expand the money supply, think 2008-2021 stimulus, quantitative easing, COVID relief, it's like opening the floodgates. More money chases the same assets, which leads to asset prices rises.

This is what drove stock markets from 2009 to 2021. It wasn't just economic growth; it was the money supply expanding dramatically. When there's more money in the system, it has to go somewhere and much of it flows into stocks, property, and other assets.

When central banks tighten the money supply (like 2022-2023), growth slows, and asset prices often fall or stagnate.

Your real wealth depends on how your assets grow compared to the money supply.

- If your portfolio grows 5% but M2 grows 10%, you've actually lost ground in real terms. The tide has risen faster than your boat.
- If your portfolio grows 8% and M2 grows 3%, you're genuinely building wealth.

This is what people mean when they say fiat currencies (USD, GBP, Euro) are losing value; they can be printed infinitely, unlike assets with fixed supply. It's why property prices and stock markets can rise even during recessions, if the money supply expands, assets inflate regardless of economic fundamentals.

What to watch:

- **UK:** M4 (Bank of England publishes this monthly)
- **US:** M2 (Federal Reserve, if you invest in US markets)

Compare your portfolio's annual growth rate to M2/M4 growth. That's your real return, the one that matters.

The uncomfortable reality is that most investors celebrate 7% returns without realizing M2 grew 8%. They're technically poorer, but they feel richer. Remember that all boats rise in a rising tide. The question is whether yours is rising faster or just floating with everyone else's.

The Growth Signals: Your Confirmation Data

Like customer satisfaction scores, these indicators confirm whether the economy is responding as expected to the Big Three. Strong GDP and employment usually mean the primary forces are balanced; weakness means something's off.

4. GDP Growth – The Economy's Heartbeat

GDP measures the total value a country produces, think of it as the economy's pulse. A strong, steady beat signals growth, jobs, and rising company profits. A weaker pulse hints at slowdown or recession.

Why it matters: GDP affects wages, company earnings, and policy decisions. When GDP grows steadily, your employer is likely hiring, your investments are probably growing, and confidence is high. When it stalls, caution makes sense.

What to watch: Quarterly GDP growth (UK: ONS). Look for trends across quarters rather than reacting to single numbers.

5. Unemployment Rate – The Economy's Oxygen

Jobs are the oxygen of the economy. When more people work, money flows and confidence rises. When unemployment grows, spending falls and central banks often step in with stimulus.

Why it matters: Employment is a lagging indicator and confirms what's already happening. It's also sector-specific: if unemployment is rising in sectors where you're invested, that may change your risk tolerance.

What to watch: UK unemployment rate (ONS, monthly). Also watch wage growth as rising wages with low unemployment signals a healthy economy and conversely falling wages with high unemployment signals trouble.

6. Retail Sales & PMI – The Early Warning Lights

These are your leading indicators, the lights on the dashboard that go on before the economy shifts.

Retail sales show consumer confidence. When people spend, the economy grows. When they hold back, a slowdown follows.

PMI (Purchasing Managers' Index) tracks business activity. Above 50 means expansion; below 50 means contraction.

Why it matters: These indicators give you advance notice. A few weak months of retail sales or PMI can warn of slowdown long before GDP confirms it.

What to watch: UK Retail Sales (ONS, monthly) and UK Manufacturing/Services PMI (published monthly by S&P Global).

The Global Context: Market Intelligence

Like competitor analysis this is useful context, but not mission-critical for UK investors.

7. Nonfarm Payrolls – The Global Shockwave

If you invest in global markets, the U.S. Nonfarm Payrolls report (released first Friday of each month) is worth watching. It's the pulse check on the world's largest economy.

A strong number signals growth and can lift markets worldwide. A weak one often prompts rate-cut talk and market volatility.

Why it matters: U.S. economic health affects global markets, however for UK-focused investors, it's context rather than essential tracking.

What to watch: U.S. Nonfarm Payrolls (Bureau of Labor Statistics, first Friday monthly). Notice market reactions rather than analysing the data deeply.

Beyond the Numbers: Volatility and Sentiment

While inflation, interest rates, and GDP tend to steal the spotlight, there are two quieter forces that shape how markets feel, and that's how you might feel about them.

Volatility → the speed and sharpness of price moves.

Sentiment → the mood behind those moves: fear or greed.

They're not economic fundamentals, but they're essential to understanding how your investments behave in real time. Sentiment acts like a magnifying glass, amplifying optimism in booms and fear in downturns.

You can't predict mood swings, but you can keep your exposure steady and respond calmly when the winds shift. Think of volatility as weather turbulence, it feels dramatic in the moment, but if your destination is years away, it rarely matters.

Your Weather Dashboard: From Theory to Practice

Reading about these indicators once won't change anything. But tracking them monthly for six months will rewire how you see the financial world.

Inside your Fearless Wealth Playbook, you'll find your Economic Weather Dashboard—a simple tracker with seven rows (one per indicator) and columns for each month. Here's how to use it:

1. Choose your sources

The Bank of England, ONS (Office for National Statistics), and Trading Economics publish all seven indicators monthly. Pick one source you'll check regularly. I use a mix of the ONS website and Trading Economics because their dashboards are clean and accessible.

2. Record the numbers

Once a month, log the current reading for each indicator. It takes about 10 minutes. You're not analysing yet, just recording.

3. Note what happened

In the comments column, jot down what you noticed: "FTSE up 3%" or "Bitcoin rallied after rate cut announced" or "Property listings down in my area."

You're building your own case study. Over time, patterns will emerge that no textbook could teach you.

Here's what this might look like in practice:

January 2025: Inflation drops from 4% to 3.2%. Interest rates hold at 5.25%. GDP growth flat at 0.1%.

What you might notice: Stock market rallies (inflation cooling = rate cuts possible soon). Property market still quiet (rates still high, but buyer interest picking up). Your savings account paying 5% feels good.

March 2025: Inflation ticks back up to 3.8%. Bank of England delays rate cut.

What you might notice: Stock market wobbles. Property market stays slow. You're glad you didn't rush into a property purchase in January.

This is financial weather literacy. Just like a CEO reviews company metrics monthly, you'll review your economic dashboard with the same discipline to understand the story.

From Weather to Wealth

You now know how to read the financial weather. You understand that inflation erodes cash, interest rates shape borrowing costs, and money supply sets the tide that lifts or lowers all boats. You know they interact, you can prepare for them, and keep your head clear when others panic.

Reading the forecast, though, is only half the story. The next step is choosing what to plant in the current climate. That's where asset allocation comes in, the art of deciding which investments thrive in which conditions. When you understand both the weather and which crops grow best in sunshine versus rain, that's when your portfolio becomes truly resilient.

Once you start reading the weather for yourself, your confidence will increase and you stop waiting for the perfect forecast and start sailing with your own compass.

That's what we'll explore next, in the next chapter: The Alchemy of Assets.

Quick Reference: Your Economic KPIs at a Glance

Inflation	Prices rising, purchasing power falling	"Hot" if inflation >4%, "Mild" if 2–4%, "Cool" if <2%	Rising inflation erodes cash → growth assets matter more
M2 / Money Supply	How much money is circulating	Expanding → fuels growth & asset prices; Contracting → slows economy	More money = potential inflation; less money = slower growth

Interest Rates	The "price" of borrowing	High → storm clouds; Low → sunny spells	High rates hurt borrowers, cool property; low rates boost spending
GDP Growth	Economic heartbeat	Strong = clear skies; Weak = cloudy, possible storms	Healthy GDP = job security & asset growth; slow GDP = caution
Volatility	How wild markets swing	Calm = smooth skies; High = turbulence ahead	Turbulence = opportunity if long-term; risk if short-term

Key Takeaways

- **Economics is your weather forecast** - you can't control it, but you can learn to read it
- **Seven indicators are your KPIs** - track them monthly, and numbers will tell you a story
- **The Big Three drive everything** - inflation, interest rates, money supply; master these and you'll understand 80% of market moves
- **Growth Signals confirm the response** - GDP, employment, retail/PMI show whether the economy is responding as expected
- **Your dashboard enables recognition** - not prediction; six months of tracking teaches more than any textbook
- **Volatility and sentiment magnify everything** - your steady hand is the real anchor
- **Personal inflation matters most** - track what you actually spend on, not official numbers

Practical Actions

1. **Check your personal inflation** - Look back over your past year's spending. Have your real-life costs risen faster than the official CPI figure? This number matters more than any headline.
2. **Set up your Weather Dashboard** - In your Fearless Wealth Playbook, start tracking just ONE indicator this month - I suggest inflation. Next month, add interest rates. Build the habit slowly.
3. **Notice the language** - This week, when you see financial news, spot one term you now understand. You'll be amazed how quickly the puzzle assembles.

Chapter 13

THE ALCHEMY OF ASSETS

Building Your Investment Toolkit

When I first started investing, I thought I knew what the toolkit looked like. Equities. Maybe bonds. Property, if you were ambitious. I'd studied economics, built a career in finance, and understood how markets worked, but in practice I kept my investing world small. Equities were familiar. Bonds were background noise. Property felt tangible, so that became my next step.

Over time, life shifted. My goals, responsibilities, and risk appetite evolved. I began looking for income that property couldn't deliver, for diversification that equities couldn't offer, and eventually for new opportunities shaped by innovation and technology.

My first real leap into something new was Bitcoin, not as a fad, but from curiosity about how technology and scarcity could redefine value. Private equity followed, which suited my lifelong love of business; getting under the bonnet of companies, helping them grow, and sharing in their success. More recently, I've added options income strategies, which give me steadier returns and the time freedom I value now more than ever. Like any good relationship, my portfolio has evolved as I have; what worked for me in my thirties doesn't quite fit the same way now.

This brings us to the assets themselves, your potential partners in building wealth. Understanding what each one does, how it behaves, and where it fits in your life gives you the confidence to design a portfolio that truly works for you.

If I am honest, my investing life, like my love life, hasn't always been tidy. Both have required patience, curiosity, and the courage to start again when things didn't work. And both reward awareness: the more you understand your assets' personalities, their strengths, quirks, and how they behave under pressure, the better choices you make and the stronger your long-term relationships become.

The alchemy lies in knowing what each one brings to the table, how they respond to economic conditions, and which ones still deserve a place in your life.

What Is an Asset?

An asset is something you own that has value, something that can generate income for you, appreciate over time, or protect what you've already built.

Not all assets play the same role. Some are designed to work quietly in the background, while others are designated to drive growth or provide stability. Knowing which is which helps you decide where to put your money, time, and attention.

Before we dive in, a quick note: not everything here is an asset in the strictest sense. Options, for example, are instruments that provide ways to access or enhance returns from underlying assets. But the point isn't perfect terminology; it's understanding that these tools behave differently and serve different purposes.

Three Families of Assets

Broadly, there are three asset classes in your investment toolkit. Think of them as characters in an ensemble cast, each with a role, each needing the right stage time.

Family	Purpose	How It Works	Examples	Typical Trade-Offs
Income Generating	Generate a steady income or cash flow	You own something that pays you regularly or grows steadily over time	Dividend-paying equities, bonds, rental property, REITs, option wheel strategy	Stable income, slower growth; capital required to start
Protectors	Preserve value and provide resilience in uncertain markets	Hedge against inflation, volatility, or economic shocks	Gold, Bitcoin, inflation-linked bonds	Lower returns in boom times; may lag during market optimism
Growth & Alternatives	Create higher long-term growth or transformative returns	Take calculated risks in pursuit of expansion or innovation	Private equity, digital assets, options strategies	Higher reward potential; more volatility and illiquidity

You don't need exposure to every type. What matters is that you recognise how each behaves, when to rely on it, when to rebalance, and how it fits your stage of life.

Early on, you might lean more toward Income. Generating assets to build stability and cash flow. Over time, as confidence and capital grow, Growth & Alternatives may play a bigger role. Protectors, meanwhile, act as the ballast, the stabilisers that keep your financial ship steady when markets change direction. Your mix will shift over time and that's exactly as it should be.

Part 1: Income-Generating Assets - Your Foundation Tools

Let's start with the most familiar tools, the ones designed to produce income and drive long-term wealth creation. They are your steady, reliable types; they might not sweep you off your feet, but they'll show up every month. They are the foundation of many portfolios.

Equities (Stocks or Shares)

This is where my journey began, managing portfolios of companies listed on stock markets, primarily in emerging Europe: Russia, Poland, Hungary, and Turkey.

What they are: Ownership stakes in companies listed on stock exchanges. You make money through share price growth (capital appreciation) and sometimes through dividends, regular payments companies make to shareholders from their profits.

Why they matter: Historically, one of the strongest long-term wealth builders. When you own equities, you own a piece of real businesses generating real profits. Over decades, this has delivered better returns than almost any other asset class.

Watch out: The biggest mistake is emotional investing: buying high when everyone's excited, selling low when panic hits.

We'll explore how to invest in equities through ETFs and index funds in the next section of this book.

Bonds (Fixed Income)

I learned about bonds by watching Turkish investors in the late '90s. Turkish T-bills were yielding 70–90%, so savvy investors borrowed in Germany at 3–4% and pocketed the difference, a massive interest rate arbitrage. It worked beautifully... until a sudden currency devaluation turned the tables.

What they are: Loans you make to governments or companies in exchange for regular interest payments (called "coupons").

Why they matter: Provide predictable income and often act as stabilisers when equity markets fall; the classic "flight to safety" trade.

Watch out: Sensitive to interest rates. When rates rise, bond prices typically fall. Also, credit risk, if the borrower defaults, you could lose money.

Property (Real Estate)

Most people are familiar with property. It can generate income through rent and growth through appreciation, which is why it's such a central part of many UK portfolios. Some people love the tangibility of owning *bricks and mortar*; others prefer indirect exposure through funds or REITs (Real Estate Investment Trusts).

It's also the asset most likely to charm you into ignoring the numbers — so stay alert.

What it is: Ownership or investment in residential, commercial, or industrial real estate.

Why it matters: Can provide steady rental income and long-term capital growth. Often linked to inflation, which adds resilience.

Watch out: Illiquid, you can't sell quickly if you need cash. Requires management and maintenance. Sensitive to interest rates and economic cycles.

Because property is such a complex and widely used asset, we're giving it a full chapter next.

Part 2: Protectors- Preserving What You've Built

Once your foundation is in place, the next question is how to protect what you've built. These are your "safe hands," the ones who keep you grounded when everyone else is losing their heads. They are designed to add stability, security, and peace of mind to your portfolio during turbulent markets.

Gold & Silver

I used to think gold and silver were just jewellery, not investments. But precious metals can play an important role as stores of value, especially during uncertainty or rising inflation. They act as insurance in your portfolio, historically maintaining purchasing power over time. Today, you don't need vaults or gold bars as apps like Glint and ETFs make it simple to own.

What they are: Precious metals traditionally used as stores of value and safe-haven assets during periods of uncertainty or inflation.

Why they matter: They act as insurance against inflation and financial instability.

Watch out: Generate no income. Can have long periods of flat returns.

Bitcoin

I treat Bitcoin differently from other cryptocurrencies because, for me, it's in a class of its own. I first discovered it back in 2017 through an article in *The Economist* on blockchain and the potential for decentralised systems to change how we transact and store value. It's a decentralised digital asset with a fixed supply cap of 21 million coins, called "digital gold."

What it is: A decentralised digital asset with a fixed supply of 21 million coins, designed to act as a store of value outside traditional financial systems

Why it matters: Often called 'digital gold' because of its scarcity and store-of-value properties. Increasingly recognised as a potential hedge against inflation and currency debasement.

Watch out: Highly volatile. Regulatory risks. Security is crucial when self-custodying.

If you want to understand Bitcoin's philosophy, I highly recommend *The Bitcoin Standard* by Saifedean Ammous.

We'll explore Bitcoin investing in more depth in the Activation section.

Part 3: Growth & Alternatives - Accelerating Wealth and Expanding Possibilities

Beyond protection lies acceleration, the part of your portfolio designed for long-term expansion. These are your adventure partners: high energy, sometimes high drama, but never boring. They are higher-risk, higher-reward, and they often require more research, more patience, and sometimes more courage.

Digital Assets (Beyond Bitcoin)

After Bitcoin, there's a wider world of blockchain-based digital assets: Ethereum, DeFi tokens, and smart contracts driving financial innovation. Extreme volatility and high failure rates make these higher-risk plays for those willing to do deep research.

Private Equity

I started investing in private equity to diversify away from property. It felt like a natural extension of my work as a business coach. I love getting under the bonnet of businesses and helping them scale. For years, this was reserved for high-net-worth investors, but platforms like Seedrs, Syndicate Room and angel networks have democratised access, lowering minimums from millions to thousands.

What it is: Investing directly in private companies, from early-stage startups to established growth businesses.

Why it matters: Offers access to high-growth opportunities unavailable in public markets. Potential for significant returns if successful.

Watch out: Illiquid with long-term horizons. Higher failure risk, especially in early-stage ventures. Requires patience and due diligence.

We'll explore private equity investing in detail in the Activation section.

Options Trading

Options are the newest tool in my toolkit. They're not an asset but an investment strategy. There are many strategies for options, ranging from very low-risk to very high-risk ways to make money. I'm using this to generate income beyond property.

What they are: Financial contracts linked to the price of an underlying asset (like equities or ETFs) that give you the right, but not the obligation, to buy or sell at a set price.

Why they matter: Offering flexibility can generate income, hedge downside risk, or express views on market movements.

Watch out: Can be complex. Leverage magnifies both gains and losses. Requires education and a clear strategy before use. Translation: learn the rules before you start flirting with leverage.

We'll explore options strategies in detail in the Activation section.

Commodities & Other Alternatives

Commodities (oil, copper, wheat) and niche alternatives (art, wine, and collectables) round out the toolkit. These are typically passion-driven plays requiring deep expertise, usually much later in an investing journey.

How Assets Behave in Different Economic Conditions

As we saw in the previous chapter, different economic conditions create distinct investment climates. Just like people, assets behave differently under pressure, some thrive in the heat, others need cooler weather. Understanding how assets perform across environments helps you stay calm when the forecast changes. Think of this as a quick reference map for when you hear about inflation, rate hikes, or recessions in the news.

Category	**Asset**	**Typical Risk**	**Inflation Hedge?**	**Tend to Perform Well When...**	**Tend to Struggle When...**
Income-Generating	Equities	High	Indirect	Growth is strong; rates are stable or falling	Recessions; sharp rate hikes
	Bonds	Low–Medium	Weak	Interest rates falling; "flight to safety"	Rising rates; inflation surprises
	Property	Medium	Often	Stable economies; low borrowing costs	Recessions, rising interest rates
Protectors	Cash & Equivalents	Very Low	Weak	Short-term uncertainty; liquidity matters	Inflation erodes value
	Gold & Silver	Medium	Strong	Inflation spikes; financial instability	Strong equity rallies; low inflation
	Bitcoin	High	Emerging (thesis dependent)	Rising demand for scarce assets; distrust of fiat	Regulatory crackdowns; liquidity crunch
Growth & Alternatives	Digital Assets	Very High	Mixed	Liquidity-driven markets; innovation cycles	Regulation tightens; sentiment turns
	Commodities	High	Strong	Inflationary shocks; supply constraints	Deflationary slowdowns
	Private Equity	High	Weak	Expansion phases; cheap credit	Funding dries up; IPO markets close

	Options Trading	High	N/A	Strategic income plays; controlled volatility	Misused leverage; unpredict-able swings
	Other Alternatives	High	Mixed	Niche booms; passion-led mar-kets thrive	Illiquid-ity bites; demand collapses

This is the dance between assets and the economy: each has its rhythm, and together they create the music of your portfolio.

Why You Rarely Win With Just One

Every asset, like every relationship, teaches you something. Some bring excitement, some bring steadiness, some bring lessons you wish you'd learned cheaper. You wouldn't build a life around one relationship, and the same goes for your money.The alchemy lies in understanding what each one brings to the table, how they respond to economic conditions, and which ones still earn a place in your life.

We'll cover that in Chapter 15, Portfolio Architect. Before then, though, we'll look at my longest investing relationship, property and how to think about it with fresh eyes in a world that's changing fast.

Key Takeaways

- **Your toolkit has three categories** - Income-Generating (foundation), Protectors (resilience), and Growth & Alternatives (acceleration)
- **Knowledge creates choice** - you don't need to master every tool, but knowing what's available gives you flexibility and confidence
- **Property is one tool of many** - it's core, but not the only option
- **Assets behave differently in different conditions** - understanding when each one shines helps you build resilience

- **The right mix creates wealth** - real wealth comes from assets working together, not from mastering just one

Practical Actions

1. **Map what you already own** - List your current investments and note which category each belongs to: Income-Generating, Protectors, or Growth & Alternatives.
2. **Spot your gaps** - note where you are concentrated and where you might be overexposed or missing entirely
3. **Choose one unfamiliar asset class from this chapter** - perhaps private equity or options and commit to reading its Activation section this week
4. **Read the news differently** - When you hear about inflation or rate changes, check the *Economic Conditions* table: which assets benefit, which struggle?
5. **Decide your next focus** - Which category do you want to strengthen first: *Income-Generating, Protectors,* or *Growth & Alternatives*?

Chapter 14

BEYOND BRICKS

How to Expand Your Wealth Strategy Beyond Property

For many of us in the UK, one tool in the investment kit looms larger than the rest: property. I get it. I really do. I have a love-hate relationship with it myself. I've made money from it, and I've lost money from it. The emotional pull is real, there's something magical about taking a tired old building and turning it into something useful and beautiful. It's why so many of us are drawn to it in the first place.

But property is just one tool, not the whole toolkit. In this chapter, we'll look at why it looms so large in our culture, how the numbers have shifted, and how to decide whether it deserves as much space in your wealth strategy as it often takes up. This is about rewriting the reflex, keeping the wisdom of property while giving your money more ways to grow.

Building Community Through Property

When I moved back to the UK about eight years ago, I landed in a small seaside town in Devon. I didn't know a soul. I'd bought a house in Seaton to renovate, so my children could go to school nearby, and to be close to my mum. It was a fresh start, and I realised quickly that I needed to build a community around me.

The only thing I really knew then was coaching and property. So, when I met my architect, I floated the idea of starting a local property meetup, and he offered the football club in Lyme Regis as a venue. And so, the Devon & Dorset Investment Group was born.

Every month, 30 or so of us would gather, from Bournemouth to Plymouth, sharing ideas, strategies, and speakers on everything from HMOs to modular builds to commercial conversions. For me, it was about so much more than property. It was about connection and creating new friends.

Looking back, that experience taught me something fundamental: investing doesn't have to be a solo sport. The right community accelerates learning, sharpens decisions, and reminds you you're not alone in the risks you take. That belief underpins everything I do now, and it's one of the reasons I created the Fearless Female Investor Collective.

Property has been a significant part of my journey, and many of the friendships and connections I've built over the years have come through it. I know how great property can be. Some of my proudest moments have come from it; from my first large conversion project in the centre of Sallanches in the Haute Savoie, to building a beautiful chalet in the Alps, to my last pub conversion development in Exeter, where, after months of setbacks, I finally achieved a valuation higher than I'd dared hope for. There's something deeply satisfying about seeing a vision materialise in brick and stone, creating something lasting and tangible from an idea and a spreadsheet.

However, there is another side. And it's not just my story, it's woven into how we think about money in this country. The same emotional pull that draws us in can sometimes derail us. We overspend, we underestimate timelines, or assume prices will always rise and when the numbers don't stack up, that "safe" bet suddenly feels a lot less secure.

The UK's Love Affair With Property

In Britain, property isn't just an investment, it's an identity. "Getting on the ladder" is seen as a rite of passage. Renting is framed as "throwing money away." Entire TV schedules are filled with shows celebrating flipping, renovating, and becoming a "developer."

The obsession isn't just financial, it's cultural. In the UK, homeownership represents stability, security, and control over one's environment. It's tied to adulthood, success, and social status, and has been reinforced for decades by policies like the *Right to Buy* scheme. Property has become a public marker of achievement, the symbol that you "made it."

While other countries also value owning homes, Britain stands out. In the US, a more transient population and flexible rental culture create more options, and in Europe, strong rental markets allow greater mobility. In the UK, though, the link between property and identity runs deeper, and it subtly shapes our financial decisions.

It's no wonder so many of us equate property with security and success. It feels tangible, familiar, and, done well, can be a brilliant wealth builder. However, some of the old assumptions need refreshing.

Why the Maths Feel Different Now

Part of the property's hold on us is that it feels real. You can touch it, live in it, or borrow against it. Leverage makes it especially appealing for those starting out with little capital.

But the landscape has shifted, and those advantages no longer guarantee success:

- **Slower nominal growth in many regions**—in several areas, prices haven't kept up with inflation, so real gains have lagged.
- **Higher costs**—materials, labour and compliance have risen meaningfully, squeezing margins, especially on small projects.
- **Regulatory complexity**—changes in tax treatment, building standards and tenant protections increasingly reward professionalism and scale.

- **Financing is cyclical**—leverage amplifies both gains and losses. In a rising market it feels like genius; in a flat or falling one, it can trap you with negative cash flow and no exit.

In several regions, house prices haven't kept pace with the cost of living in recent years. Even where values rose, purchasing power sometimes fell. That doesn't make property "bad"; it just means you should compare what your equity could earn elsewhere before you lock it up. In other words, the old "buy, hold, do nothing" approach still works in some niches, but it's no longer a free ride.

Selectivity and skill matter more. You really have to know how to add value to property. The good news is, opportunities still exist; they just look different. Today, the best returns tend to come from adding value you control, not waiting for the market to rise. That could mean securing planning gain, extending short-term leases, reconfiguring layouts to unlock extra rental income, or focusing on niches such as short-term lets, build-to-rent, or co-living spaces where demand remains strong. Property can still shine, but only when you bring skill, creativity, and clear numbers to the table; when leverage is appropriate, cash flow is sustainable, and risk is diversified.

Four Numbers to Run Before You Buy

Numbers aren't here to scare you, they're how we translate intuition into clarity. If you're actively investing in property, these four calculations are non-negotiable. If you're not, focus on the principle: every investment needs clear numbers, not just a good feeling.

Once you run them a few times, it becomes second nature. Whether you're buying to rent or to flip, strip away the emotion and check these.

1. Net Yield (Buy-to-let/HMO/Serviced Accommodation)

Net Yield = (Annual rent – running costs – mortgage interest) ÷ purchase price.

If the net yield is under 5%, should I consider a simple ETF or REIT that pays me the same income (or more) with less hassle?

2. Return on Equity / Return on Invested Capital (ROE/ROIC) (Buy-to-let and flips)

This is the real test. It measures how hard *your money* is working for you. It looks at how much *you* have left in the property after a refinance or sale.

> ROIC = return on the cash you still have left after refinance.
>
> ROE = return on your equity tied up (what's still locked in the bricks).

Seasoned investors track both; ROE stops you from kidding yourself that "nothing left in" means "infinite return." If your ROIC is under 10%, you may be better off in equities, ETFs, or even private equity deals where your capital works harder.

3. Tax and Opportunity Cost

Where you hold your property matters. For personally held BTL, mortgage interest isn't fully deductible; cash flow can be tight after paying interest.

And every pound of equity locked in a wall could be working elsewhere, which is an opportunity cost.

4. Flips: Count Everything

With flips, many people compare headline figures to calculate a projected profit. In reality, stamp duty, fees, finance, overruns, CGT, and your time all eat substantially into profits. The headline "£50k" often shrinks to a much smaller number.

Worked Example: Buy at £190k, Add £20k, Revalue at £250k

Assumptions

- Purchase price: £190,000
- Refurbishment: £20,000
- Total spent: £210,000
- Revalued price: £250,000
- Refinance: 75% LTV → new mortgage = £187,500
- Rent: £15,000/year (£1,250/month)
- Costs (insurance, management, maintenance, voids): £3,000/year
- Mortgage interest (5%): £9,375/year

Step 1: Capital in and out

- Initial deposit (25% of £190k): £47,500
- Total cash in (deposit + refurb): £67,500
- Cash released at refinance: £45,000
- Cash left in deal: £22,500
- Equity left in property (£250k – £187.5k): £62,500

Step 2: Income

- Annual rent: £15,000
- Annual costs: £3,000
- Annual mortgage: £9,375
- **Net cash flow: £2,625/year**

Step 3: Returns

- **ROIC (cash left in):** £2,625 ÷ £22,500 = **11.7%**
- **ROE (equity tied up):** £2,625 ÷ £62,500 = **4.2%**

Could this still be worth doing? Absolutely, if you have a clear plan, a genuine edge (sourcing, building a team, or niche), and a reason to hold that specific asset. The point isn't "don't buy"; it's "know what you're really earning on *all* the capital tied up."

On paper, this looks like a strong deal, nearly 12% on cash left in. However, once you factor in the equity still tied up (£62.5k), the true return is just over 4%. That's less than a simple dividend ETF with daily liquidity. This is the opportunity-cost trap: what looks like 'nothing left in' can still mean your capital is working at a low rate.

Track ROIC *and* ROE: ROIC shows how your leftover cash is working; ROE shows how all your tied-up equity is working, and whether it could earn more elsewhere.

You've seen this in your Freedom Number and Conscious Spending work: every pound you tie up in one place has an opportunity cost. The question is always the same: could my money work harder somewhere else?

It's also worth stress-testing these numbers. If interest rates rise, rents fall, or if you have an extra month of voids, the picture can change quickly. Keep revisiting your ROIC and ROE as conditions shift; they're living numbers, not a one-off calculation.

Bottom line

- Gross yield is marketing; **net** is what you spend.
- ROIC tells you how hard your **cash** is working.
- ROE tells you how hard your **equity** is working.
- Always sanity-check against a simple ETF/REIT alternative.
- If a simple, diversified option pays you as much (or more) with less effort, pause and reassess.

For deeper numbers: You'll find the full comparison tables, regional price trends, buy-to-let vs flips vs REITs vs ETFs, ROIC/ROE worksheets, and extra worked examples in the **Fearless Wealth Playbook**.

Use them to stress-test your deal and benchmark it against simple, liquid alternatives before you commit.

In practice, a small buy-to-let can deliver modest net income and low liquidity; flips can produce lumpy gains with high effort and risk; and a dividend ETF offers lower effort with daily liquidity. None is "best," the question is which mix fits your goals, time, and tolerance for mess.

Property Without the Headaches: Alternative Paths

Not everyone wants to deal with tenants, repairs, or regulatory headaches. And not every investor wants all their capital locked up in bricks and mortar. The good news is that there are other ways to gain exposure to property, or compare it to other investments, without the same level of risk or hassle.

Lending to Developers: Higher Returns, Higher Risks

One route many investors explore as a hands-off alternative to buying property themselves is lending to developers, often tempted by promises of high returns, 10%, 15%, even 25% annually. Lending can be brilliant in the right hands and brutal in the wrong ones. My own experience taught me to upgrade due diligence, protections, and partners before I chase a headline rate.

In 2018, I lent nearly £300,000 through my SSAS to a developer converting a pub in Exeter into a 22-room HMO. On paper, it looked solid. In reality, poor management led to the project's collapse. I spent 2020 in court, then another two years and significant additional funds trying to salvage my pension investment.

Eventually, I succeeded with the project and recovered my capital, and more. But the emotional stress and cost of those two years were enormous. Looking back, I'd do it differently. And I am not alone: many investors I know have similar stories of lending money to property developers who promised great returns but failed to deliver.

The lesson is simple: if you're considering this path, do extreme due diligence. Understand the project, the developer's track record, the risks and, most importantly, how you'll get your money back if things go wrong. Minimums I now insist on: independent QS or monitoring surveyor, step-in rights, first-charge security (or clearly documented risk if not), ring-fenced build budgets, and a sober exit plan that isn't "hope".

REITs: Property Without the Hassle

Another option, for those who want property exposure without the headaches or single-borrower risk, is Real Estate Investment Trusts (REITs). These are:

- Listed companies that own or finance property portfolios.
- Traded on the stock market, so your money stays liquid.
- At times, traded at discounts to Net Asset Value (NAV), so you can buy £1 of assets for, say, 75–80p.

Some examples:

- AEW UK REIT — value-oriented UK commercial.
- Supermarket Income REIT — long leases, inflation-linked.
- Impact Healthcare REIT — healthcare/care homes exposure.

REITs aren't risk-free; they're sensitive to interest rates and market cycles, but they offer diversification, liquidity, and passive income without the full-time commitment. REIT share prices can trade at discounts to their underlying net assets when rates are high or sentiment is gloomy. That can be an opportunity, or a value trap, so look under the bonnet (leverage, tenant quality, lease lengths).

REITs make most sense when you want property exposure with liquidity, diversification across multiple properties, and professional management, essentially treating property like any other asset class rather than a hands-on project.

Beyond Property: Smarter Alternatives

This is where my own thinking has shifted dramatically. I used to believe property was the best, maybe the only way to replace income and create financial freedom through rental yields. But over time, I realised my money could work harder elsewhere.

Moving from being a "property investor" to simply being "an investor" was harder than I expected. Property had been part of my identity for years; my business, my lifestyle, my community. Letting go of that and choosing to sell most of my properties wasn't just about the money; it was emotional.

I'm in the process of selling down my properties. As those sales are completed, I gain liquidity, flexibility and freedom. And I want to give you the same tools to make choices based on numbers, not narratives.

One strategy I am now moving to is the options wheel, which we'll explore in detail in Section 3. The principle is simple: it's like 'renting out' your shares, generating around 1.5–2% monthly while keeping your capital liquid and available to deploy.

Returns vary, and there's a learning curve, however, I treat it like running a small business with clear rules, written records, and defined risk limits. The consistency matters far more than the excitement.

When I look at how experienced family offices allocate capital, property is a meaningful slice but certainly not the whole pie. They balance illiquid assets with liquid strategies, enabling them to pivot when conditions change. We can do the same.

Pulling It All Together

For years, my identity was bound up with property. I lived it, breathed it, and even now I sometimes feel the pull to dive back in. It's familiar, tangible, and for many of us, it feels safe. But I've also learned that safety can be an illusion, and that real wealth comes from giving your money more ways to grow.

Property isn't 'wrong.' If you're already investing in it, I want to acknowledge your courage and craft; it takes boldness to build anything real. There are genuine advantages - mortgage interest relief in limited companies, capital gains rollover relief, but these benefits need to be weighed against liquidity constraints, concentration risk, and the alternative returns available elsewhere.

The freedom comes when you see it as part of a bigger, more resilient strategy, not the whole plan. We'll explore how to balance illiquid assets like property with liquid investments and income strategies when we reach the Investment Strategies spokes of the Wheel of Wealth later in the book.

Next, we'll take everything you've learned so far about property, the power of compounding, and navigating economic shifts, and start building. In the next chapter, you'll learn how to create a portfolio that blends property with other investments, how to think about asset allocation, and how to design a strategy that's balanced, resilient, and aligned with the life you want to create.

Let's start to construct the foundations of your portfolio.

Key Takeaways

- **Property is powerful but harder now** - the easy wins are rarer
- **Edge and execution matter most** - in today's market, these determine success
- **Always check the numbers** - ROIC and ROE, and compare with simple alternatives
- **Balance liquidity** - match illiquid assets with liquid ones so you can pivot
- **Your skills transfer** - you already have what you need; now apply them beyond bricks

Practical Actions

1. **Run the numbers on every deal** - Calculate net yield, ROIC, and ROE before committing to any property.
2. **Stress-test your mortgage** - Model your cashflow if interest rates rise by 2–3% and make sure the deal still works.
3. **Benchmark against the simple alternative** - Compare any property opportunity against a straightforward ETF or REIT before taking on the complexity.
4. **Review your property weighting** - If property is more than around 50% of your net worth, build a rebalance plan.
5. **Take one property skill and apply it elsewhere** - Identify one transferable skill — deal analysis, project management, cashflow reading and put it to work in a liquid strategy.

Chapter 15

THE PORTFOLIO ARCHITECT

From Portfolio Theory to Personal Power

In the last chapter, we explored property as a powerful wealth builder but it also has its limits. Bricks and mortar can be a cornerstone of financial freedom, yet a house alone doesn't make a portfolio. True resilience comes from balance: different assets, each with its own role, working together. The moment you start thinking beyond bricks, you step into the role of architect, designing a portfolio that reflects not just returns but your values, confidence, and future freedom.

You are about to learn how to become the fund manager of your own wealth.

What You Actually Need (And It's Not What They Tell You)

I spent years learning portfolio theory. Morgan Stanley kindly paid tens of thousands for me to get a Master's in Finance from London Business School. I became a fund manager. I worked with quantitative analysts running complex risk models. I learned about efficient frontiers, Sharpe ratios, and optimal portfolio construction.

If portfolio theory ever made you feel out of your depth, you're not alone; most of the industry makes it sound far more complicated than it really is. The quiet truth is that you don't need any of that. What you need is curiosity, discipline, and patience: the ability to observe, think clearly, and not panic when markets move.

The brilliant thing is that as women, we are generally better equipped with these qualities. In my experience, women ask better questions than most fund managers I've worked with. Women are less likely to panic-sell or chase shiny objects. Women understand that good things take time.

What women often lack isn't capability, it's recognising that finance is often presented as being complex and hard to understand; it isn't.

So stick with me. This chapter will give you everything that matters from my expensive education, stripped of the nonsense.

Diversification: The Simple Truth Hidden Behind Complex Theory

Back in the 1950s, an economist named Harry Markowitz won a Nobel Prize for proving mathematically what good investors already knew: by holding a mix of investments that don't all move together, you can lower your overall risk without lowering your returns. He called it Modern Portfolio Theory. The academics loved it: Greek letters, optimisation models, and Nobel Prizes.

However, Charlie Munger, Warren Buffett's long-time partner, would tell you most of that is unnecessary complexity. The essence is simple:

- Don't own things that all crash together
- Know what you own
- Be patient

That's it. That's diversification.

However, many people don't understand this. They get swept up in the excitement of a specific asset class. They attend a property seminar, get enthusiastic about the returns, and pile everything into say serviced accommodation. Or they discover crypto and go all-in on Bitcoin. Or they read about gold and put their entire portfolio into bullion.

Sometimes this works brilliantly, for a while. But when the market turns, and it always does, they're exposed. No other income streams, no way to rebalance without selling at the worst moment.

The problem isn't the asset itself. The problem is the concentration: building a one-legged stool and hoping gravity works differently for you.

Diversification Happens at Multiple Levels

Think of diversification as happening in layers, like Russian dolls:

Layer 1: Your Life Portfolio

If you have a job and you have capital invested, you are already diversified at the life level. You have human capital (your earning ability) and financial capital working in your favour. This is why a salaried doctor with £200,000 in equities is in a different position than a retired person with the same £200,000, with different life diversification.

Layer 2: Your Strategy Focus

You might choose to focus deeply on one approach: property investing, options trading, or value stock picking. That's not a lack of diversification if you're doing it intentionally and you understand what you own. Focus can be powerful.

Layer 3: Diversification Within Your Strategy

This is where it gets interesting. A property investor might own 5-7 buy-to-let properties across different cities and tenant demographics. They're only in property but diversified across location and risk profile.

An options trader running the Wheel strategy might hold positions in indices, precious metals, and tech stocks, or choose different strike prices. They're "only doing options," but they're diversified across sectors and correlation patterns.

Layer 4: Asset Class Correlation

At the broadest level, you're looking at how different asset types behave relative to each other. We looked at a table on this in the previous chapter, and how assets behave in different economic conditions. This is where traditional diversification thinking lives: equities, bonds, property, cash, and alternatives.

The key is being clear which layer you're talking about when you discuss diversification, because someone asking "Am I diversified enough?" might be perfectly balanced at Layer 3 but dangerously concentrated at Layer 4.

It is absolutely possible to be over-diversified, for example buying 40 random stocks or 10 different asset classes you don't understand just because someone told you to spread your risk. This is not diversification, this is ignorance.

This type of diversification feels safe because you're "spread out," but you're actually diluting any potential outperformance, paying unnecessary costs and fooling yourself that you're protected

The goal isn't to own everything. It's to own enough different things that one disaster doesn't destroy you, but few enough that you can actually pay attention.

As one of my mentors once said: "Diversify enough to sleep at night, concentrate enough to stay awake during the day."

Understanding Correlation: Why Your Investments Need Different Personalities

Now let's talk about why asset correlation matters, because this is where the "protection" part of diversification actually works.

Think of correlation like your circle of close friends. Some friends always react the same way to your news, panic when you panic, and celebrate when you celebrate. That's high correlation. Other friends respond differently: one stays calm, another reassures you, and a third has an alternative view. Those are low-correlation friends, and they balance you out.

Your investments work the same way. If all your assets behave identically under stress, you're not diversified; you've just labelled the same risk five different ways. True diversification comes from owning investments that respond differently to change. Correlation isn't static, it shifts. That's why you need to understand how things move together, not just trust that diversification magically works.

From Theory to Garden: A Practical View

Let's make this even more tangible. Imagine your portfolio as a living ecosystem, a garden that needs balance, care, and diversity to thrive.

You wouldn't plant only roses or only tomatoes. You'd mix perennials with shrubs, herbs with fruit trees. Some grow fast, some take years. Some need pruning, others thrive with neglect.

- Equities are your sun-loving plants, high growth potential, but sensitive to economic weather
- Bonds are your shade-tolerant shrubs, steady, reliable, not flashy but dependable
- Property is your fruit tree, slow to mature, but rewarding over time with regular income
- Cash is the soil, essential foundation, but not where the magic of growth happens

Different plants need different conditions. Your job as a gardener isn't to make every plant the same; it's to create an ecosystem where they support each other. Your financial portfolio works in exactly the same way.

Asset Allocation: The Strategic Journey

Asset allocation is where science meets art, where your analytical mind meets your intuitive wisdom. It's not about creating the "perfect" portfolio; it's about finding the right mix for your unique situation, goals, and emotional truth.

Asset allocation is the process of deciding how to split your money across assets. It's shaped by three things:

- Your goals (growth, income, stability)
- Your time horizon (when you'll need the money)
- Your emotional and financial risk tolerance

When I was designing my own portfolio strategy, I realised that traditional age-based advice didn't fit my life. The standard IFA formula of "100 minus your age in equities" would have had me reducing risk just as I was building momentum in my business and feeling most confident about taking calculated risks.

Instead of mapping asset mixes to life stages, I've developed what I call confidence-based allocation, where portfolios are designed around your investor confidence and intentionality.

The Four Investor Archetypes

Using my passion for skiing, here are four possible investor archetypes. These are starting points and suggestions, not rigid rules. Like learning to ski, you might spend time on different pistes as you build confidence, and you can always adjust your approach as your situation changes.

Some of you reading this will think "that's too aggressive for me," perfect, adjust down. Others will think "that's too conservative," also perfect, adjust up. The goal is to give you a framework to think through YOUR situation, not a one-size-fits-all formula.

1. The Stabiliser (Building Confidence) Like learning to ski on blue pistes

Mindset: "I'm learning the fundamentals and building my foundation"

Focus: Understanding markets, building emergency funds, taking first confident steps

When I was starting out in finance, this was me. I needed to understand how markets moved before I could take bigger risks. I had a mix of equity funds and property. There's no shame in starting here; every expert was once a beginner.

2. The Accelerator (Gaining Control) Red piste skiing, more speed, more technique

Mindset: "I understand the game and I'm ready to compound aggressively"

Focus: Growth, learning about different asset classes, building wealth momentum

This is where I was about 10 years ago. Having built a strong income-generating property portfolio, I felt ready to explore investing beyond property and equity funds. I started focusing on accelerating my wealth-building rather than preserving it.

3. The Freedom Seeker (Skilled Navigation) Black piste territory, technical, bold, strategic

Mindset: "I'm designing my portfolio for both growth and income"

Focus: Diversification across asset classes, generating passive income, strategic risk-taking

Over the past two years, I have focused on learning option-income-generating strategies to move beyond property income. I have also been exploring other options to diversify my portfolio.

4. The Architect (Full Autonomy) Off-piste skiing, powder, exhilaration, and bespoke routes

Mindset: "I'm building wealth with intention and impact"

Focus: Complex strategies, tax optimisation, legacy building, alternative investments

This is where I am moving next: building wealth with intention, exploring new opportunities and continuing to diversify my portfolio. My current focus is on tax optimisation and legacy planning.

Another key factor in portfolio design is liquidity: how quickly you can access your money if life throws you a curveball. ETFs and listed shares can usually be sold within days; property or private equity may lock up capital for years. Neither is 'better': it depends on your goals. Being clear on how much of your wealth is liquid versus tied up is part of building confidence in your strategy.

Maintaining Your Portfolio: The Art of Rebalancing

Once you've built your portfolio, the work isn't over but it's simpler than you think. Your job isn't to constantly tinker or chase performance. It's to maintain your intended balance as markets move.

This is an example of what happens naturally: Your £10,000 in equities grows to £15,000 while your £10,000 in bonds stays at £11,000. Suddenly, you're more equity-heavy than you intended, not because you made a decision, but because markets moved.

Rebalancing means selling some of what's grown (equities) and buying more of what's lagged (bonds) to return to your target allocation. You're systematically selling high and buying low, the opposite of what emotions tell you to do.

When to rebalance:

- Set a threshold: when any asset class drifts more than 5-10% from your target
- Or calendar-based: review quarterly, rebalance annually
- When your life circumstances change significantly

When not to rebalance:

- Because markets dropped and you're scared

- Because something performed well and you want "more of the winner"
- Because you read a headline

This connects directly to the monthly review practices we'll explore in the AAA framework later in the book. Regular reviews help you spot when rebalancing is needed before small drifts become major imbalances.

Addressing the Fear: There's No Perfect Portfolio

Here's something the financial industry doesn't always tell you: there is no right or wrong portfolio. Just like life, investing is an iterative process.

You might be thinking: "But what if I choose wrong? What if I lose money? What if I'm not smart enough for this?"

These fears are completely natural. Every investor has felt them, including me. The biggest risk isn't making a "wrong" choice; it's making no choice at all, keeping your money in cash and letting inflation erode your wealth away.

This is also the moment to remind you to separate two concepts that often get muddled: volatility and risk. Volatility is the movement of prices; the ups and downs that make headlines. Risk is the chance of permanent loss of capital. They are not the same.

Private equity, for example, often appears stable because prices don't move day to day, but the underlying risk can be high. Bitcoin, on the other hand, has been wildly volatile, yet the best-performing asset of the last decade. Sometimes the greatest risk lies not in the swings, but in missing the upside.

Remember:

- You can adjust your portfolio as you learn and grow
- Starting with a simple, diversified approach is better than perfect paralysis

- Every professional investor makes mistakes; it's part of the learning process
- Your portfolio should evolve as your confidence and circumstances change

The goal isn't perfection. It's progress. You're building skills, confidence, and wealth simultaneously.

See the ETF chapter: "When Should I Actually Buy?" for a practical step-by-step guide on when to invest and the chapter on Emotional Money Mastery on managing your emotions when investing in the next section, Activation.

The Real Cost of Outsourcing: Taking Back Your Power

For many women, the default has been to hand control of their investments to an Independent Financial Adviser (IFA). Like most of the financial industry, the IFA industry is still largely male; however, it is slowly changing, and there are some brilliant female advisers who truly understand our lived experiences.

This isn't intended as a takedown of the IFA industry. IFAs absolutely have their place, particularly for specialist projects such as setting up a trust, structuring legacy plans, managing cross-border assets, or creating complex liquidity strategies. The right adviser, in those situations, is worth their weight in gold. I've used them myself and will continue to do so.

What few people talk about though, is the impact on your wealth of giving someone else your portfolio to manage. If you're paying an IFA 1–1.5% a year plus another 1–1.5% in fund manager fees, you're giving away 2–3% of your returns every single year.

That might not sound like much... until you see what it really costs:

Starting with a £100,000 investment.

The Long-Term Impact of Fees on Investment Outcomes

Metric	DIY Investor	ISA + Fund Fees
Gross Annual Return	10.0%	10.0%
Total Fees (p.a.)	~0.25%	~2.5%
Net Annual Return	9.75%	7.5%
Value After 20 Years	~£700,000	~£450,000
Value After 30 Years	£1.8 million	£1million

That's a £800,000 difference over 30 years, the price of outsourcing decisions you are perfectly capable of making yourself. And that's conservative. If markets return 12% instead of 10%, the gap widens to over £1 million.

This isn't about cutting advisers out of your life. It's about being intentional: choosing where to pay for expertise and where to reclaim your own power.

By learning to manage your portfolio yourself, you keep more of your returns working for you. And perhaps most importantly, you step into full ownership of your financial future.

Because no one, not even the best adviser in the world, will care about your wealth, your goals, and your freedom quite as much as you do.

Designing Your Investment Strategy

By now, you've seen that building a portfolio isn't about complexity; it's about clarity. You already have the qualities of a great investor: curiosity, discipline, and patience. Your next step is to design a portfolio that truly reflects *you*, your goals, your confidence, and your values.

In your Fearless Wealth Playbook, you'll find tools to help you put this into action and bring your strategy to life.

For now, pause and reflect: *What kind of architect do you want to be?* One who plays by someone else's blueprint, or one who designs her own financial freedom on her terms?

Bringing It All Together: Your Portfolio as Life Philosophy

You now understand what finance professionals won't always tell you: you don't need expensive degrees to build a resilient portfolio. You need curiosity, discipline, and patience; qualities you already have.

The most powerful portfolios aren't built from spreadsheets; they're built from self-awareness and alignment. In the next chapter, we'll add the final layer: your Investment Values Compass, a framework for mapping your values onto your investments so that your money doesn't just grow, it guides you.

Key Takeaways

- **You already have what you need** - curiosity, discipline, and patience matter more than finance degrees
- **Diversification is contextual** - it happens at multiple layers: life portfolio, strategy focus, within-strategy, and asset correlation
- **Smart diversification is focused** - owning enough different things that one setback doesn't destroy you, but few enough to actually monitor
- **Correlation is protection** - true balance means holding assets that behave differently in different conditions
- **Over-diversification dilutes returns** - 40 random stocks isn't smart diversification, it's expensive noise
- **Confidence beats formulas** - build a portfolio that reflects where you are now, not what a rule tells you
- **Volatility isn't risk** - price swings don't always mean danger, and stability doesn't always mean safety

- **Keep costs low** - check what you are paying for
- **Ownership is power** - managing your portfolio is easier than managing a household budget

Practical Actions

1. **Identify which layer of diversification you're thinking about** - Life portfolio? Strategy focus? Within-strategy? Asset correlation? Be specific.
2. **Choose your archetype honestly** - Stabiliser, Accelerator, Freedom Seeker, or Architect - where are you right now, not where you wish you were?
3. **Assess what you're optimising for** - Growth, income, or capital preservation? Your answer shapes everything.
4. **Decide your liquidity needs** - How much needs to be easily accessible versus locked up long-term?
5. **Write your one-page investment philosophy** - Your objectives, your chosen strategy focus, your diversification approach, and your guiding principles. Keep it simple.

Chapter 16

THE INVESTMENT VALUES COMPASS

Money And Meaning: Aligning Wealth With Who You Are

Now that you've learned how to design your portfolio, it's time to ask a more unexpected question: Does it feel right?

Not "is it diversified?" or "will it grow?" The question now is deeper: When you look at your investments, do you feel energised or drained? Curious or bored? Connected or detached? A portfolio can be perfect on paper and yet still feel wrong. When something feels wrong, we don't stick with it.

Up to this point, you've uncovered your values, built your financial knowledge, and explored the tools and strategies that can grow your wealth. This last step is about integration, checking that your outer wealth (what you're investing in) and your inner wealth (what matters to you) are speaking the same language: strategy and soul, money and meaning.

Think of Alignment as preparation: building the foundation and finding your true north. The next stage, Activation, is ignition, switching something on, bringing energy and momentum, putting your clarity into consistent motion.

That begins here, with one simple lens: the Investment Values Compass.

My "Aha" Moment

The Investment Values Compass came to me not through research or systematic testing, but through a moment of clarity about my own portfolio. I'd been making choices for years without understanding why some strategies lit me up whilst others drained me, even when they were equally profitable.

When I finally mapped my investments against my core values, I discovered something unexpected: alignment isn't about perfection. It's about consciousness.

Learning

I've known for quite a while now that my top three values are Learning, Connecting, and Achieving, but it wasn't until I understood how those values related to my investing decisions that everything clicked into place.

I've always been endlessly curious. I love discovering how things work and diving deep into new ideas. That's what drew me into property investing early on; there were so many strategies and so much to learn. In 2017, my curiosity led me into Bitcoin and cryptocurrency. I was fascinated by the potential of blockchain technology and wanted to understand it from the inside out.

As property became less about growth for me, I noticed myself naturally gravitating towards new strategies, exploring private equity, venture funds, and emerging themes. For me, learning isn't a tick-box exercise; it's how I stay energised and connected to my wealth journey.

Connecting

Relationships are everything to me. Engaging deeply with people energises me: sharing stories, building trust, being part of something bigger. That's why private equity has become one of my largest investment themes.

Unlike listed companies, where investment decisions are mostly made based on numbers and reports, private equity is personal. Over 60% of any decision comes down to the management team and assessing if they can they deliver what they promise.

For me, that means getting to know founders, having honest conversations, asking questions, and feeling their passion. Those relationships feed my need for connection, and when I invest this way, it doesn't just feel strategic; it feels fulfilling.

Achieving

I've always been driven to make things happen. I love seeing results, moving things forward, and creating momentum. That's why I'm drawn to investing in businesses that want to scale, innovate, and grow, companies that match my energy and ambition.

Private equity again ticks that box for me. When I back founders who are hungry to build, I feel aligned. Their vision becomes part of mine, and I get to contribute to creating something meaningful.

When Misalignment Isn't Actually Misalignment

When I mapped my investments against my values, options trading stuck out like a sore thumb. It didn't serve Learning, once I'd learnt the strategy, it was just repetition. It was me, a screen, and rules to follow so didn't serve Connecting. It felt structured, rigid, and the opposite of how I like to work.

By every measure, options trading looked like a misalignment. And my first instinct was: "I should stop doing this."

Then I paused and asked a different question: "What is this giving me?" That's when I saw it: Achievement.

Options trading can generate substantial, consistent income. Money that gives me freedom to do what matters to me without worrying about paying the bills.

The strategy itself didn't excite me, however, what it enabled certainly did. That changed how I viewed options trading and I made a conscious choice to stick with it. Not because I loved it, but because I was clear about which value it served and why that mattered.

That was my big "aha" moment: Alignment isn't about only doing what you love. It's about making conscious choices based on what matters most.

The sophisticated truth about alignment is that you don't have to love everything in your portfolio. You just need to know why you're doing it and which value it serves.

Introducing the Investment Values Compass

The Compass below isn't a research-based methodology or a framework I've tested with hundreds of clients. It's a tool that emerged from my own aha moment and acts as a filter to help bring your true self into the centre of your financial decisions.

I've grouped common values into eight broad clusters and suggested possible links between each cluster and investment strategies that might naturally align. These aren't prescriptions, they're prompts. Use what resonates, ignore what doesn't.

Think of this as a lens for reflection, not a system for optimisation.

When your investments honour your values, or at least one important value, you stay engaged during market ups and downs. You feel energised instead of overwhelmed. You build wealth in a way that feels authentic and sustainable.

The Investment Values Compass

Below is a simple guide to explore how different values might express themselves in your investment choices.

Use it as inspiration, not instruction. The goal isn't to fit yourself into a box, but to see where energy flows naturally and what truly lights you up.

Value Cluster	What Drives You	Aligned Investment Styles / Asset Classes	Why It Fits
Learning & Growth	Curiosity, exploration, discovery	Startups, private equity, blockchain, emerging markets, thematic ETFs	You thrive on researching trends, technologies, and new opportunities.
Connection & Community	Relationships, people, trust	Private equity, angel investing, property partnerships, mastermind groups	Success depends on shared journeys and human dynamics.
Freedom & Autonomy	Independence, flexibility	Dividend portfolios, trading strategies, crypto, REITs, and direct property	It lets you design your lifestyle and stay in control of your time.
Security & Stability	Safety, predictability	Bonds, blue-chip stocks, long-term real estate, diversified ETFs	You prioritise consistency and peace of mind.
Impact & Contribution	Purpose, meaning, legacy	ESG funds, green bonds, social impact investments, and community investment funds	Your money creates measurable good whilst growing sustainably.
Achievement & Influence	Progress, leadership, results	Direct private equity, scaling businesses, and active property development	You want to shape outcomes and help drive growth.

Simplicity & Ease	Clarity, calm, minimal effort	Robo-advisors, passive ETF strategies, and multi-asset funds	You value financial freedom without complexity.
Thrill & Discovery	Risk, novelty, adrenaline	Crypto trading, frontier markets, venture capital, disruptive tech	Fast-moving and dynamic, perfect for explorers and innovators.

Spotting Misalignments (And Understanding Them)

When no values are being served, we feel it in our bodies, our energy, even our sleep. If your top value is Security but you're day-trading crypto with money you can't afford to lose, sleepless nights. If you value Simplicity but you're juggling five property developments with no support, overwhelm. If Connection drives you but your entire portfolio is passive ETFs you never think about, disengagement.

Sometimes though, what feels like misalignment is actually partial alignment. Check this by asking: "Which of my values does this serve? And is that enough?"

My options trading serves Achievement through income generation, and that's enough for me, even though it doesn't serve Learning or Connecting.

Genuine misalignment is when nothing connects. When you can't find a single value being met. That's when you need to change something.

Partial alignment is when at least one is being served, and you're conscious about that and why it matters.

How to Use the Compass

This isn't a complex process. It's insight work, not system work.

1. **Reconnect with your top three values** (from Chapter 8).

2. **Look at your current investments and ask for each one:** Which of my values does this serve? Not "does it match perfectly?" but "what's it actually giving me?"
3. **Notice the patterns:**
   - **Strong alignment:** Multiple values are being met. This energises you.
   - **Partial alignment:** One value is being met. Understand your why.
   - **No alignment:** Nothing connects. Consider changing something.
4. **Make one conscious choice:** Reaffirm what's working, reframe what you've misunderstood, or identify what needs to shift.

That's all the Compass is: a lens to check whether your money is flowing in a direction that makes sense and feels right to you.

Permission to Not Change Everything

This chapter is not saying that you should only invest in things you love that every strategy should light you up, or that misalignment means you're doing it wrong.

Real life has constraints. You might need income now, even if the strategy isn't thrilling. You might have investments you inherited that don't match your values but are doing their job. You might be in a season where simplicity matters more than optimisation.

The power isn't in having a perfect portfolio. The power is in knowing why you've made each choice and which value it serves. Sometimes one value is enough. Sometimes "not now, but I'm working towards it" is enough. Sometimes "this doesn't match my values, but it matches my circumstances right now" is the honest answer.

What drains us isn't imperfect alignment. What drains us is unconscious drift, doing things we don't understand, for reasons we can't articulate, towards goals that don't actually matter to us.

Consciousness is the goal. Choice is the power.

Your Two Portfolios: The Wealth Audit

Before we move to Activation, let's pause for a moment. The last few chapters have been deeply practical, assets, strategies, portfolio construction. Your head might be full of financial mechanics.

I want to remind you why we're doing this. Building wealth isn't just about the money. It never was.

Reflection: The Wealth Audit

As you use the Compass, remember you are always managing not one, but two portfolios in life.

Material Finance (Outer Wealth)

- Assets: savings, investments, property, income
- Liabilities: debts, expenses, obligations
- Currencies: money and time
- Flow: how money moves through your life

Spiritual Finance (Inner Wealth)

- Assets: relationships, resilience, skills, wisdom, joy
- Liabilities: limiting beliefs, fears, toxic patterns, emotional debts
- Currencies: energy, attention, love, presence
- Flow: how you invest yourself: your focus, energy, and heart

When both portfolios, inner and outer wealth, reinforce each other, that's when alignment becomes sustainable. Financial success without spiritual alignment feels hollow. Spiritual fulfilment without financial stability feels fragile. Together, they amplify each other, and money becomes what it was always meant to be: a tool to live the life you want.

Keep coming back to the questions:

- Where do I already feel wealthy in my life: in energy, relationships, purpose, or time?
- Do my financial goals align with what matters most to me?

From Alignment to Activation

The Compass gives you direction; the Wheel of Wealth gives you traction.

This chapter completes the Alignment stage of your journey. You've uncovered your values, explored the mechanics of building wealth, and examined your Investment Values Compass to ensure your money decisions stay true to who you are. You've even paused to reflect on your two portfolios, inner and outer wealth, so that you can hold meaning and money together.

Clarity is key; however, commitment is what builds wealth. Which is why the next stage of your journey is Activation. Activation is more than just taking action. It's about switching something on, igniting your momentum, bringing energy to your plans, and creating systems that keep you moving forward.

In the next chapter, you'll meet the Wheel of Wealth, your blueprint for financial freedom. This tool breaks your wealth into clear, practical areas you can strengthen; one spoke at a time. From there, you'll design your 90-Day Wealth Activation Plan, introduce the AAA Framework (Authority, Accountability, Acknowledgement), and learn how to turn clarity into consistent progress.

You've built the financial understanding, designed your freedom vision, and aligned your values. Now it's time to step forward, to move from knowing to doing, and from dreaming to building.

Key Takeaways

- **Your values are your compass** - they help you understand where you thrive and where you're just going through the motions
- **Alignment is consciousness, not perfection** - knowing why you're doing what you're doing
- **Partial alignment is valid** - sometimes one value being met is enough, as long as it's the right one

- **Genuine misalignment demands change** - when nothing connects, that's your signal
- **You don't have to love every strategy** - you just need to know which value it serves
- **Sustainable wealth integrates both** - financial growth and personal fulfilment, your two portfolios working together

Practical Actions

1. **Do a Values Compass check-in** - Choose one investment and ask: "Which of my values does this serve?"
2. **Carry out a wealth audit** - Identify where you feel strong and where fragile, financially and personally.
3. **Write down one insight** - What did you discover about how your values show up in your investment choices?
4. **Set a 6-month reminder to repeat this** - Alignment is ongoing practice, not a one-time event.

PART 3

ACTIVATION

Chapter 17

THE WHEEL OF WEALTH

Your Complete Wealth Ecosystem

The distance between dreams and reality is called action. - Unknown

Knowing isn't enough.

There's a huge gap between knowing and doing. Like knowing you need to go to the gym. Knowing you should eat the apple instead of that chocolate biscuit. And actually doing it. It's the doing that moves the needle.

You can know all there is to know about money and finance. You can have the perfect plan mapped out in your head. But the reality is that none of this matters a jot unless you start taking action. That's the only thing that actually makes a difference and builds wealth.

And that's what this section is about: moving from understanding to doing.

The first two parts of this book were critical because, without awareness and alignment, you can take action but may end up being a busy fool. Those sections were the groundwork. Now you have enough knowledge and information to get started. What you need now is a system and a plan to start putting it into action.

I'm passionate about this book being more than shelf development. That would waste both our time. So we're starting this section by returning to a powerful tool you've already used: the Wheel. As you have already seen in Chapter 5 with the Wheel of Authenticity, this tool is powerful, incredibly simple and effective for helping you take those first steps.

Overwhelm to Clarity: How the Wheel Works

Before we dive into the Wheel of Wealth, let me show you how this simple tool transformed a completely different area of my life and how that experience shaped my approach to building wealth.

Years ago, when I was building my coaching business, I hit a wall of pure frustration. I believed deeply in what I was creating, but I was paralysed by the tech side: websites, email systems, social media, online trackers. Every time I fixed one thing, three new problems appeared. I was completely overwhelmed.

One day, in complete exasperation, I drew a wheel. Around it, I wrote down every area that was blocking me from an IT perspective. I scored each one out of 10 based on where I was at that point. Then I decided to write a new mindset to go with my wheel: "IT enables and empowers me to create a thriving coaching business."

This small thing made such a difference. I went from struggling to clarity, and it helped me see where to start. Instead of drowning in tech, I could see that I'd scored my website at 3 and my email system at 4. So I knew I should start with my website.

Within weeks, I'd hired the right person to help me. Within a month, I had my new website up and running. I went from confusion to clarity, which led to commitment.

I've used the wheel tool countless times since, with clients, teams, businesses, and schools. The Wheel transforms overwhelm into insight, and insight into action. It works for IT challenges, business strategy, teaching quality, and any area where complexity creates paralysis.

So when it came to building wealth, I realised the same principle applied: clarity first, then courage, then consistent action. That's how the Wheel of Wealth was born.

If you feel overwhelmed about where to start building your wealth, this will help you get started.

Introducing The Wheel of Wealth

The Wheel of Wealth is designed to help you see your whole financial life at once, rather than making decisions in isolation. Each spoke represents a distinct function of wealth, and if one spoke is underdeveloped or over-stressed, the entire wheel wobbles.

This is not about doing everything at once. It's about knowing where you are, what matters now, and what needs strengthening next. Aligned wealth isn't built by chasing the "best" investment. It's built by creating balance, coherence, and momentum across the whole system. That's how wealth becomes something you *live with*, not something you manage anxiously from a distance.

For the Wheel of Wealth, I've identified eight key areas for creating financial wealth. These aren't set in stone; you can adapt them, but I'd encourage you to start here. This framework comes from decades of experience in finance, coaching, and investing.

Before we dive in, though, let's reconnect with something important: your Freedom Number.

Back in Chapter 10, you designed your financial freedom vision and calculated your Freedom Number: the annual income that would give you complete choice about how you spend your time. Then I asked you to park it while we built your knowledge and explored different wealth-building strategies.It's time to bring that number forward again.

Everything we're about to explore, the eight wealth builders, the assessment, and the action planning, is in service of closing the gap between where you are now and that Freedom Number.

That gap is your Freedom Gap, and this Wheel shows you the different levers you can pull to close it. Earning more income. Building financial knowledge. Addressing pension planning. Developing emotional mastery to stay steady when markets wobble.

The Wheel of Wealth isn't just an assessment tool. It's a strategic map showing you which areas need attention to close your Freedom Gap and build the wealth that gives you choice.

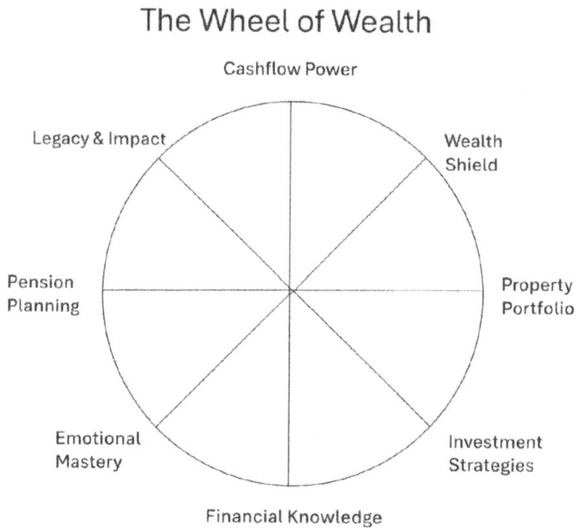

The Eight Wealth Builders

1. Cash Flow Power

Cash Flow Power is the first spoke on this wheel, and there's a reason for that.

You cannot build wealth without conscious command of your cash flow.

This isn't about earning a six-figure salary. Maybe you're a high earner, but you have zero cash flow power because money drains away unconsciously. Or maybe you're a modest earner, but you've mastered the practices we explored earlier - awareness (knowing exactly where you are), discipline (spending consciously), and direction (paying yourself first) and you're building genuine wealth.

Cash Flow Power integrates four dimensions:

1. **Clarity** – Your Blue Dot (Chapter 7): knowing your exact cash flow position
2. **Consciousness** – Spending deliberately (Chapter 9), not letting money drift
3. **Commitment** – Paying yourself first (Chapter 9), making wealth-building automatic
4. **Creation** – Building multiple income streams: salary, bonuses, business income, dividends, rental income, or income from investment strategies

Without the first three, the fourth is just more money to spend unconsciously. With all four, you have genuine cash flow power.

This is why Cash Flow Power sits first among the eight wealth builders. Not because it's more important than the others but because without it, you can't fund pensions, build investment strategies, or create legacy. There's no money consciously flowing toward these goals.

If you haven't yet completed your Blue Dot exercise (Chapter 7) or installed the consciousness practices (Chapter 9), do that first. Then return here. The Wheel will make far more sense when you're working from clarity, not confusion.

This is often the most direct lever for closing your Freedom Gap. Growing your income: negotiating a raise, building a side business, generating rental income accelerates wealth-building. Combine income growth with the first three dimensions, and you have more money consciously directed toward building investment assets that eventually create income to replace your salary.

Cash flow power isn't just about how much comes in, it's about conscious command of the entire system.

Questions to consider as you score this:

- Do you know your exact monthly cash flow, not roughly, but precisely?
- Are you spending consciously based on values, or unconsciously from comparison?
- Are savings and investments non-negotiable, or what's left over?
- After covering essentials, how much can you allocate to wealth building each month?

2. Wealth Shield

This is your financial protection system: the foundation that lets you take smart risks and weather storms without derailing your long-term plans.

It includes:

- **Emergency cash** (3-6 months of expenses in accessible accounts)
- **Tax efficiency** (ISAs, pension contributions, and other tax-advantaged structures)
- **Protection** (income protection, life insurance, critical illness cover where appropriate)

This spoke is about creating structural resilience, so when life throws curveballs, your wealth-building momentum continues.

Tax rules and optimal structures change frequently. For current guidance on ISAs, allowances, and tax-efficient strategies, the Fearless Female Investor Collective provides updated resources and expert sessions.

Questions to consider as you score this:

- Do you have 3-6 months of essential expenses in accessible cash?
- Are you maximizing tax-advantaged accounts like ISAs and pensions?

- Do you have appropriate protection in place if you couldn't work?
- Would an emergency force you to liquidate long-term investments?

3. Property Portfolio

For many people, property is where significant wealth sits; sometimes by design, sometimes by default (inherited properties).

This spoke covers everything from buy-to-let investments to more sophisticated property strategies. Property can provide both capital growth and rental income, but it's also illiquid, requires active management, and comes with costs.

Understanding how property fits into your overall wealth picture, and whether it's working for you or against you, is essential.

Questions to consider as you score this:

- Do you understand how much wealth is tied up in property versus other assets?
- Is your property working for you (generating income or growth) or just sitting there?
- Do you have a clear strategy for property, or has it just... happened?

4. Investment Strategies

This is your long-term growth engine: the asset classes you invest in and the strategies you use to build wealth over time.

As we explored in Chapter 13, The Alchemy of Assets, there are many different asset classes you can invest in: from equities and bonds to commodities, property, and alternative assets. Within each asset class, there are multiple investment strategies you can deploy.

This is where wealth compounds, gradually closing your Freedom Gap through both income generation (dividends, interest) and capital growth (the value of your investments increasing).

This isn't about getting rich quickly; it's about consistent, strategic allocation across different asset classes and approaches. In the chapters ahead, we'll dive deep into four powerful strategies: **ETFs, Bitcoin, Private Equity, and Options Trading**. I've chosen these because they represent different risk profiles, accessibility levels, and wealth-building approaches, and together, they show you the range of what's possible.

Questions to consider as you score this:

- Do you have investments beyond cash and property that are growing for your future?
- Is your investment strategy deliberate and diversified, or reactive and patchy?
- Do you understand what you're invested in and why?

5. Financial Knowledge

This is what you understand about how finance works. It's a broad and evolving landscape, from the fundamentals like compound interest to more sophisticated strategies around tax efficiency, asset allocation, and beyond.

Throughout this book, you've been building financial knowledge, and that journey continues. The more you understand, the better decisions you make, and the less dependent you are on others to manage your wealth. Without it, you're either doing nothing or dependent on advisers, and you can't evaluate whether their advice is sound.

Knowledge is power, but only when it's applied. This spoke measures how well you understand the financial landscape you're navigating.

Questions to consider as you score this:

- How confident do you feel about your financial knowledge, from basics to more advanced concepts?
- Can you evaluate financial advice and make informed decisions, or do you just trust and hope?

- Are you actively learning and expanding your understanding, or have you plateaued?

6. Emotional Money Mastery

This is how your relationship with money, your behavioural patterns, your discipline, and resilience are.

You can have all the financial knowledge in the world, but if you panic-sell when markets drop, or chase returns when things feel hot, or avoid looking at your statements when things feel scary, knowledge won't save you.

This spoke is about emotional regulation, sticking to your strategy through volatility, and making decisions from clarity rather than fear or greed. It's the inner game of wealth, and it's just as important as the outer game.

Questions to consider as you score this:

- How do you respond when markets drop? Panic, or stick to your plan?
- Do you avoid looking at your finances when things feel uncomfortable?
- Can you separate your emotions from your financial decisions?

7. Pension Planning

Your pension is likely to be one of your largest assets, yet it's often the most neglected.

This includes workplace pensions, personal pensions, SIPPs (Self-Invested Personal Pensions) and SSASs (Small Self-Administered Scheme) in the UK, and any long-term tax-advantaged retirement savings. The power here lies in compound growth plus tax relief, but the challenge is the lack of visibility and control.

Many people don't know what they have, where it is, or whether it's on track to give them the retirement they want. This spoke is about getting clear, getting consolidated, and getting strategic.

Questions to consider as you score this:

- Do you know how much is in your pension(s) and where they are?
- Are you on track for the retirement you actually want?
- When did you last review your pension contributions or investment choices?

8. Legacy & Impact

This is about living your legacy now, not just leaving one behind. It's using your wealth as a force for meaning and change, through how you show up, what you protect, and the impact you create today.

Legacy has three dimensions: *who you are* (your values and wisdom in action), *what you build* (estate planning, wills, trusts, and how you steward wealth), and *how you give* (the causes you support and the conversations you have with the next generation).

This isn't something to think about "later." The choices you make today, from protecting what matters to having money conversations with your children to supporting causes you care about, are shaping your legacy right now.

Questions to consider as you score this:

- Do you have a will and Lasting Power of Attorney in place?
- Are you having wealth conversations with the next generation?
- Have you identified causes or communities you want to support—and started doing so?
- Does your wealth reflect your values in action, or is it just sitting there?

A Word on Cash

Before we move into the exercise, I want to address something about cash that often gets misunderstood.

Many investors treat cash like a dead weight, especially when markets are rising and FOMO kicks in. But as a fund manager, we always held cash strategically; it was never an accident or a failure to be "fully invested."

Holding cash can feel uncomfortable, but patience is a position. It gives you options when everyone else is forced to sell. Warren Buffett said it perfectly: "The stock market is the device for transferring money from the impatient to the patient." His partner, Charlie Munger, added: "It takes character to sit with cash and do nothing."

Cash won't compound like equities, but it protects your plan, your sleep, and your ability to act when opportunities arise.

So, as you score your Wealth Shield, also consider: am I making intentional decisions about cash allocation across my broader wealth? Or is cash just where money sits when I haven't decided what to do with it?

Cash is a position, not a mistake.

Your Turn: The Wheel of Wealth Exercise

Now that you understand the eight Wealth Builders, it's time to assess where you are today across all of them.

Before we start, I want to be clear: this isn't a test. There's no perfect score you're supposed to reach. It's a tool to help you create distinctions, spot patterns, and build clarity so you can choose where to focus.

Here's how it works:

Step One: Create Your Wheel

Grab a blank sheet of paper and draw a large circle. Divide it into eight equal segments, like pie slices.

Label each segment around the outer rim:

- Cashflow Power
- Wealth Shield
- Property Portfolio
- Investment Strategies
- Financial Knowledge
- Emotional Money Mastery
- Pension Planning
- Legacy & Impact

You can download a printable template from the website if you prefer, but I recommend doing it by hand. Pen to paper connects you more deeply to the process.

Step Two: Score Yourself

Before you start scoring, go back to the financial freedom you want. Use that as your benchmark, not someone else's impossible standard. If you haven't yet calculated your Freedom Number, revisit Chapter 10 now: it's your essential reference point for this exercise.

Now ask yourself: Where am I today in each of these eight areas and score yourself from 1 to 10.

Mark your score on the spoke itself, with 1 near the center and 10 at the outer edge.

> 1 - this area is completely neglected, far from where you want it to be.
>
> 10 - this area feels strong, aligned, exactly where you want it to be.

Trust your instincts. This is subjective. There are no right or wrong answers. No one else will see this but you.

Your scores might cluster high, low, or anywhere in between. All starting points are valid. The power is in your honesty and the decision to focus.

Step Three: Connect the Dots

Once you've scored all eight areas, connect the dots to create your personal Wealth Wheel snapshot.

What shape does it make? Is it relatively round, or wildly uneven? Where are the high points? Where are the low points?

Just notice, don't judge.

Step Four: Reflect

Now take a moment and ask yourself:

- What jumps out at me straight away?
- What surprised me?
- Where am I thriving?
- Where do I feel uncomfortable?
- What insights am I taking from this exercise?

Sometimes the patterns you see will be obvious. Sometimes they'll surprise you. Either way, the clarity is powerful.

Step Five: Choose Your Priorities

This is the most important step.

Look at your Wheel and ask: "If I could focus on one or two areas that would make the biggest difference across my entire financial life, which would they be?"

Ask yourself: which area, if I strengthened it, would have a ripple effect across the others? Which feels most urgent? Which excites you most? Write them down.

These are your focus areas and will guide which chapters in this Activation section you tackle first. You don't need to read them sequentially, let your Wheel show you where to start.

The clarity from both wheels is power. Now you know where to start. The rest of this section builds your Wheel of Wealth: the strategies, tools, and action steps to strengthen your financial foundation.

In the next chapter, we'll map out exactly how to develop these areas and close your Freedom Gap. You'll see which wealth builders we're diving deep into, why I've chosen them, and how to navigate the rest of this section based on your priorities.

Key Takeaways

- **Clarity creates movement** - the Wheel of Wealth turns overwhelm into a clear plan of action
- **Awareness and alignment come first** - without them, action can make you a busy fool
- **Focus beats perfection** - strengthening one or two areas creates more progress than trying to fix everything at once
- **Your Freedom Number is your target** - every spoke on the Wheel helps you close the gap between where you are and where you want to be
- **Each spoke is connected** - progress in one area lifts the whole system
- **Insight without action changes nothing** - this is where knowledge becomes movement

Practical Actions

1. **Draw or print your Wheel of Wealth -** Label each of the eight spokes with the wealth builders.

2. **Score each area from 1–10 -** Be honest rather than aspirational; this snapshot reflects where you are today, not where you want to be.
3. **Connect your scores -** Step back and look at the shape — notice where your wheel feels strong, and where it looks uneven.
4. **Reflect on what the wheel is telling you -** What surprises you? Where are you thriving, and where do you feel resistance or discomfort?
5. **Choose one or two areas to focus on -** Pick the spokes where improvement would make the biggest difference to your overall wealth picture.
6. **Keep your Freedom Number visible -** Use it as your north star to stay connected to the bigger purpose behind the work.

Chapter 18

THE FEARLESS INVESTOR'S TOOLKIT

How to Navigate the Rest of This Book

You've completed the Wheel of Wealth. You've assessed where you are across all eight wealth builders. You've identified your one or two focus areas, the spokes that will make the biggest difference to closing your Freedom Gap.

Now what?

This is where many investing books leave you: inspired, informed, but standing at the threshold, wondering which door to walk through first.

Not this book.

In this chapter, I'm going to show you exactly how the rest of this section works, which wealth builders we're diving deep into, why I've chosen these four, and how to navigate the chapters ahead based on your priorities from the Wheel.

Think of this as your strategic roadmap. You've done the assessment. Now let's talk about activation.

The Four Wealth Builders We're Covering

In the chapters ahead, we're going deep into four specific spokes from your Wheel of Wealth:

Investment Strategies — This is where most wealth gets built over time. I'll show you four different strategies (ETFs, Bitcoin, Private Equity, Options) that range from completely beginner-friendly to more sophisticated. You don't need all four, but you need to understand your options.

Emotional Money Mastery — The inner game that keeps you steady when markets wobble. You can have a perfect strategy, but if you panic-sell in downturns or chase hot returns, knowledge won't save you. This chapter helps build the emotional resilience that separates successful investors from those who quit.

Pension Planning — Likely one of your largest assets, yet often the most neglected. This chapter shows you how to review, consolidate, and maximise this wealth builder that compounds in the background.

Legacy & Impact — How to protect what you're building and structure it to reflect your values. This includes estate planning, charitable giving structures, and using wealth as a force for meaning beyond your lifetime.

What We're Not Covering

You'll notice four wealth builders aren't getting dedicated chapters:

Cash Flow Power — You've already mapped this in Chapter 8 (Where You Are Now). The work here is ongoing: optimise your spending, grow your income streams, allocate intentionally. If this is one of your focus areas, your action is to revisit Chapter 8 and implement the cash flow strategies we covered there.

Wealth Shield— Your emergency buffer, tax structures and insurance protection work quietly in the background. You've already assessed this in your Wheel. If your score was low, your action is straightforward: build 3-6 months of expenses in accessible savings, review what tax efficient investing schemes are open to you (e.g. ISAs in the UK) and explore insurance coverage (life, critical illness, income protection). No dedicated chapter needed, just systematic action until you hit your targets.

Financial Knowledge — You're building this throughout the entire book. Every chapter adds to your understanding. There's no single "knowledge chapter" because knowledge is the foundation underneath everything we're exploring together.

Property Portfolio — Property is complex, personal, and regional and needs its own book, not a chapter. If property was one of your focus areas from the Wheel, I'd recommend seeking specialised property investment education or working with advisors who understand your local market.

Timeline Matters: Choosing Your Focus Strategically

Before we dive into these four wealth builders, there's one more critical lens to apply: how much time do you have to close your Freedom Gap?

Your priorities aren't just about your lowest scores on the Wheel; they're also shaped by your timeline.

If you're in your 30s with decades ahead of you, focus on building financial knowledge and starting to invest regularly. Compounding has decades to work in your favour. Your Investment Strategies speak more than Pension Planning at this stage.

If you're 50+ and closer to your target date, Pension Planning becomes critical. You need to be strategic about every pound and every tax advantage. Consolidating old pensions, maximising contributions, and aligning your pension investments with your timeline becomes urgent.

If you have strong cash flow but low investment knowledge, your priority is building that financial knowledge quickly so you can put your cash flow to work effectively.

If you have solid knowledge but struggle with emotional mastery, focus on the behavioural side, developing the discipline to stick to your strategy when markets feel scary or euphoric.

Your age, your Freedom Gap, your current resources, and your timeline all shape which spokes deserve your focused attention right now. This is your wheel, reflecting your situation and your journey to financial freedom.

Keep your timeline in mind as you read the chapters ahead. It will help you make smarter, more strategic choices about where to focus your energy.

Two Pathways Through This Section

You have two options for how to move through the rest of this book:

Pathway 1: Deep Learning First

Read the detailed chapters on Investment Strategies, Emotional Money Mastery, Pensions, and Legacy and Impact. Build your knowledge first, then create your Wealth Activation Plan in the final chapter.

Choose this if you want a comprehensive understanding before committing to action, or if you're naturally methodical and like having the full picture first.

Pathway 2: Action Planning First

Jump to Chapter 23 (the AAA Framework) and build your action plan now based on your Wheel priorities. Then circle back to the detailed chapters as you implement.

Choose this if you're ready to move now and prefer learning by doing, or if you want structure and accountability in place immediately.

Both pathways work. Choose what feels right for you.

Insight without action changes nothing. This is where understanding starts to show up in real decisions

Four Ways to Build Wealth with Confidence

Investment Strategies is one of the core spokes of the Wheel, and for most people, it's where significant wealth gets built over time.

I also know this may be where many of you want to close the book and come back "when you're ready."

I get it. This is where you have to separate yourself from your money. Where theory becomes practice. Where reading becomes doing.

This is why this matters: you've already done the work most people skip. You've examined your relationship with money, dismantled the myths about investing, reframed risk, learned about different asset classes, and designed your portfolio strategy.

You're no longer starting from fear; you're starting from clarity, and clarity builds confidence.

The four strategies we're about to explore are the same ones I use to build my own wealth. Not because I've done it perfectly, but because I've lived it. I've made expensive mistakes, learned from them, and kept going. What I'm sharing here isn't theory; it's what I know works, because I'm living it.

Understanding Your Four Investment Options

These four strategies range from completely beginner-friendly to approaches requiring dedicated learning. Let me show you what each one does, then we'll compare them.

The Four Strategies: What Each One Does

You've already met these asset classes in Alchemy of Assets. Now we're going deeper, into exactly how to use them.

ETFs (Exchange-Traded Funds): Your foundation. Broad market exposure, owning tiny slices of hundreds of companies in one simple, low-cost product. Perfect for beginners and busy people looking to build long-term wealth without becoming full-time investors. Complete and actionable, you can start this week.

Bitcoin: Your hedge. Digital scarcity, a decentralised monetary network, a store of value outside traditional systems. Volatile, controversial, but also the best-performing asset of the past decade. Small allocation (5-10%), long time horizon, proper security practices. Complete and actionable, you can start this week.

Private Equity: Your growth accelerator. Investing directly in private companies before they go public, capturing growth before IPO or trade sale. Higher potential returns (I've seen 10x), higher risk, longer timeframes (5-10 years). Requires both capital and conviction. This chapter shows you what's possible, but executing requires dedicated learning beyond this book.

Options (Wheel Strategy): Your income generator. The only active strategy here. Done properly, it can generate 1.5–3.5% monthly income and compound powerfully. Simple to grasp, disciplined to manage. Requires structured training before you start.

How These Strategies Compare

Each strategy requires different levels of money, time, knowledge, and flexibility. Here's how they compare:

Investment Require-ments	ETFs	Bitcoin	Private Equity	Options
Ease of Access	Start today with £100 — zero prior knowledge	Start this week with £50 and basic research	Requires £5,000+ and months of learning	Requires £10,000+, structured training
Capital Required	£100–£1,000+	£50–£500+	£5,000–£25,000+	£10,000+

Time Required	Truly passive: set and forget	Mostly passive after setup	10–20 hrs research per deal, then passive	30–60 min weekly, disciplined
Money Tied up	Fully liquid	Highly liquid	Locked for 5–10 yrs	Moderately liquid; positions manageable

ETFs and Bitcoin are genuinely beginner-friendly; you can start safely with small amounts. Private Equity and Options require more capital, more learning, and active management.

You don't need to learn all four. Choose one or two that fit your current situation.

How to Approach These Chapters

- **If you're brand new,** start with ETFs. Invest your first £100. Get comfortable watching your money move. Nothing else yet. Return to Bitcoin in a few months when you're confident.
- **If you're experienced with property,** you already understand returns, risk, and leverage. These strategies add diversification and liquidity, tools that property alone can't offer.
- **If you have significant capital (£50k+ available to invest):** Read all four to understand your options, but still begin with ETFs to learn market mechanics.
- **If you love systems and rules,** the Options chapter will fascinate you. Master ETFs and Bitcoin first; then progress with structure and discipline.

Here's what applies across all four strategies: only invest money you won't need to live on, diversify across strategies (not just within them), and start small. Your first £500 is education, not retirement planning. Mistakes are part of mastery.

I've lost money investing. Those lessons taught me due diligence, position sizing, and emotional discipline. These chapters will teach you how to invest so losses become education, not devastation.

What Happens When You Do This

Here's what unfolds when you move from learning about investing to practising it:

- You shift from cautious to intentional living. Wealth-building stops being something "other people" do. You claim sovereignty over your own money.
- You'll watch your wealth grow in meaningful ways that compound over time far more than a savings account.
- Most importantly, you move from an age-old taboo to mastering something that genuinely isn't that complicated. You feel empowered knowing your money is working for you, on your terms

These four strategies are different ways to make your money work for you. I'm showing you all four because I believe in giving you options, not prescriptions. Your wealth journey is yours to design. I'm showing the map and sharing routes I've walked.

The courage isn't in choosing the "right" strategy. The courage is in choosing one and starting.

Key Takeaways

- **Strategic focus beats trying everything** - Your Wheel results plus your timeline determine which 1-2 wealth builders deserve attention now

- **Two valid pathways exist** - Deep learning first or action planning first; choose based on how you naturally operate, not what you "should" do
- **The four investment strategies serve different needs** - ETFs and Bitcoin are beginner-friendly; Private Equity and Options require more capital and learning. Start with what fits your current situation

Practical Actions

- **Review your Wheel results and timeline** - Which 1-2 focus areas matter most? How many years until your Freedom Number? This determines your chapter priorities
- **Choose your pathway -** Do you want to do deep learning first (read all wealth builders chapters) or action planning first (jump to the AAA Framework)? Trust your natural approach
- **If Investment Strategies is your focus** - Use the comparison table to identify which strategy (ETFs, Bitcoin, Private Equity, Options) fits your current capital, time, and knowledge level

Chapter 19

YOUR FIRST INVESTMENT

A Beginner's Guide to ETFs

I'd like to start with a confession.

When I landed my first job at Schroders as an "Assistant Fund Manager," I had no idea what a fund manager actually did. Not a clue. I was 23, armed with an Economics degree and a shiny new suit, but no one had thought to explain the basics.

I honestly thought *fund management* meant something entirely different, you know, "fun" management. Cocktail parties, champagne lunches, the glamorous City life...

Nope. Turns out it meant being responsible for other people's millions. No pressure.

On my first day, I actually asked someone what a fund manager *was*. They looked at me like I'd asked where babies come from. Apparently, it was "obvious." Spoiler: it wasn't. Not to me, and probably not to most people reading this book either.

So, if you feel like you "should" already know this stuff, let me reassure you: there are no stupid questions here. If 23-year-old me had to research "FTSE" on my lunch break, you are absolutely allowed to start wherever you are.

Everyone starts somewhere, and the moment you begin to learn is the moment you stop feeling left out of the conversation. You don't need to know the language yet; you'll pick it up as you go.

So let's start with the absolute basics, what the stock market actually is and how it works.

What You Need to Know About the Stock Market

The stock market is where you can buy shares in publicly listed companies that anyone can invest in. When you own a share, you own a tiny slice of that business.

Share prices go up and down based on supply and demand - that's volatility, and it's completely normal. What matters is your time horizon: if you invest money you don't need for at least three to five years, you give your investments time to recover from those inevitable dips.

The key thing is that you are not betting on tomorrow's price; you're building wealth over years and decades. Every successful investor has lived through dozens of dips and learned that staying invested through the noise is what builds real wealth

Your Three Main Options for Investing

When you invest in the stock market, you have three main options. I'm going to recommend ETFs, and here's why:

- **ETFs (Exchange-Traded Funds)** give you instant diversification - hundreds or thousands of companies bundled into one simple product. Low cost (often under 0.1% annually), you can buy and sell anytime, and because your risk is spread across the entire basket, you're not dependent on any single company succeeding.
- **Individual shares** (buying Apple, Nike, or Tesco directly) can deliver big gains, but if that company fails, you lose everything. If you remember Kodak this was a huge brand that totally collapsed. This is for experienced investors comfortable with research and concentrated risk.
- **Mutual funds** offer professional management and diversification, but charge higher fees (often 1%+ annually) and trade only once daily. You're paying for hands-on management you may not need.

ETFs are where most people should start. They give you instant diversification without researching dozens of companies yourself. As they hold hundreds of companies, they're not going to zero - every single company would have to collapse. Yes, prices go up and down (that's normal volatility), but your risk is spread across the entire basket.

Understanding ETF Basics

ETFs come in different types: equities (stocks), bonds, commodities, and specific sectors like technology or healthcare. For now, focus on equity ETFs; they're beginner-friendly and give you broad exposure to the stock market.

For example, VUSA tracks the S&P 500 (500 biggest U.S. companies) with an annual fee around 0.07%. VUKE tracks the FTSE 100 (top UK companies) at around 0.09%. EQQQ tracks the Nasdaq 100 (U.S. tech leaders) at around 0.30%. These aren't recommendations - just examples to show you how ETFs work.

The annual fee (called the OCF - Ongoing Charge Figure) is automatically deducted from the fund. Compared to typical mutual fund fees of 1% or more, ETFs are far cheaper, which makes a huge difference over time.

A note for UK investors: If you're using platforms like Trading 212, Freetrade, or AJ Bell, you'll be buying UK-listed ETFs even when they track U.S. markets. This is due to UK regulatory protections. For example, you can't buy the U.S.-listed QQQ directly, but you can buy EQQQ, which tracks the same Nasdaq 100 index and is approved for UK investors.

When Should I Actually Buy?

This is the question that stops most people. You've chosen your ETF, you're ready to invest... but what if you buy at the top and it crashes tomorrow? This is where even confident people hesitate and that's completely normal. Money decisions always stir emotion; the goal isn't to have no fears, it's to take one small, informed step anyway.

In reality, nobody knows what the market will do tomorrow. Not me, not fund managers, not the "experts" on TV. Anyone who claims otherwise is selling something.

The approach you take depends on how you've come to have money to invest.

Scenario 1: Building Wealth from Monthly Income

Your approach: Pound-Cost Averaging ("Set It and Forget It")

If you're investing from your salary or business income, invest a fixed amount regularly - weekly, monthly, whatever works for you. We covered this in Chapter 11 on Compounding when the market is high you buy fewer shares, when it's low you buy more, and over time this averages out your entry price.

Most importantly, it gets you in the market instead of sitting on the sidelines waiting for the "perfect" moment that never comes.

Just start. This week. Set up the automatic contribution and then go live your life.

Scenario 2: You Have a Lump Sum

This is where people freeze. You've suddenly got £10,000, £50,000, £100,000 to invest and you're terrified of getting it wrong.

If the amount feels manageable to you:

Do a simple check: pull up your chosen ETF on TradingView or your broker app, zoom out to a 6-month view, and look at the overall trend.

If it's generally trending upward → invest now and get on with your life If it's clearly falling or just had a massive spike → wait a few weeks, or split it: half now, half in a month

This isn't timing the market perfectly: it's avoiding the obvious mistake of buying when everything's clearly falling. Think of it like checking the weather before a picnic.

If the amount feels significant to you, enough that a 15% drop would genuinely sting:

Here's a practical way to reduce the emotional load while you get started.

Start with a small amount, for example £1,000, and invest it now. Pick your ETF, open your account, and press buy.

This lets you feel what it's like to be in the market. Watch it go up. Watch it go down. Feel the flutter of anxiety on a red day. Notice yourself checking it too often. Experience the urge to sell when the news gets scary.

That £1,000 is your education fee. Not because you'll lose it (you probably won't), but because it teaches you how you react emotionally to market movements. That's crucial information you need before you invest the rest.

After 2-3 months, you'll know how you react to volatility and whether this ETF feels right. Then phase in the rest in tranches - maybe thirds over three months, or halves over two months. There's no perfect formula. You're not trying to time the market; you're managing your own psychology.

Example: Caroline inherited £50,000

Month 1: Invested £1,000 in VUSA. It immediately dropped 3%. She panicked, checked it daily, and nearly sold. But it recovered within two weeks. Lesson learned: volatility is normal.

Months 2-3: She watched her £1,000 bounce around and got comfortable with the movement. She decided to diversify between VUSA and VWRL.

Month 3: Invested £15,000 / Month 4: Another £15,000 / Month 6: Final £19,000

By month 6, she'd averaged her entry across different price points and could weather market dips without panic because she'd already lived through them with her initial £1,000.

What you're avoiding is the classic mistake: putting everything in at the peak, watching it drop 10-20% (normal market behaviour), panicking, and selling at the bottom. That's not a market problem; that's an emotional management problem.

Summary:

- Building wealth monthly → Automate it and forget about timing
- Amount feels manageable → Quick trend check and invest
- Amount feels significant → Start small, learn while you're in, phase in the rest over 3-6 months

How to Actually Buy Your First ETF

Here's exactly how to invest your first £100 (or £1,000).

Step 1: Open Your Brokerage Account

Beginner-friendly platforms in the UK:

- Trading 212 → Free, easy to use, ISAs available
- Freetrade → Clean app, no-fuss investing, ISAs available
- AJ Bell → Well-established, trusted, good for larger portfolios

Safety note: UK brokers are FCA-regulated, meaning your investments are held separately from the broker's own funds. You're covered by the Financial Services Compensation Scheme (FSCS) up to £85,000 per platform.

Step 2: Choose Your First ETF

Start by picking a broad-based ETF that fits your goals and risk tolerance. A simple way to do this is to use an ETF screener, such as justetf.com, to explore options and compare features like diversification, cost, and underlying holdings.

Step 3: Place Your Trade

On your brokerage platform:

1. Search for your ETF by name or ticker
2. Click Buy
3. Enter your amount (e.g., £100 or £1,000)
4. Select Market Order (buying at the current price)
5. Confirm the purchase

Step 4: Keep Going

Set up automatic monthly contributions if your broker allows it. Consistency matters more than timing.

Your First Win and the Bigger Journey Ahead

Once you've made your first ETF investment, take a moment to celebrate. You've taken a powerful step towards financial independence.

Wealth isn't built in one leap; it's built one decision at a time. From here, you can explore more strategies in the Fearless Female Investor Collective - diversification, chart reading, stop-losses, and moving averages are all waiting when you're ready.

Right now, the most important thing is simple: you've started. That's how wealth is built.

Key Takeaways

- **You don't need to know everything to begin** - you learn by doing, one small step at a time.
- **ETFs give you instant diversification at low cost** - a smart, simple place to start.
- **Volatility is normal** - it's just the market breathing in and out.
- **Time in the market beats timing the market** - every single time.

- **Automate consistency** - regular investing builds wealth far more effectively than chasing perfect timing.
- **Start with one ETF you understand and trust** - simplicity wins.

Practical Actions

- **Open a brokerage account** - (Trading 212, Freetrade, or AJ Bell are all good starting points).
- **Do a little research** - explore one or two broad ETFs such as the S&P 500, FTSE 100, or a global all-world fund.
- **Make your first small investment** - even £100 is enough to begin and build confidence.
- **Set up a simple plan** - decide how often you'll add money and stick with it through ups and downs.
- **Celebrate starting** - that single action is the bridge between learning and wealth-building.

Chapter 20

BITCOIN: FREEDOM, SOVEREIGNTY & THE FUTURE OF MONEY

How to Start Small, Stay Steady, and HODL for the Long Term

Part 1: From Curiosity to Conviction

I hadn't planned to become a Bitcoin advocate. Back in 2017, it wasn't even on my radar.

But that summer changed everything. I was reading *The Economist* when I came across a special pullout titled *What If.* One scenario explored blockchain becoming the dominant infrastructure for global transactions. Estate agents replaced by smart contracts, property tokenised and traded without middlemen. I was captivated.

Blockchain is extraordinary as a secure, transparent way to record data, which is changing how we do business. It allows smart contracts, ownership tracking, and systems without middlemen. Even if you never buy a single Satoshi (bit of Bitcoin), understanding blockchain matters as it's shaping the future of finance, property, and identity

My curiosity led me to Bitcoin. I made my first investment at around £4,000 per coin, and within a matter of months, it had doubled. I was hooked. Like so many newcomers, I got caught up in the excitement, and then life took over. I stopped paying attention.

Fast forward to 2022, when I logged back into my account and discovered that my modest investment had grown to over £30,000. I was elated until, a year later, I looked again, and I realised my account had been emptied.

It was a painful lesson, a £30,000 wake-up call about security and self-custody. It taught me more than any book could have about why Bitcoin is different, why understanding wallets matters, and why this isn't an investment to dabble in casually.

That experience taught me why this chapter matters. For clarity: I hold a small position in Bitcoin, but I'm not a maximalist. My real passion lies in private company investing, which we'll explore in the next chapter.

What excites me isn't Bitcoin itself, it's what Bitcoin represents: proof that we can have money and systems not controlled by central authorities. Behind Bitcoin lies blockchain technology, tokenisation (fractional ownership of real assets), stablecoins (digital currencies without volatility), and decentralised finance or DeFi (financial services without banks), innovations reshaping how we think about ownership and control.

This chapter focuses on Bitcoin because it's the simplest entry point to understanding digital sovereignty. That's what I'm passionate about.

Part 2: Why Bitcoin Exists

Before we dive into Bitcoin, we need to understand the problem it solves. Most people assume money has intrinsic value. It doesn't. Today's pounds, euros, and dollars are *fiat currencies:* valuable simply because governments declare them so.

The reality is that governments can print as much money as they want: there's no hard limit on how much can be created. As we explored in the economics chapter, this causes real devaluation of fiat currency; your money literally melts away over time through inflation. This isn't a conspiracy theory; it's how modern monetary systems work.

Bitcoin was designed as an alternative to exactly this problem, a monetary system with fixed scarcity built into its code. It's built on three principles:

- **Scarcity** → Unlike the pounds or dollars in your bank account, there will only ever be 21 million bitcoins. No central bank can decide to "print" more because the markets need stimulus. The scarcity is baked into the code itself.
- **Decentralisation** → No single government, company, or person controls it. It's maintained by thousands of computers around the world, all following the same mathematical rules.
- **Transparency** → Every transaction is recorded on the blockchain, and anyone can view it.

This is why Bitcoin matters. It challenges the assumptions we've held for decades about how money works, and who gets to control it.

Part 3: Bitcoin 101 – What You Need to Know

Let's strip away the jargon. Bitcoin is digital money you can send anywhere, instantly, without asking permission, a network where rules are set in code, not by politicians.

Bitcoin has been the best-performing asset over the past decade. Between 2014 and 2024, Bitcoin delivered a 26,931% return: meaning £100 would have grown to £27,000. Here's how it compares:

To put that in perspective, here's how other major assets stacked up over the same 10-year period:

10-Year Asset Performance (2014-2024)

Asset	**10-Year Return**
Bitcoin (BTC)	26,931%
S&P 500	193%

5-Year Treasuries	157%
Gold	126%
10-Year Treasuries	87%
Crude Oil	4%

Source: Bloomberg, CoinGecko, Goldman Sachs, Federal Reserve

Of course, Bitcoin's journey hasn't been smooth, volatility is part of the story, and we'll explore this later in the chapter.

Part 4: Bitcoin Myths & Truths

Bitcoin also comes with baggage: myths, misunderstandings, and media noise. Let's clear the air on three common misconceptions:

"Bitcoin is a scam."

Scams exist *around* Bitcoin, but the Bitcoin network itself is open-source, decentralised, and secure. It's been running for 15 years without a single day of downtime.

"Only criminals use Bitcoin."

Bitcoin is pseudonymous, not anonymous, every transaction is publicly recorded. In reality, cash remains the preferred choice for illegal activity.

"You need to buy a whole Bitcoin."

You can start with £1, £100, or £10,000, whatever feels aligned. These fractional units are called satoshis, and they're your entry point. The important thing isn't how much you buy, it's starting small, learning, and building confidence step by step.

Bitcoin isn't just for "tech bros" or traders. It's for anyone ready to rethink what money can be.

Part 5: Bitcoin vs "Crypto"

Bitcoin and "crypto" are not the same thing. You'll hear them lumped together, but that's like saying gold and penny stocks are the same because they're both investments.

Bitcoin is completely different because no one owns it. It's truly decentralised: no CEO (Satoshi Nakamoto, the founder, disappeared), no company, no government controls it.

Most cryptocurrencies are owned by companies or foundations and serve specific purposes within their platforms. Projects like Ethereum, Solana, and XRP are fascinating and may play significant roles in the future of digital infrastructure.

Bitcoin's primary function is to act as digital gold, a store of value with absolute scarcity. Only 21 million will ever exist. This fixed supply is what makes Bitcoin fundamentally different from other digital assets, which can have unlimited or flexible supply mechanisms. Think of it as Bitcoin and everything else, that's the meaningful distinction.

Part 6: Security First

As you read, I learned this the hard way: security matters.

In the beginning, keep it simple. When you first buy Bitcoin, it sits in a "hot wallet" on the exchange, which is fine for small amounts, like cash in your physical purse or wallet. As holdings grow, you'll want to self-custody, which means moving Bitcoin into a "cold wallet" you control directly, such as Trezor, Ledger, or Tangem devices.

One phrase you will hear a lot in the digital world is: "Not your keys, not your coins". This isn't just a slogan, it's a reminder that if you don't control your private keys (ie leave your Bitcoin on a digital platform), you are trusting someone else to keep your Bitcoin safe. This is fine to begin with, but over time, learning self-custody becomes part of your empowerment journey.

What "learning gradually" actually looks like:

- **Months 1-3:** Keep your Bitcoin on the exchange. Focus on understanding how to buy, track, and observe price movements without panic.
- **Months 3-6:** Once you're comfortable and your holdings reach £500-£1,000, research hardware wallets. Read reviews, watch YouTube tutorials, and understand the basics.
- **Months 6-12:** Purchase a reputable hardware wallet (Ledger, Trezor, Tangem). Transfer a small amount first to test the process. Get comfortable with the mechanics.
- **12+ months:** As your confidence and holdings grow, move the majority to cold storage while keeping a small amount on the exchange for flexibility.

Security scales with your investment. You don't need to master everything on day one. Just start and be in the game.

Part 7: Should Bitcoin Be in Your Wealth Plan?

The technology that underpins Bitcoin, blockchain, is worth understanding, even if you decide Bitcoin itself isn't for you.

Bitcoin has a fixed supply, which is one reason it's often discussed as a potential hedge against inflation. In practice, however, it has behaved more like a high-volatility risk asset, amplifying broader market moves rather than offsetting them. Because it behaves differently from traditional assets, some investors still find that even a small allocation can add diversification to a portfolio.

Bitcoin offers portability and control: you can send value across borders without intermediaries, hold wealth that transcends geography, and control access through your private keys. For some investors, this sovereignty is compelling. For others, the volatility and complexity outweigh the benefits.

If You Decide to Allocate, How Much?

If Bitcoin resonates with you, here's a simple framework some investors use to think about proportion, not prescription. This isn't about finding the "right" number; it's about understanding how different levels of exposure can feel, given Bitcoin's volatility.

- **If you want to explore cautiously:** 1–3% of your investable assets
- **If you're comfortable with the ups and downs:** 5–10% of your investable assets
- **If you have high conviction and a long time horizon:** 10–15% of your investable assets

Start small. You can always add more as your confidence and conviction grow. The goal isn't to bet the farm, it's to participate in something you find compelling while protecting your downside.

This is entirely a personal decision. Only invest what you can afford to hold through significant volatility, ideally over a five-year or longer time horizon.

Part 8: How to Buy Your First Bitcoin

If investing in Bitcoin is of interest, let's look at how to take your first confident step into doing so:

Step 1 – Choose Your Platform & Verify

Pick an FCA-regulated platform like Coinpass (Oanda), Coinbase, or Kraken. Complete ID verification (KYC): it takes minutes and ensures you can buy, sell, and store crypto safely.

Step 2 – Fund Your Account

Bank transfers are cheaper; debit cards are faster. Choose based on your priorities, and remember you're in control of how much you invest.

Step 3 – Make Your First Purchase

Enter the amount (£100, £1,000, whatever you're comfortable with) and click Buy. There's no "perfect" entry point. The key is starting.

Step 4 – Build Your System

Track your investment using TradingView or your platform's dashboard. Zoom out for perspective: daily moves are noise; long-term trends tell the story. Consider setting up monthly contributions to build discipline and reduce emotional decisions.

Step 5 – Evolve Your Security

Start with platform storage. As your holdings grow and confidence builds, explore hardware wallets.

A common strategy among investors is to take their original capital back once their Bitcoin holding has grown. This means you're now playing with "free money," profits only, which removes much of the emotional weight. You can hold the rest long-term without the pressure of having your own cash at risk. There's no shame in taking profits when your life circumstances change. This is about your wealth plan, not proving a point.

Part 9: Volatility Reframed and the HODL Philosophy

Bitcoin's price has seen dramatic dips, like the 65% slide in 2022. As we have discussed previously, volatility is simply the price you pay for being in the market. What's fascinating is that Bitcoin has actually become less volatile over time as institutional adoption has grown.

The most powerful tool I use to navigate volatility is the same for ETF investing: investing small, consistent amounts on a regular basis, regardless of price. This strategy smooths out the highs and lows over time and allows compounding and consistency to do the heavy lifting.

I used to check the Bitcoin price obsessively, but eventually I made a conscious shift. I began treating Bitcoin like a pension contribution, money I invest regularly and don't plan to touch for years. This mindset means volatility becomes background noise and the emotional rollercoaster has flattened out. I have stopped reacting and started trusting.

This approach is what the Bitcoin community calls "HODL"; originally a typo from 2013 that became a rallying cry for long-term conviction. Some say it stands for "Hold On for Dear Life," a nod to the emotional grit required to stay the course.

But HODLing isn't just about stubbornly clinging to an asset. It's about clarity, discipline, and belief in a bigger picture. It's about zooming out, tuning out the noise, and remembering why you started. For me, HODLing is a philosophy, one that mirrors how I approach life and long-term transformation.

Traditional investing often rewards control and perfect market timing. Bitcoin invites a different rhythm. The HODL philosophy isn't about control; it's about conviction. It asks us to surrender the illusion of perfect timing and trust in long-term participation. Just as Bitcoin offers financial sovereignty, it invites emotional sovereignty, the confidence to trust your own timing, choices, and voice.

Why Now?

If you've made it this far, you understand what Bitcoin is, how to buy it, and how to hold it for the long term. There's one more piece of context worth noting: Bitcoin is no longer fringe.

BlackRock launched a Bitcoin ETF in 2024 that attracted over $50 billion in months, one of the most successful ETF launches in history. The UK's FCA lifted its retail ban in October 2025, making regulated Bitcoin exposure accessible through ISAs and pensions. Companies like MicroStrategy are holding Bitcoin as treasury reserves on their balance sheets. This institutional adoption doesn't mean you should buy, it means the experiment has reached a new phase of legitimacy worth understanding.

Important note: owning an ETF isn't the same as owning Bitcoin. You're buying a financial instrument, not the asset itself, which means you lose the benefits of self-custody and sovereignty.

I'm not here to make predictions or create urgency. I'm here to show you the landscape and let you decide whether this asset deserves a place in your wealth plan.

A Balanced View

Not everyone shares my interest in Bitcoin, and that's healthy. Before you invest a single pound, you should understand the strongest cases against it.

The Regulatory Risk

Governments have shut down or severely restricted Bitcoin in China, and regulatory uncertainty remains high globally. The UK's recent FCA approval could be reversed. If major economies coordinate to restrict Bitcoin ownership, its value proposition weakens significantly.

The Utility Question

Warren Buffett calls Bitcoin "rat poison" because it produces nothing, no dividends, no earnings, no intrinsic cash flow. When you own shares in a company, you own something that produces goods and profits. When you own property, you can rent it. Bitcoin, by contrast, does not produce income or cash flow. Its value depends entirely on someone else being willing to pay more for it later.

This isn't just an old investor dismissing new technology, it's a fundamental critique every serious investor must grapple with.

The Competition Threat

Bitcoin was first, but thousands of cryptocurrencies have followed with faster speeds, lower energy consumption, and more sophisticated capabilities. If a superior alternative emerges, or if central banks successfully launch digital currencies with government backing, Bitcoin's first-mover advantage could evaporate.

The "Too Late" Problem

At current prices, Bitcoin has already appreciated massively. The 26,931% returns of 2014-2024 cannot repeat from these levels - the mathematics don't work. Early adopters captured the asymmetric upside. You're arguably late.

Where I Land

These critiques are fair. Here's my response:

On utility: Bitcoin isn't competing with companies or rental properties. It's competing with gold - which also produces nothing, yet has been valued for millennia because of scarcity and durability. The question isn't "what does Bitcoin produce?" but "does digital scarcity have value in an increasingly digital world?" I believe it does. You might not. That's okay.

On regulation and competition: Yes, governments could restrict Bitcoin, and better alternatives could emerge. But Bitcoin has survived 15 years of challenges. Its simplicity is its strength.

On timing: Even from current levels, a small allocation (1-5%) offers asymmetric risk/reward. If Bitcoin fails, you lose 1-5% of your portfolio. If it becomes a reserve asset, that position could be transformative.

Bitcoin isn't for everyone, and it shouldn't dominate your portfolio. But the question worth asking is: "What if I'm wrong about dismissing this?" That question alone might justify a small position.

Final Thoughts

I hold a small position in Bitcoin, enough to participate in what I believe is an important technological shift, but not betting the farm. My core passion remains private company investing, which we'll explore in depth in the next chapter.

Bitcoin proved something profound: we can create systems of value that don't require central intermediaries. That proof has unleashed innovations in tokenisation, stablecoins, and decentralised finance - topics too dynamic and evolving for a printed book, but worth understanding as they reshape ownership and control.

What excites me isn't Bitcoin's price - it's the sovereignty these technologies enable. The ability to truly own your assets, control your wealth, and participate in systems that don't require permission from gatekeepers.

Start with Bitcoin if it resonates. Hold a small position. Learn gradually. This is not about chasing returns or predicting the future. It's about understanding a system that is reshaping money, ownership, and control and deciding, for yourself, how (or whether) it fits into your wealth journey.

Recommended Resources

If you want to dive deeper:

- **Joe Bryan - "What's the Problem?"** *(YouTube)*
- **The Bitcoin Standard** by Saifedean Ammous (essential)
- **What Bitcoin Did** - Peter McCormack's podcast

Key Takeaways

- **Bitcoin is powered by blockchain** - a technology reshaping business and finance
- **You don't need a whole Bitcoin** - start small
- **Bitcoin is not equal to "crypto"** - it's unique, scarce, and decentralised
- **Security matters** - start simple, learn gradually, own your keys later
- **Price volatility is normal** - zoom out and HODL
- **Bitcoin offers optionality** - sovereignty and participation in the future of money

Practical Actions

1. **Educate first** - Watch Joe Bryan's video. Read The Bitcoin Standard. Understand the "why" before the "how."
2. **Choose and verify** - Select an FCA-regulated platform. Complete KYC verification. Fund your account.
3. **Start small** - Buy your first £50-£500 worth. Focus on learning, not timing the market.
4. **Automate if possible** - Set up monthly contributions to remove emotional decisions.
5. **Track wisely** - Check quarterly, not daily. Use TradingView's 5-year chart for perspective.
6. **Learn security gradually** - Start with exchange storage. Research hardware wallets, and wait until your holdings reach £500-£1,000. Self-custody is a skill built over time.

Chapter 21

BACKING THE FUTURE

Private Equity: Investing in the Ideas, Founders, and Futures You Believe In

Business has always been one of my greatest passions.

After decades analysing companies as a fund manager, coaching founders to scale their businesses, co-founding a SaaS platform now valued at over £20 million, and serving as a founding director in a company heading towards a NASDAQ listing, I've seen the full lifecycle: from idea to IPO, vision to value. I love business. I love watching someone spot an opportunity and make it real. I love the moment when a founder's vision clicks into sustainable growth.

Private equity, investing directly in private companies before they go public, has become one of the most powerful ways I've built wealth. While your money in the stock market might grow steadily over time, private equity lets you back specific companies in their growth phase, capturing returns before the public markets get access. It's not for everyone, and it requires serious capital and patience, but for those who do it well, the potential is transformative.

I've also observed something that's shaped my conviction about this space.

Female-founded companies receive less than 3% of venture funding, even though research shows they deliver higher returns and greater capital efficiency. Only around 20% of PE capital and 22% of industry roles are held by women.

This creates an unusual opportunity. If you've built wealth through property, business, or professional success, and you understand how to evaluate risk and reward, you're already qualified to participate in private equity investing. The old barriers (£500,000 minimums, insider-only deal flow) have largely fallen. What remains is simply the question: do you want to?

When women become investors, they change their own lives. When women become capital allocators, they change which businesses get funded and which innovations reach the market. This isn't a manifesto; it's simply an observation about what happens when those with capital choose to deploy it directly.

For decades the Rose Review has shown us the same story: female founders are systematically underfunded not because they lack potential, but because the people writing the cheques rarely look like them. The solution isn't simply to campaign for fairness: it's for more women to sit on the other side of the table. Private equity is one place where that shift can happen.

This is why I'm including this chapter, even though it's the most complex strategy in this book. Some of you reading this have successfully built and scaled your own businesses, so you understand what it takes to grow a company. You have the financial capacity to invest in private companies.

I want to invite you to consider whether this belongs in your wealth strategy. I believe that private equity isn't just an investment opportunity: it's a way to gain agency over which businesses grow and which innovations reach the market.

Passion doesn't override reality, though. PE comes with genuine risks, requires serious capital, and demands rigorous due diligence. My job in this chapter is to show you both what's possible and what's required, so you can make an informed decision about whether this fits your goals.

Why This Fits My Values (And Might Fit Yours)

Remember the Investment Compass from earlier in this book? The values shape which strategies resonate with you?

Private equity aligns powerfully with two specific values: relationships and achievement.

If you value relationships, PE offers something no other investment strategy does: a direct connection to founders building businesses. You're not buying anonymous shares on a stock exchange. You're backing specific people with specific visions. Over the 5-7 year journey, you watch them navigate challenges, celebrate wins, and build something meaningful. When I invested in one of my brewing companies, I got to know the founders over coffee, watched them navigate their first major retailer deal, and celebrated when they hit their revenue targets. That relationship made the investment meaningful in ways that owning ETF shares never could.

If you value achievement, PE gives you front-row seats to companies scaling from small teams to significant operations. You're not just watching, you're enabling it. Your capital gives founders a runway to hire, expand, and execute their vision. The achievement isn't just financial returns; it's the satisfaction of seeing something grow from idea to impact.

If you value agency, having a say in which businesses grow and which innovations reach the market, PE offers something the stock market never can. You're not accepting whatever companies happen to be in your index fund. You're actively choosing where your capital flows. For some investors, particularly those who've built wealth and now want it working towards outcomes they believe in, that sense of participation in shaping the economic landscape is deeply satisfying. You're not just building personal wealth; you're backing the founders and solutions you want to see succeed.

What *Is* Private Equity? The Landscape

Private equity covers everything from pre-revenue start-ups to billion-pound buyouts, and the risks vary wildly across that spectrum.

Stage	What It Means	Typical Investment	Risk Level	My Focus
Seed/ Pre-seed	Very early stage, often pre-revenue. Proving the concept.	£5,000-£25,000	Extremely high - most fail	Occasionally, not my focus
Scale-ups	3-5 years from exit. Already delivering product/service. Revenue is flowing or about to launch after years of development.	£10,000-£50,000	Moderate - most survive, but returns vary widely	**This is my sweet spot**
Growth Equity	Series A, B, and C+ rounds. Established companies and raising larger amounts.	£50,000+ typically	Lower but requires significant capital	Outside my range
Buyouts	Acquiring established profitable companies.	£100,000+	Different game entirely	Not relevant here

My focus is firmly on scale-ups. These are companies that have already done the hard early work; they've developed their product, proven demand, and built their team. They're not raw start-ups hoping to find product-market fit. They're 3-5 years from a trade sale or IPO, they've got cash flow coming in (or they're tech companies ready to launch after years of development), and they're raising capital to scale, not to survive.

This distinction matters enormously for risk. Start-up failure rates can hit 80%. Scale-up failure rates are lower because these companies have already survived the most dangerous early phase.

When I talk about private equity in this chapter, I'm talking about scale-ups. That's the opportunity I see for experienced investors who want growth without gambling on completely unproven concepts.

Why This Is Possible Now

For decades, private equity was closed to most people, not because you lacked skills, but because of high minimums (often £500,000) and exclusive deal flow.

That world has changed. Platforms like Seedrs and Crowdcube let you invest from £10, while private investment clubs offer access from £5,000–£10,000. Information that once required insider connections, financials, market analysis, and founder backgrounds is now available in pitch decks and online databases.

The old barriers have fallen. The question is just whether you want to learn the evaluation skills.

My Journey Into Private Equity

I didn't start here. I came from traditional fund management, analysing companies and sitting across tables from CEOs. That gave me skills, but not access to early-stage private companies.

In 2020, I invested £20,000 in two seed-stage companies: a luxury cat brand and a beauty app. Both are still operating, but initial forecasts haven't materialised. They taught me that seed-stage investing is high risk.

By 2022, after refinancing a property project, I had capital to deploy more strategically. I joined several investment clubs, where deals come pre-vetted, and I shifted my focus to scale-ups rather than seed-stage opportunities.

By this point, I wasn't just analysing companies from the outside. I'd moved from fund manager to founder, raising initial capital for the SaaS platform and serving as one of five founding directors at Fenix Battery Recycling. At Fenix, I raised our first funding round and later became Financial Director. The company was acquired based on the strength of the founding team and our access to the UK market, and that business is now part of a company heading towards a NASDAQ listing.

I've sat in rooms raising capital, negotiated valuations, built financial models, and watched companies move from concept to seven and eight-figure valuations. I know what product-market fit actually looks like, not just on paper. I understand what scaling really takes. That dual perspective, founder and investor, fundamentally changed how I evaluate opportunities.

A Reality Check: Risk, Patience, and Possibility

I'd be dishonest if I painted this as guaranteed riches. Private equity has taught me expensive lessons.

One company I invested in was valued at £12 million when I came in. By early 2024, it was valued at £150 million. My £25,000 investment looked set to be worth £300,000. I was mentally spending that money, imagining what that kind of return could do, thinking about the next investments I'd make.

Then, weeks later, the company collapsed into bankruptcy due to regulatory intervention. I lost the entire investment.

Even with EIS tax relief caps, my actual 40% loss was a gut punch. I'd believed in the founders, championed them to others. The failure felt personal.

But it taught me something critical: nothing is guaranteed until it's money in the bank. Paper valuations mean nothing. Even companies that look unstoppable can collapse overnight. This is why diversification matters so much in PE; even scale-ups can fail, though less often than start-ups.

That said, focusing only on the downside misses an important part of the picture.

Private company investing is one of the few places where genuinely outsized outcomes are possible, not because they're common, but because ownership in growing businesses allows value to compound in a way that most traditional assets simply can't replicate.

Some of my private investments have progressed steadily over time, with businesses maturing, strengthening their fundamentals, and increasing in value as they scale. Others are still in progress, moving forward in uneven ways that reflect the reality of private markets. A few have not worked at all.

This mix is normal. It's not a flaw in the strategy: it is the strategy. The logic only works at the portfolio level, where a small number of strong performers can more than compensate for disappointments and losses elsewhere.

This is why private equity isn't about picking a single "winner". It's about backing multiple businesses thoughtfully, doing proper due diligence, and giving time and execution room to work. When it does, the outcomes can be materially different from what's achievable through income or public markets alone, not guaranteed, but possible.

That possibility, approached with patience, discernment, and humility, is why private investing has a place in my own wealth strategy.

What This Strategy Requires

Now that you've seen both the potential and the reality of private investing, let's talk about what private equity actually demands from you, because this is fundamentally different from ETFs or Bitcoin.

Long-term thinking: This is how family offices build generational wealth. They think in decades, not years. Private equity requires a minimum 5-10 year horizon, but the real mindset shift is bigger than that. This is about building wealth for yourself, your children, potentially your children's children. You're not looking for quick wins or exits you can time. You're backing businesses that will mature over the long arc of their development. If you're someone who thinks "I need returns within three years," this isn't your strategy. However, if you can embrace truly long-term wealth building, the way established family offices do, this becomes one of the most powerful tools available.

Capital requirements: Unlike ETFs, where £100 gets you diversification, PE requires enough capital to absorb complete losses on individual companies without destroying your overall portfolio. Whilst platforms like Seedrs and Crowdcube let you invest smaller amounts, these tend to focus on earlier-stage, higher-risk companies. If you want to focus on scale-ups with better survival rates, you'll typically need a minimum of £5,000-10,000 per deal, often £25,000 or more, so you will need a much larger pot to build a diversified portfolio.

Liquidity: Zero. Once invested, that money is completely inaccessible until exit (a trade sale or an IPO). I've had moments where I've thought, "If I could just access £20,000 of that fintech holding for the house renovation..." But I can't. Neither can you. This means when unexpected expenses arise, when opportunities present themselves, when life happens, this money simply doesn't exist for those purposes. This only works if you genuinely won't need these funds for a decade and you have other liquid reserves for life's surprises.

Involvement level: Research-heavy upfront (10-20 hours per deal reading pitch decks, assessing founders, evaluating markets), then mostly passive for years except occasional updates. You're not managing properties or rebalancing portfolios. You read, decide, invest, and then wait. For some personalities, this is perfect. For others who need to "do something" with their investments, it can feel frustratingly passive.

Patience and information gaps: This is perhaps the most challenging aspect. You often don't know what your investment is actually worth between funding rounds. Getting information from companies can be difficult. Exits that are "coming in three months" regularly take 12-18 months longer than expected. My aerospace liquidity event was expected in early 2025. As with many private investments, timelines shifted repeatedly, and I have spent months sitting with uncertainty about when, or if, it will complete. The anxiety isn't market volatility, it's the lack of transparency and the constant delays. You need genuine patience and the ability to sit with uncertainty without becoming obsessive about checking for updates.

However, if you're someone who values deep relationships, loves watching companies scale, has capital you won't need for years, and gets excited about backing founders building the future, then this might be exactly your opportunity.

The Skills You Already Have

If you've succeeded in property investing or built your own business, you already have most of what PE requires:

Your Experience	PE Application
Assessing locations, developers, and tenants	Assessing markets, founders, and management teams
Managing multi-year cash flows and projections	Managing multi-year growth plans and burn rates
Creating value through renovation	Creating value through scale and strategy
Due diligence on properties	Due diligence on companies and competitive landscape
5-10 year investment horizons	5-7 year investment horizons

If you've built and sold your own business, you have even more relevant skills. You understand cash flow vs. profit. You know what "product-market fit" looks like. You've navigated regulatory challenges. You can smell the BS in a financial forecast. You know the difference between a visionary founder and a dreamer who can't execute.

The mindset is the same: find value, back competent people, be patient, and think long term.

Private equity isn't a leap from property or business; it's a pivot using skills you've already developed.

The UK's Secret Weapon: EIS and SEIS

If you're a UK investor, HMRC actively encourages investment in small private companies. So they've created tax incentives that dramatically reduce your downside while letting you keep all the upside.

EIS (Enterprise Investment Scheme):

- Claim back 30% of your investment against income tax
- Keep profits tax-free after three years
- Offset losses against other income or gains
- Invest up to £1 million per year

SEIS (Seed Enterprise Investment Scheme):

- Claim back 50% of your investment
- Tax-free growth after three years
- Offset losses against other income
- Invest up to £200,000 per year

Here's how it works in practice: If you invest £10,000 into an EIS-qualifying company, you can reclaim £3,000 straight away through your tax return. Your real risk is £7,000, but you keep 100% of any upside.

If the company fails completely, you can offset that £7,000 loss against other income or capital gains. If it succeeds and you make a £50,000 profit, you pay zero capital gains tax.

This is why private equity can be so powerful for UK investors, you're reducing the downside but keeping all the upside. It's one of the best-kept secrets in British investing.

For readers outside the UK, the US offers a broadly comparable incentive through the Qualified Small Business Stock (QSBS) exemption, which can make gains on eligible early-stage company investments tax-free after a five-year holding period. Check local guidance or speak to your tax adviser for details.

The Risks You Need to Understand

Private equity carries specific risks that differ from ETFs or Bitcoin. You need to understand what you're taking on:

- **Company risk** (the business fails)
- **Timing risk** (exits take longer than expected)
- **Liquidity risk** (your money is completely locked)
- **Valuation risk** (paper gains evaporate)
- **Regulatory risk** (as happened with my £150m loss)
- **Concentration risk** (each investment is a big bet on one company, unlike ETFs, where you own hundreds).

The risk you're not taking: market volatility stress. There's no price to watch, no temptation to panic sell. Once invested, you wait for the exit, which suits some personalities perfectly and drives others mad.

You're equipped to manage these risks if you have business evaluation skills, can afford to lose 100% of any single investment, won't need this money for 7-10 years, and can maintain a portfolio of 5-10 companies to diversify properly.

Getting Started: What You Actually Need to Know

If you're intrigued, you'll need to understand due diligence, platforms, and red flags. You can find companies through family and friends, angel networks, investment syndicates, or platforms like Seedrs and Crowdcube.

Additional resources to help you explore private equity further are available in the Fearless Wealth Playbook. For comprehensive due diligence training, live deal analysis, and community support, the Fearless Female Investor Collective offers a deeper exploration of private equity investing.

The Mechanics Are Simpler Than You Think

After all the talk about due diligence frameworks and learning curves, the actual transaction of buying shares in a private company is remarkably simple.

You've already learned how to open brokerage accounts or buy Bitcoin through exchanges; that's far more technical than this. When you invest privately, you simply say, "Yes, I'd like to invest £10,000." The company calculates how many shares it's based on the valuation, you sign a shareholders' agreement (setting out everyone's rights), transfer the money, and you're done. The company updates its cap table, and you own shares.

It's essentially a deal between two parties, you and the company. Sometimes a lawyer is involved; often not. I've completed private share purchases that took less time than opening a brokerage account.

The complexity isn't in the paperwork; it's in the decision-making beforehand. Once you've done your homework, executing is refreshingly simple.

Learn Through Community

If this resonates, don't learn in isolation. My best opportunities haven't come from browsing platforms like Seedrs, though they're a great place to start exploring. They have come through relationships:

investment clubs, angel networks, and introductions from other investors.

Attend pitch events. Watch how experienced investors interrogate a founder's plan. Listen for the red flags they spot that you might miss. You'll learn more in one room of investors than from months of reading online.

So start with curiosity: browse Seedrs or Crowdcube to see what's out there. Use the Fearless Wealth Playbook resources to understand the framework. When you're serious about actually investing, join an angel network or investment syndicate. Go to pitch events. Watch how it's done. Build relationships with other investors who can share deal flow and due diligence.

That's where the real learning and opportunities happen.

A Personal Perspective

As you'll have gathered from this chapter, private equity plays an important role in my own wealth strategy. Not because it's easy or predictable, it isn't, but because it offers something most other asset classes don't: meaningful wealth creation through ownership in growing businesses.

That potential is precisely why I believe private equity is something more women should understand and consider. For many women, the assumption is that real wealth comes either from building a business yourself or from accumulating assets slowly over time. Private investing offers a third path; one where you participate in the growth of businesses without carrying the operational burden of running them.

But I'd be lying if I said this was only about building personal wealth. It's bigger than that.

When you invest in private companies, you stop being a bystander in the economy. You become a capital allocator, someone who decides which ideas, which founders, and which solutions receive funding. And those decisions shape what actually gets built. Right now, the people making those decisions are overwhelmingly men, which is one reason female founders still receive a fraction of available investment despite consistently delivering strong returns. The problem isn't that women can't build great companies. The problem is that we're not at the table when the capital gets allocated.

This is what I mean by wealth reimagined. It's not just about growing your portfolio, though private equity can absolutely do that. It's about recognising that capital allocation is power, and that when more women hold that power, the economic landscape shifts. Different problems get funded. Different founders get backed. Different futures become possible.

Think about what's happened in women's rugby. Women didn't wait for permission. They got off the sidelines, got on the pitch, and started redesigning the game on their own terms. We can do exactly the same thing with capital. We don't need to ask for a seat at the table. We can build the table.

So yes, learn private equity because it can build wealth. But also learn it because every woman who evaluates a deal, backs a founder, or joins an investment syndicate is doing something quietly revolutionary: she's becoming one of the people who decides what gets funded. And collectively, that changes everything.

Key Takeaways

- **Private equity spans a wide spectrum** - from seed-stage startup companies to scale-ups, growth equity, management buyouts, and late-stage investments; each offers different risk/return profiles and entry points
- **Scale-ups are not start-ups** - Lower failure rates than seed investment, but still real risk; diversify across 5-10 companies
- **PE is patient capital** - Your money is locked for 5-10 years; returns are lumpy and arrive at exit

- **Do the work upfront** - The transaction is simple; the judgement is not. Your edge is diligence and pattern recognition
- **Use your existing strengths** - Property/business skills transfer: underwriting teams, markets, cashflows, and execution risk
- **UK tax relief is a force multiplier** - EIS/SEIS reduce downside and preserve upside; get competent tax advice early
- **Community compounds judgement** - Angel clubs, syndicates, and investor rooms accelerate learning and improve deal flow
- **Invest with a thesis** - Back the sectors and problems you want to see solved: returns and meaning travel together

Practical Actions

1. **Assess your readiness for private equity** - You need capital you won't need for 7-10 years, comfort with risk and illiquidity, genuine interest in evaluating businesses and people, desire to back innovation (not just buy shares), and belief that wealth is built with patience and purpose. If these conditions fit, continue; if not, revisit when circumstances change.
2. **Understand your tax advantages** - Speak with your accountant about EIS or SEIS reliefs and how they could reduce your downside risk.
3. **Get curious, safely** - Spend 30 minutes browsing platforms like Seedrs or Crowdcube. Notice which founders and sectors excite you. No action yet, just observation.
4. **Expand your knowledge in the Fearless Wealth Playbook** - Access private equity strategy resources,and frameworks to help you evaluate opportunities and build your investment approach.

Chapter 22

FROM INTIMIDATION TO INCOME GENERATION

How I Discovered the Surprisingly Simple Strategy That's Replacing My Property Portfolio

If you'd told me back in business school that one day I'd be obsessed with options trading, I'd have laughed you out of the lecture theatre.

We were studying the Black-Scholes model, an options pricing equation so complex it looked like something NASA might use to launch a rocket. My brain shut down. I remember thinking: "This is ridiculous. There's no way I'm investing using options. Ever."

I filed them away under "things I'll never touch."

Fast forward to 2023. I was in my SSAS pension investor group, surrounded by smart people earning 1.5% to 2% per month, selling options. I was sceptical until their trainer explained the strategy in plain English. In ten minutes, my fear turned into fascination.

I joined his coaching programme, and I can honestly say it's been eye-opening. Nearly two years later, I've been learning, paper trading, attending in-person workshops, and watching dozens of people in my investor group execute this strategy month after month. I've seen it work in bull markets, sideways markets, and yes, even bear markets.

I haven't gone fully live yet, not for lack of trust but lack of liquidity. My capital has been tied up in property and private equity. When that money lands, this is exactly where it's going.

This chapter isn't me posing as a veteran trader; it's me holding the door open and sharing why I'm convinced enough to allocate my property proceeds to doing this.

What Are the Options? (The Simple Truth)

An option is a contract giving the buyer the right, not the obligation, to buy or sell a stock at a set price within a set timeframe. The buyer pays a premium; the seller collects it.

Think of a call like locking in a holiday price with a deposit. A put is like travel insurance; you pay a small premium for protection.

Most people think about buying options to bet on big moves. There's another way: selling options to generate income. No predictions, no complicated maths, you're simply being paid to make the offer. Forget anything complex like butterflies, iron condors, strangles or understanding "the Greeks" (delta, theta, gamma). We're keeping this practical. We are going to explore the basic Wheel Strategy.

If terms like *puts*, *calls*, *strikes*, and *assignment* feel like a secret code, you're not alone. Once you learn what they mean, it becomes logical fast. There's a glossary at the back if you want to check a term as you go.

The Wheel Strategy: A Cycle That Keeps Turning

The Wheel Strategy is a cycle that keeps turning, generating income at each turn. For this example, we'll assume you have cash to buy shares.

Here's how it works:

Step 1: Sell a Put

Offer to buy shares at a price below today's level and collect a premium. If the market stays above your price, you keep the premium and nothing else happens. If it drops, you are assigned the shares at the price you were happy with anyway.

Step 2: Own the shares.

Once assigned, you hold the shares at your chosen price and prepare for the next step

Step 3: Sell a covered call.

Offer to sell those shares at a higher price and collect another premium. If the price stays below, you keep the premium and the shares. If it rises above, your shares are "called away," you sell at a profit and keep the premiums.

Step 4: Repeat

Once your shares are sold, you get your cash back, plus the two premiums you have collected, and you can start the cycle again by selling a put.

Round and round it goes. Each turn generates income.

The Property Analogy That Changed Everything

Let me show you when this really clicked for me. I was explaining this to a property investor friend and realised: this is exactly like running a rental portfolio.

Property Investing	Wheel Strategy
Make an offer below the asking price, get paid for making the offer	Sell a put, collect premium
Buy the property if the price drops to your offer	Get assigned shares at your chosen price
Rent it out monthly	Sell calls, collect premium
Sell property when the price rises	Shares get called away at a profit
Start over with a new property	Repeat the wheel

The beauty is no tenants, no toilets, no midnight broken-boiler calls. No solicitors, no stamp duty, no void periods. Just premiums quietly dropping into your account.

The Mechanics: How This Actually Works

I spend a few minutes a day checking TradingView for specific signals. If there's a signal, I place the trade, update my tracker, and carry on. Most days there's no signal. Once a trade is placed, it runs itself until expiry.

I know I like to ski off-piste in other parts of life, but here I stay very much on-piste. That discipline is why the income is consistent.

Why I Use ETFs, Not Individual Stocks

You'll see this strategy discussed online using individual stocks; however, individual companies can and do blow up, so I use ETFs for this strategy. You learned about Exchange Traded Funds in Chapter 19 and how ETFs spread that risk across a basket of companies. You can even use broad commodities or metals ETFs, and as these are tied to underlying assets, the chance your ETF will go to zero is far lower. It removes unnecessary single-company risk from a strategy that's already designed to be conservative.

Let's Talk About Risk (Because We Must)

The biggest risk: you can end up holding shares during a market drop.

In March 2020, the NASDAQ fell by 34% in weeks. If you'd been assigned shares at what looked like a fair price, you'd have watched them fall further. Like property that drops below your mortgage, you don't panic-sell. You keep selling calls, collect income, and let time work for you.

Golden rule: don't sell when you don't have to.

If your shares are underwater, you can keep generating income with calls and, where appropriate, use rolling/management tactics. With additional capital, you can also sell puts lower to acquire more shares and average down, still collecting premiums as you go.

The harder part is emotional. Seeing shares down 20–30% and *still* selling small calls requires conviction. Another human wrinkle is that there will be months with no signal. If you rely on this for income, a good strategy is to keep several months' expenses aside so that quiet periods without signals don't put pressure on you.

This isn't passive income, but the time commitment is minimal. The real work is mostly psychological, follow the rules!

Why Doesn't Everyone Do This?

It requires learning. Most people are intimidated by options terminology and never get past that fear.

It requires capital. You need enough to buy 100 shares of an ETF, anywhere from a few thousand pounds to £10,000+.

It requires discipline. You have to follow the rules, even when your gut tells you otherwise, and sit on your hands when there's no signal.

It requires emotional resilience. Can you keep executing when your shares are underwater?

And many people don't believe it until they understand it. That was me.

Why I Trust This Enough to Commit My Property Proceeds

All those years ago, sitting in that business-school lecture theatre staring at the Black-Scholes equation, I'd have bet my life that I would *never* write this chapter.

And yet, here we are.

I haven't gone fully live yet, not from doubt, but from being capital-constrained. My money's been locked in property and private equity. But I've spent two years preparing for when I do have liquidity: understanding the mechanics, paper trading through real market conditions, watching this work month after month in my investor group. When my property capital lands, I'll be deploying it here with confidence built on rigorous preparation, not hopeful guesswork.

Making It Real: The Numbers

Let's keep this grounded and use an example:

Take £100,000 from a property sale and run the Wheel, aiming for an average monthly return of 2%.

- **Average annual income:** approx. £24,000 a year. No agents, no leaks, no maintenance.
- **Reinvest and compound monthly:** approx. £128,000 after a year, roughly £28,000 in income.*

  **Illustrative only, this is not advice or a guarantee.*

It won't be 2% every month. Some months are higher; some months there will be nothing. However, over 18-24 months, the people I've watched consistently land around 1.5–3% using the simplest version of this strategy. No fancy tweaks, no complex analytics, just following the rules. And for me, that's the appeal: it's not about being clever; it's about being consistent.

The Real Point

I'm not trying to turn you into a trader. I'm sharing this because it's completely changed how I think about generating income.

This strategy is calm, repeatable, and fits around life. This will become my main income-generating strategy, not because it's flashy, but because it's practical, empowering, and proven enough to commit my own money.

I can't show you a year's worth of my results yet as my capital's still tied up. But I've done the work, asked the questions and seen enough. I'm not asking you to take my word for it; I'm inviting you to explore for yourself. Learn, paper-trade, practise, verify. And if you want company, that's what the Fearless Female Investor Collective is for.

Creating income doesn't need to be complicated. It doesn't have to consume your life.

It asks for curiosity, courage and the willingness to try the thing you once swore you'd never do.

This isn't about chasing excitement or getting rich quickly. It's about building something reliable, an income that compounds quietly while you live your life.

And if I, the woman who once rolled her eyes at the Black-Scholes equation, can get here… so can you.

Key Takeaways

- **Options aren't mysterious or reckless** - they're simply contracts that can create steady monthly income
- **The Wheel Options Strategy takes minutes daily** - once you understand it
- **Average returns of 1.5-2% per month** - achievable with discipline and patience
- **It's rule-based and repeatable** - adaptable to almost any market
- **The smartest move is learn first** - test slowly, then scale with confidence

Practical Actions

1. **Start learning** - Tastytrade.com offers brilliant, free beginner lessons.
2. **Read - The Options Playbook by Brian Overby** explains everything clearly, without jargon.
3. **Paper trade first** - Open a simulator account with Interactive Brokers. Treat it like a flight simulator for your finances.
4. **Start small when you go live** - Begin with one position, then build gradually over 6-12 months.
5. **Join a community** - Learn with others.

Chapter 23

MASTERING THE INNER GAME

Courage, Commitment & the Conscious Investor's Edge

When I was learning to ski, my instructors would shout instructions as I hurtled down the slope: "Bend your knees! Press into the ski! Weight forward!"

I was overthinking every move, stiff, awkward, and slightly terrified.

Then I discovered The Inner Game of Skiing. It talked about the two players inside you, the one who acts and the one who judges. The only way to ski well was to quieten that inner critic and trust your body's natural intelligence.

That insight changed everything for my skiing, and the same applies to investing and life.

In earlier chapters, we explored how emotions drive financial decisions (Chapter 3), how your emotional state shapes risk tolerance (Chapter 4), and how mindset is the source code behind it all (Chapter 6).

This chapter brings those ideas together, showing you how to run that new code under pressure. Because without emotional mastery, all the financial knowledge in the world won't help you build lasting wealth.

You can read every finance book on the shelf, earn a master's degree, learn the formulas and ratios, but none of it matters if your emotions hijack you when the market falls, or when FOMO whispers that everyone else is getting rich faster. I learned this the hard way in the City: all the models in the world can't help you when your nervous system is in panic mode.

Money mastery, I've learned, has two sides: the outer game (knowledge, systems, and strategy), and the inner game (self-awareness, emotional mastery, and courage under pressure).

The outer game is what most of us study. The inner game is what most of us stumble through. Yet it's the inner game that decides whether all that knowledge ever turns into wisdom, wealth, or peace of mind.

Nowhere have I seen that truth more vividly than on a mountain in Chamonix, watching my six-year-old daughter face her own edge of fear.

Standing at the Edge

"I'm scared, but I'm going to do it anyway."

That wasn't a seasoned fund manager staring at crashing markets or a property developer facing bankruptcy.

That was my six-year-old daughter, Charlotte, sitting at the top of what looked, to me, like a small mountain in Chamonix, about to launch herself off a towering ski jump.

The air was sharp and thin at that altitude. Around us, teenage members of the French ski team were watching, genuinely impressed by this tiny girl in her pink salopettes.

I stood before a group of smoking ESF instructors in their iconic red jackets, asking whether my daughter could possibly jump off that.

They looked at me, looked at her, and shrugged.

"We 'ave never 'ad a six-year-old who wanted to jump off that," one said.

"Mais pourquoi pas?" (But why not?)

Charlotte had been working up to this moment all day, first on gentle slopes, then small jumps, then bigger ones. Each time, her confidence grew. And now, she wanted to test herself at the next level.

So up we went.

From below, the jump hadn't looked too intimidating. From the top, it was a different story.

The in-run stretched steeply ahead, long parallel grooves carved perfectly straight into the snow, leading to a lip that launched you into open air. Charlotte edged onto the seat and slid her skis into the tracks, edges flat, no turning, no snowploughing. Once she pushed off, there'd be no stopping. She was committed.

The Moment Before

She peered down at the enormous drop, then turned to me.

Her voice was small but steady.

"Mummy, I'm really scared."

My heart was hammering. My hands pressed together almost unconsciously in prayer.

"Sweetheart, we don't have to do this," I whispered. "We can walk back down. There's no shame in that."

She paused, balancing perfectly on the edge, skis locked into the tracks.

And then, calmly: "I'm going to do it anyway, Mummy."

The Leap

Before I could respond, she pushed off.

Time slowed. The hiss of her skis built into a rush as she accelerated down the in-run, and then… silence… as she launched into space.

For one long, suspended moment, gravity released her completely.

I whispered a desperate prayer: Please, please, please let her land.

A cheer erupted from below before I even saw her. She'd done it. Landed perfectly.

Relief hit so hard my knees almost buckled. But alongside it came something else, a realisation so sharp it's never left me.

Charlotte had just taught me one of the most profound lessons about courage, commitment, and backing yourself. That lesson, backing yourself and trusting your plan, sits at the very heart of emotional money mastery.

But you can't back yourself if you don't know yourself. Emotional mastery starts with self-awareness, noticing what triggers you, what shakes your confidence, and what pulls you off track.

Standing at the top of that ski jump, little Charlotte was fully present, fully focused. She wasn't rushing, panicking, or second-guessing herself. She was in a high-frequency state: calm, clear, and committed.

As investors, that's exactly what we need to cultivate. The decisions we make from panic or scarcity almost always cost us. The decisions we make from clarity and confidence, even when we feel fear, set us up for success.

For me, it's often noise, endless opinions, analysis, and predictions. For you, it might be comparison, FOMO, or fear of making a mistake. When you can spot your patterns, you can change them. That's where emotional mastery begins.

The Lesson

When you're standing at the edge of fear, whether it's a ski jump, an investment decision, or a life-changing choice, there is no halfway. You have to commit fully.

Charlotte showed me that day that courage isn't the absence of fear. It's acting despite it.

What she taught me applies to every investment decision I've made. Every market crash. Every time my portfolio has been in freefall. Every moment you're staring into the unknown, stomach tight, heart racing.

And then… You take the next step anyway.

Every single time you choose courage over certainty.

The deeper truth, as we explored in Chapter 3, The Frequency of Money, is that the emotional mastery required to navigate market volatility is exactly the same skill set you need to ride the waves of life itself.

The consciousness. The emotional frequency. The emotional resilience we're about to dive into, these aren't just investment strategies. They're life strategies. They're the foundation of true wealth.

The Price of Admission to Extraordinary Returns

Standing at the top of that ski jump with Charlotte, I realised something: fear isn't a signal to stop; it's an invitation to grow.

As we explored in Chapter 4, volatility isn't danger; it's simply movement, the market breathing in and out. The real challenge isn't what prices do, it's what *we* do when they move.

Many people, especially women, shy away from investing because volatility looks chaotic. But volatility is just the price of admission to extraordinary returns. The danger isn't in the swings themselves; it's in how we react to them, panic-selling at the bottom, chasing FOMO trades at the top, or abandoning a solid plan when our nervous system screams, "Do something!"

That's where investors lose wealth, not because the market moved, but because of how they responded. Mastering the inner game means learning to stay conscious in motion, trusting your process while everything around you fluctuates.

Why It Feels So Hard

The reason volatility feels like danger has less to do with markets and more to do with biology.

Your nervous system is built for survival, not wealth. When markets plunge, your brain reacts as if you've seen a predator, adrenaline surges, your heart races, and rational thinking shuts down.

This ancient wiring kept our ancestors alive but sabotages us in modern markets. The behaviours that once protected us now lead us to panic-sell at the bottom or chase performance at the top.

Think of a rollercoaster: the drops, twists, and stomach-lurching turns are engineered into the ride. When you understand the design, fear transforms into exhilaration. Volatility is no different. Once you see it clearly, everything changes.

The Four Faces of Fear (and What Happens When They Collide)

You've already met these fears in earlier chapters; they're the emotional fingerprints of risk. Seeing them clearly is how you stop them from quietly running the show.

1. Fear of Missing Out (FOMO) – The buzz when everyone else seems to be making money and you're not. It convinces you that opportunity is running out.

Just last year, despite decades in finance, I fell for this. I invested £10,000 in an FX trading scheme promising double-digit monthly returns. My gut screamed "no," but it seemed like everyone I knew and respected was getting in. I ignored my own analysis and followed the crowd. Within weeks, it collapsed.

The reality is that these fears don't disappear with experience. They rise up again and again. The key is learning to notice them, manage your response, and when you do get caught out, move on with wisdom rather than shame.

2. Fear of Loss – Opening a portfolio of red numbers can feel like a physical blow. Loss aversion makes us sell too soon just to stop the pain, turning temporary dips into permanent losses.

3. Fear of Being Wrong – When money and identity tangle, mistakes feel personal. Back in my fund-manager days, I once doubled down on a losing position simply to avoid admitting I'd misjudged it. I threw good money after bad because the alternative - walking into the Investment Committee meeting and saying "I got this wrong" - felt unbearable. Ego can be expensive.

4. Fear of Irrelevance – The nagging sense that everyone else knows more, moves faster, or has access to better information, which makes you doubt your own judgement and overreact to external noise.

Shiny Penny Syndrome: when two or more fears collide, usually FOMO and Irrelevance, you end up chasing every new idea and abandoning what was already working.

As a fund manager, I'd drown in analyst reports: "buy," "sell," "hold", often conflicting recommendations for the same stock. When I developed conviction on a position, sometimes doubt would creep in: Goldman has 47 analysts tracking this sector full-time with proprietary models I'll never see. Morgan Stanley has access to management teams I can't reach. How can my analysis possibly compete with that? That's the trap. You stop trusting your own judgment and start trusting noise instead. That's how you lose your edge.

The antidote is focus. As Warren Buffett, one of the best investors ever, shows, real mastery isn't about finding the right opinion; it's about protecting your mental bandwidth so you can stick to your strategy, cancel the noise, and trust yourself.

Recognising these fears is half the battle. The other half is learning to pause, a practice we'll explore next, where you notice the trigger, breathe, and act from clarity instead of reaction.

The Five Pillars of Emotional Investment Mastery

What I have learned over the years is that successful investing (and life!) is 80% emotional mastery and 20% strategy. The good news: emotional mastery isn't something you either have or don't have. It's a practice. Every time you pause before reacting, you're building it. Every time you notice your fear and choose clarity anyway, you're strengthening it. Charlotte didn't wake up brave, she practised on small jumps first. Here is a framework that can form your foundation for staying calm, intentional, and resilient as an investor.

1. Emotional Awareness

When your portfolio drops 20%, fear screams louder than logic. Emotional awareness doesn't mean ignoring your feelings; it means learning to observe them without letting them control your actions. Mark Douglas, author of *Trading in the Zone*, calls this neutral thinking, treating each outcome as feedback, not a verdict on your worth.

Awareness on its own isn't enough. As we explored in Chapter 3, money is energy, and the state you're in when you make decisions matters. Acting from fear, scarcity, or desperation leads to reactive, short-term choices. High-frequency states, curiosity, calm, confidence, and gratitude, produce very different results.

Before I make any investment decision, I pause and ask: "Am I making this choice from fear… or from clarity?" If the answer is fear, I wait. Because decisions made from low-frequency energy nearly always cost me. That simple check-in - what I call Investment Therapy - has saved me thousands of pounds in reactive decisions. It's using each money decision as a conscious moment to notice your state before you act.

Investment Therapy in Practice: The Three-Step Pause

This is where emotional awareness becomes actionable.

1. **Name the Emotion:** Not "I feel bad" but "I'm experiencing FOMO" or "This is loss aversion speaking." Simply naming it separates you from it and takes away its power.
2. **Pause and Breathe:** Take one conscious breath. Sometimes that's all it takes to shift from reaction to response.
3. **Respond, Don't React:** Check back with your investment framework. Has anything fundamentally changed, or is this just noise?

That tiny pause between stimulus and response is where emotional resilience is built. Every time you run **Name → Pause → Respond,** you're strengthening the muscle. The first few times feel awkward. By the tenth time, it becomes instinctive.

Markets don't create your emotions; your beliefs about money do. Two people can experience the same portfolio drop: one panics, the other stays calm. The difference? The story they're telling themselves.

Practical actions:

- Keep an emotion log during volatile periods. Write down exactly what you're feeling before making a decision.
- Build a 24-hour rule for emotional decisions. If you're triggered, pause, breathe, and revisit the decision the next day.
- After any major market move, ask yourself: "What am I making this mean?" The meaning, not the movement, drives your reaction.

2. Disciplined Consistency

"Time in the market beats timing the market" isn't just a cliché; it's a mathematical truth. Long-term wealth doesn't come from "getting it right" once; it comes from showing up consistently.

As we explored in earlier chapters on ETF and Bitcoin investing, consistency is the quiet force underlying all meaningful transformation. Just as £100 invested monthly for 40 years can grow to over £600,000 (assuming the Nasdaq's historical 10% average return), your consistent actions compound over time, building not just wealth, but the emotional resilience that makes the next decision easier.

Practical action: Automate wherever possible, monthly contributions, pension payments, and portfolio rebalancing. Automation removes willpower from the process and ensures you stay the course.

3. Backing Yourself

This is perhaps the hardest pillar to build because it requires something counterintuitive: you have to back yourself *before* you have proof you're right. Charlotte didn't know she'd land perfectly, she just knew she'd done the preparation and made a decision.

In investing, you'll never have complete certainty. Markets are probabilistic, not deterministic. Backing yourself means trusting your research, your risk assessment, and your ability to adapt if things don't go as planned. It's not blind faith, it's earned confidence in your process.

Practical action: Start your investment thesis journal. For each major decision, write down: Why you're investing, your time horizon, and the risks you've considered. When emotions flare, revisit it.

4. Intentional Flexibility

The key to successful investing is having your own strategy and sticking to it; your own rules, your own framework, your own process. This is what protects you from being swept away by noise, FOMO, or fear.

However, markets evolve. Economic conditions shift. Strategies that worked five years ago don't always work today. The crucial skill is knowing the difference between thoughtful strategic adaptation (responding to genuine fundamental changes) and emotional reactivity (panicking at headlines or abandoning your plan mid-course).

Your strategy should be firm, but not rigid. The danger isn't in adjusting your approach when circumstances genuinely change; it's in reacting emotionally to every market swing.

Practical action: Define your core strategy and adjustment criteria in advance. For example:

> "I invest monthly in global ETFs and rebalance annually" (your strategy)
>
> "I'll only adjust my asset allocation if my time horizon or risk tolerance fundamentally changes" (your flexibility boundary)

"I'll sell an individual holding if revenue falls below X for two consecutive quarters" (your exit rule)

Clear rules give you the freedom to adapt intentionally without being hijacked by emotion.

5. Strategic Rest & Noise Blocking

You don't need to monitor your investments daily. In fact, constantly checking prices, headlines, or analyst reports keeps your nervous system in fight-or-flight mode and amplifies anxiety. It also makes you far more vulnerable to shiny-penny syndrome, which distracts you from every new idea, prediction, or "hot tip."

Strategic rest is about protecting your attention as much as your time. Set no-check days, unsubscribe from unnecessary market alerts, and curate where you get your information. Protect your focus. Protect your process.

Practical action: Designate "no-check days" or even no-check weeks during periods of high volatility. Trust the system you've built and reclaim your mental bandwidth.

Mastering your Inner Game

Over time, through practice and plenty of mistakes, I've built what I call compound emotional resilience. Every time you notice your fears and navigate volatility without panicking, you strengthen your capacity. Every time you pause rather than react, you deepen your inner control.

This emotional compounding is worth more than any single market win. You could take away all my money tomorrow, but I'd still have something far more valuable: emotional sovereignty.

This isn't just about market volatility. It's about becoming someone who can ride the waves of life itself with clarity, grace, and unshakeable inner stability.

The inner game isn't separate from the outer game - they're two sides of the same coin. Your investment strategy is only as strong as the emotional foundation supporting it. And your emotional mastery grows every time you practise it under pressure.

Charlotte wasn't special because she was fearless. She was instructive because she felt the fear fully, acknowledged it honestly, and moved forward anyway. Volatility will come. Fear will whisper. Markets will swing wildly, and your emotions will try to follow. But like Charlotte at the top of that ski jump, your job isn't to eliminate fear, it's to act wisely in its presence.

Volatility, FOMO, and shiny-penny distractions are just mirrors showing us where our old code still tries to run. Every conscious pause, every act of Investment Therapy, is how you strengthen the new one. That's true money mastery - staying the course, no matter what's happening around you.

That's the essence of investing. That's the essence of living.

"I'm scared... but I'm going to do it anyway."

Sometimes the most profound teachers come in the smallest pink salopettes.

Key Takeaways

- **Volatility isn't a problem** - it's the price of admission to extraordinary returns
- **Market noise isn't wisdom** - process beats prediction every time
- **Emotional triggers are normal** - but mastering your response is everything
- **Your job isn't to avoid volatility** - it's to build stability within yourself
- **True wealth isn't about money** - it's about freedom from reactivity

Practical Actions

1. **Set up automatic investing** - remove emotion from regular investment decisions.
2. **Start an investment thesis journal** - write down your reasoning for each decision.
3. **Practice Name → Pause → Respond daily** - build emotional regulation skills.
4. **Keep a "fear log" during market volatility** - simply naming emotions creates distance.
5. **Celebrate small emotional wins** - notice when you successfully pause instead of reacting.

Chapter 24

PENSIONS, REIMAGINED

Turning the Most Overlooked Asset into Your Most Powerful Wealth-Builder

In the last chapter, we explored the inner game of wealth, the emotional mastery you need to navigate volatility, manage fear, and stay steady when markets swing. You learned how to back yourself, trust your plan, and act with courage even when you're scared.

That's the foundation. Now let's return to the outer game and talk about one of the most powerful and most overlooked containers for building your wealth: pensions.

But before we dive into pensions themselves, let's question the entire framework we've been sold.

Let's talk about retirement.

Actually, let's start by questioning whether "retirement" is even the right word anymore.

The concept of retirement was invented in the late 19th century during the Industrial Revolution. Governments needed a way to move older workers out of factories to make room for younger, cheaper labour. So they created an arbitrary age - originally around 65 - when you'd be eligible for a state pension.

It was an industrial-age solution to an industrial-age problem.

That model assumes you work until you're physically unable, then stop entirely at a government-determined age (currently 67 for UK women and rising), and live out your remaining years on whatever you saved.

Retirement, as traditionally conceived, doesn't serve most of us, especially women. We retire with pension pots worth 35% less than men. We live longer with significantly less money. In some demographics, over half of women have less than £10,000 saved for retirement.

This is what I want to disrupt: the problem isn't just that women have smaller pensions. The problem is that we're all still thinking about "retirement" as something separate from the rest of our financial lives.

Your Freedom Number IS Your Retirement Number

In Chapter 10, you calculated your Freedom Number, the annual income giving you complete choice about how you spend your time. That's your retirement number. They're the same thing.

Your Freedom Number is when work becomes optional, when you have enough wealth to cover your lifestyle without a salary. That could be 35, 45, 60, or never if you love what you do.

"Retirement" at 67 is an arbitrary government date that may not align with when you've built enough wealth to have choice.

Throughout this book, we've built a framework for material and spiritual wealth. The outdated retirement model forces a false separation: work (often unfulfilling) until 67, then finally do what you want - except by then you may lack the health, energy, or money to live the life you've deferred for decades.

That's not freedom. That's deferred living.

What if we reimagined the entire concept? What if "retirement" wasn't about stopping, but about reaching the point where you have *choice*? Where work becomes something you do because it's meaningful and aligns with who you are, not because you need the money to survive.

I'm in my fifties. I don't expect to "retire" in the traditional sense. I expect to keep doing work that matters to me on *my* terms, not because I'm trapped by financial necessity.

That's what your Freedom Number gives you. And your pension - when structured properly - is one of the most powerful vehicles for getting there.

Why Your Timeline Matters

The closer you are to your Freedom Number target date, the more urgent pension planning becomes.

If you're in your 30s: You have time for compounding to work magic. Start contributing now, get the employer match, understand your options. Even small amounts now become significant over 30+ years. Your focus should be on building the habit of consistent contributions and learning about investing so you can make informed choices as your pension grows.

If you're in your 40s: This is a strategy decade. Review what you have, consolidate scattered pots from previous employers, increase contributions if possible, and ensure your investments match your risk tolerance and timeline. If you're planning to reach your Freedom Number at 55, your pension shouldn't be automatically shifting into conservative bonds at 50 just because the default fund assumes you're retiring at 67.

If you're in your 50s: This is the execution decade. Every year matters now. If you have scattered pensions with high fees or poor performance, the cost of inaction is real and measurable. If you run a business, maximising tax-efficient contributions becomes critical. You don't have three decades of compounding ahead - you have 10-15 years to optimise everything.

If you're 60+: You're in preservation and drawdown planning mode. This chapter still matters because understanding your pension structure affects how you access it tax-efficiently.

Whatever your age, the principle is the same: your pension deserves the same strategic attention as the rest of your wealth-building. It's not separate from your Freedom plan and it's arguably the most tax-efficient vehicle for closing your Freedom Gap.

Pensions - One Powerful Spoke on Your Wheel

Pension Planning is a crucial spoke on your Wheel of Wealth because tax efficiency is unmatched (relief on contributions, tax-free growth, 25% tax-free withdrawal), and you can't access it until 55, protecting you from short-term impulses.

Your pension isn't separate from your Freedom plan; it's arguably the most tax-efficient vehicle for closing your Freedom Gap. Understanding how to use pensions strategically can transform your wealth-building.

The Sexiest Investment Vehicle You Never Knew You Had

My pension fund has become the sexiest thing in my financial life.

I know, you're probably thinking, "Isabel has finally lost it!" Pensions aren't supposed to be exciting. But when you understand how powerful these structures are, you realise they're the quiet engines that make the exciting stuff possible.

Eight years ago, I was sitting in a property investing workshop. The trainer asked a simple question: "Hands up if you'd like more equity to buy property?" Every hand shot up, mine included. Then came the game-changer: "If you've got pension funds from previous salaried work, you may be able to use them as equity in your next property project."

I nearly fell off my chair.

That's when I first learned about the SSAS pension, the Small Self-Administered Scheme. And setting up my SSAS has been one of the biggest turning points in my financial journey. It unlocked capital, allowed me to invest in everything from property to private equity, and gave me a level of control over my future I didn't even know was possible.

The best part is that by owning a SSAS I am connected to a group of incredibly savvy SSAS owners, men and women who are all taking their financial futures into their own hands. Like me, they have discovered that pensions aren't boring retirement products; they're powerful wealth-building engines that give you choices and opportunities you never imagined.

The conversations in my SSAS group are honestly some of the best I've had, people genuinely expanding their investment knowledge, pushing boundaries on how to build wealth, sharing opportunities and insights. When I was young, I thought pensions were deadly dull. Now that I manage my own, I find it incredibly exciting.

My pension is now an integral part of my wealth-building strategy, and it is the most tax-efficient part of it. Very few people talk about their pensions, or fully understand how powerful these structures can be for building wealth.

The thesis of this chapter is simple: pensions can be exciting, but first, you need to know what you actually have.

Getting Clear - Your Pension Audit

Before we talk about SSAS and SIPP structures, let's start with where you are today, because you can't optimise what you aren't aware of.

If you did the "Know Your Numbers" work earlier in this book, you may have already tracked down your pensions. If not, here's your starting point:

Find them all: Use the government's Pension Tracing Service (find it online at gov.uk/find-pension-contact-details), check old payslips, and contact previous employers. Every job you've had where you were auto-enrolled in a workplace pension has created a pot somewhere.

List them: For each pension, note the provider, current value, annual fees, and what it's actually invested in. Create a simple spreadsheet to track everything in one place.

Calculate your total: Add them all up. This is your current pension wealth.

Most people are shocked by two things: how much they have scattered across different providers, and how little attention they've been paying to it. One woman in my community discovered she had £47,000 sitting with a provider charging 2.5% annual fees - that's over £1,000 a year just in charges. Another found three pensions she'd completely forgotten about, totalling £23,000.

Your pension is likely one of your largest assets. Yet for most people, it's the asset they know least about. Once you know what you have, you can make informed decisions about what to do with it.

If You're Currently Employed: Optimise What You Have First

Before exploring SIPP and SSAS options for old pensions, let's talk about what you should do if you're currently employed with a workplace pension.

The Pension Power Check

This takes 20 minutes and could be worth thousands of pounds over your working life. Find your last pension statement and work through these six checks:

1. The Employer Matching Question

How much does your employer match? If they match contributions up to 5% and you're only contributing 3%, you're leaving free money on the table. That's an immediate guaranteed return.

Look at your statement or ask HR: "What's the maximum employer contribution I can receive?" Then check: "Am I contributing enough to get the full match?"

If you're not maximising the match, increase your contribution. It's the single best return you'll get anywhere.

2. The Higher-Rate Taxpayer Advantage

If you're a 40% or 45% taxpayer, every £100 you contribute only costs you £60 or £55 after tax relief. That's a 40-45% immediate return before any investment growth.

Can you afford to increase your contribution by even 1-2%? Over decades, this compounds dramatically. A 1% increase on a £70,000 salary is £700 annually - but it only costs you £420 from your take-home if you're a higher-rate taxpayer, and it could grow to over £35,000 by retirement with compound growth.

3. The Fee Check

Find the section on your statement showing annual charges. If your total annual fees exceed 0.75%, you're paying too much. This compounds against you for decades.

Example: A £50,000 pension with 1.5% annual fees costs you £750 per year. That's £22,500 over 30 years before you even account for the compound growth you've lost on those fees. A pension with 0.3% fees would cost you £4,500 over the same period - an £18,000 difference.

Check if your employer offers lower-cost fund options. Many workplace pensions have both expensive "active" funds and cheaper "passive" index funds. You might be in the expensive option by default.

4. The Default Fund Trap

Most workplace pensions put you in a "default lifestyle fund" that automatically shifts towards bonds and cash as you approach retirement age. The assumption is that you'll retire at the state pension age, currently 67 for women.

What if your Freedom Number date is 55 though? That default fund could shift you into low-growth conservative investments a decade too early, costing you significant growth during your final high-earning years.

Check your statement to see what fund you are in. Check when it starts shifting to a more conservative investment portfolio structure. Does that align with *your* timeline, not the government's?

If your Freedom Number is earlier than the state pension age, you may want to opt out of the lifestyle fund and choose investments that match your actual timeline.

5. The Freedom Number Gap

Your statement should show a projected income at retirement. Compare that against your Freedom Number from Chapter 10.

If there's a significant gap, your workplace pension is just one spoke on your Wheel of Wealth. You'll need other strategies - ISAs, property, business equity - to close that gap.

This isn't discouraging news. It's clarity. Knowing the gap means you can create a plan to fill it, rather than reaching 60 and discovering you're decades away from having choice.

6. What Are You Actually Invested In?

Fund names like "Global Equity Growth Fund" or "Balanced Lifestyle Fund" mean nothing without looking deeper.

Go to your pension provider's website and search for the fund factsheet. You'll discover what you're actually invested in. You might find you're funding fossil fuels, weapons manufacturers, or companies with poor labour practices - things you'd never consciously choose to support.

This matters both for values alignment and for performance. Some default funds are expensive, poorly diversified, and underperforming.

Your Action This Week

Pick one of these six checks and address it. For example increase your contribution by 1%, switch out of an expensive fund, or find out what you're actually invested in.

One action creates momentum. Once you've optimised what you currently have, you'll be ready to think strategically about those old pensions from previous employers.

A Quick Note on Pension Types

If you work in certain public sector roles - NHS, armed forces, teaching, civil service - you may have a defined benefit pension where your retirement income is guaranteed based on your salary and years of service. These pensions have different rules and limited flexibility. The options I'm about to share apply primarily to defined contribution pensions - the type most private sector employees have, where your pension pot grows based on contributions and investment performance.

If you're unsure which type you have, your pension statement will tell you, or you can ask your provider directly.

Now, let's talk about what to do with those old workplace pensions from previous employers.

Your Options: Conscious Pension Management

For twenty-five years in finance, I received annual pension statements and filed them unread. I assumed "someone" was handling it. When I finally looked properly, I discovered I had over £500,000 scattered across seven different providers; significant wealth I'd been completely unconscious about.

That discovery was a turning point for me. I realised I had considerable assets that I could manage myself and deploy in ways that would generate far better returns than the 4-5% my fund managers were delivering. I knew I could invest in property, in my own business, in opportunities that aligned with my knowledge and values, and I've since proven that instinct right.

This wasn't about becoming a day trader or obsessing over market movements. It was about recognising that I could make more informed decisions about my own money than distant fund managers who'd never met me.

Here's what I see happen with most people: they hold one of two mental constructs about pensions. Either "someone else is handling it, so I don't need to think about it" (passive abdication), or "if I take control, I'll need to become a financial expert managing everything myself" (active overwhelm).

Both are false. There's a middle path.

Conscious pension management simply means taking what you've learned from your audit - you now know what you have, where it sits, what fees you're paying and making deliberate choices about what to do next.

It means asking: given my knowledge, my goals, my timeline, and my capacity, what's the right structure for me?

Not what's most sophisticated. Not what everyone else is doing. What's right for *you.*

Here's what conscious pension management looks like in practice:

Option 1: Stay with Current Providers (But Get Strategic)

Staying with your current workplace pension can be the right choice if:

- You're employed with a good workplace pension offering employer matching
- Your fees are reasonable (under 0.75% total)
- You understand what you're invested in and it aligns with your strategy
- You've done the Pension Power Check from the previous section and optimized what you have

But even if you stay, conscious management means:

- Consolidating multiple old pensions into one provider to reduce complexity and make monitoring easier
- Reviewing your investment choices annually - do they still align with your values and risk tolerance?
- Checking fees regularly - they compound against you over time

- Actually understanding what you're invested in - "default life-style fund" often means nothing concrete

Staying with current providers is perfectly valid, as long as it's an informed, intentional choice rather than passive inertia.

Option 2: Move to a SIPP (Self-Invested Personal Pension)

A SIPP gives you significantly more control over your pension investments without requiring you to become a full-time fund manager. It's ideal for employed people, self-employed individuals without a company structure, and anyone wanting to consolidate scattered pensions into one place they actively manage.

How it works: You transfer existing pension funds into a SIPP with a provider like Hargreaves Lansdown, AJ Bell, or Interactive Investor. Most SIPP providers handle the transfer process from your old providers, and ongoing fees are typically lower than managed workplace pensions.

What you can invest in: A SIPP opens up a much broader investment menu than workplace pensions offer - individual company shares, ETFs and index funds using all the strategies we explored in earlier chapters, investment trusts, bonds, and diversified portfolios you design based on your Investment Values Compass.

Why this matters: A SIPP transforms your pension from something that happens to you into something you actively manage. Instead of hoping a fund manager makes good choices with your money, YOU make the choices. You apply your financial knowledge. You align it with your values. You take responsibility.

And here's what often surprises people: managing your own SIPP isn't harder than choosing from a limited workplace pension menu. In many cases it's simpler, because you're making conscious decisions rather than trying to decode confusing fund names.

Option 3: Set Up an SSAS (For Business Owners)

If you run a limited company, an SSAS deserves serious attention. This is where conscious pension management becomes genuinely powerful.

How it works: Your company sets up a Small Self-Administered Scheme. You and other directors/employees become members and trustees. The company makes contributions (which are a tax-deductible business expense), and you gain extraordinary investment flexibility.

What you can invest in: Everything a SIPP offers, plus commercial property (including premises for your own business), loans to your business under proper commercial terms, private equity, cryptocurrency through approved platforms, and sophisticated investment structures most pension vehicles don't allow.

The tax efficiency is extraordinary: Company contributions are pre-tax (reducing your corporation tax bill), everything inside the SSAS grows tax-free, the SSAS can receive rental income from commercial property tax-free, and 25% can be withdrawn tax-free from age 55.

The borrowing power: One of the most powerful SSAS features is that your SSAS can borrow up to 50% of its fund value. A £100,000 SSAS could borrow £50,000, giving you £150,000 to invest in commercial property that generates rental income tax-free inside the pension.

Who it's best for: Business owners with a limited company generating sufficient profit, property investors wanting to use pensions for commercial property, and those who want maximum control over sophisticated wealth-building strategies.

The setup: More complex than a SIPP, with setup costs of £2,500-£5,000 and annual administration fees of £800-£2,000+. You'll need an SSAS provider to handle administration and compliance, and should consider using an IFA with SSAS experience for initial setup.

Why this matters: A SSAS isn't for everyone. The costs only make sense if you have sufficient pension value or company profits to justify them. But for business owners serious about building wealth tax-efficiently, an SSAS can be transformational.

My SSAS isn't some passive pot sitting with a provider I've never met. It's an active, strategic, powerful part of my wealth-building system. I can invest in alignment with my values, use it for property, invest in startups I believe in - all within a tax-advantaged structure that compounds wealth faster than almost any other vehicle available.

Consolidation Transforms Strategy

Whether you choose to stay put, move to a SIPP, or set up an SSAS, consolidation is powerful. I had seven different pensions scattered across providers - small pots with high fees that I never looked at. Consolidating them meant moving from scattered, ignored, expensive pots to one substantial fund I consciously manage and strategically invest.

Your IFA or SIPP/SSAS provider can handle the consolidation process.

Taking Control Means Taking Responsibility

Moving to conscious pension management - whether that's optimising your current workplace pension, consolidating into a SIPP, or setting up an SSAS - is empowering. However, it also means taking responsibility.

You're responsible for the choices you make and their outcomes. This isn't meant to scare you; it's meant to ensure you go in with eyes open.

What Responsibility Looks Like

You need sufficient financial knowledge or professional support. If you don't understand what you're investing in, don't invest in it - even inside a tax-advantaged pension. This book has given you foundational knowledge. But ultimately, you're making the decisions.

You must maintain diversification. Don't put your entire pension in one property, one company share, or one investment, no matter how convinced you are it's a winner. Your pension is likely one of your largest assets and you can't access it until 55. It needs to be protected through diversification.

You need to follow the regulations. Pensions have significant tax advantages, but those come with rules. SSAS and SIPP structures have regulatory requirements. Breaking them can result in tax penalties that wipe out your advantages. Work with qualified advisers who understand pension regulations.

You're committing to ongoing management. A pension isn't "set and forget" - you need to review performance, rebalance, adjust as your circumstances change, and stay informed about your investments.

Self-directed doesn't mean reckless. It means informed, strategic, and intentional.

If you're not ready to actively manage investments, there's no shame in choosing a well-structured workplace pension or consolidating into a low-cost platform pension with diversified funds. That's still a conscious choice - you're choosing appropriate management for your current capacity.

The question isn't "What's the most sophisticated pension structure?" The question is "What's the right choice for me given my knowledge, capacity, timeline, and goals?"

Answer that honestly, and you'll make the right decision.

Looking Ahead: Legacy

Now that you understand pensions as one of the most powerful wealth-building engines alongside the other strategies you're exploring, a natural question arises: what happens to all this wealth you're creating?

What do you want your money to make possible for you, for your family, and for the world around you? What impact do you want it to have?

In the next chapter, we'll explore Legacy and Impact, not just estate planning and passing on wealth, but something far deeper: the legacy of meaning, values, and continuity you want to create.

Key Takeaways

- **Retirement is an outdated construct** - Your Freedom Number is your retirement number
- **Timeline matters** - The closer you are to your Freedom Number date, the more critical pension planning becomes
- **Pensions are wealth-building engines** - Tax efficiency and control make them powerful
- **You have options** - Stay put strategically, SIPP, or SSAS, but make it an informed choice
- **Consolidation transforms strategy** - Move from scattered pots to strategic management
- **Responsibility comes with control** - Self-directed means informed, strategic, and intentional

Practical Actions

1. **Audit your pensions** - Track down all old workplace pensions (use Pension Tracing Service), list providers, values, and fees.
2. **Check what you're paying** - Hidden fees compound against you; call providers if not obvious.
3. **Research your options** - SIPP providers if consolidating, SSAS consultations if you run a business.
4. **Review alignment** - Do your pension investments reflect your Investment Values Compass?
5. **Calculate contributions** - How much could you contribute this tax year to maximise tax relief?

6. **Consolidate strategically** - Move scattered pots to one actively managed vehicle.
7. **Get support** - Work with an IFA who specialises in SSAS/SIPP, or join the Women's SSAS Group in the collective for provider comparisons, setup guidance, and community support.
8. **Review regularly** - Half yearly or annual checks to rebalance and assess performance.

Chapter 25

YOUR LIVING LEGACY

Building Richness, Not Just Riches

In the last chapter, we talked about pensions as powerful wealth-building engines, how your Freedom Number is your retirement number, and how structures like SSAS and SIPP can transform your financial future.

A natural question follows: What happens to all this wealth you're creating? What do you want your money to make possible?

Most people think of legacy as something you leave behind when you're gone. That's not how I see it.

Legacy is a way of living now. It's the way you show up in the world. The wisdom you share. The energy you bring to every decision, including how you build, use, and protect your wealth.

Legacy isn't about how much money you have. It's about what that money means, what it enables, who it supports, what continues because of you.

The Dash That Defines Your Life

There's a famous poem called The Dash. On a gravestone are two dates: the year you were born, the year you died. Between them is a small dash. That tiny dash represents your life, every choice, every conversation, every risk, every love.

Your dash is your legacy.

Yet so many of us live as though that dash will last forever, as though we have unlimited time to figure out what matters and make the impact we want to make.

Legacy isn't something that begins later. It's being shaped right now.

Writing this book has made me think about my own dash.

What am I here for? What will my children remember? What ripple do I want to leave? The answer isn't just about money. It's about living authentically, with intention, and meaning.

When you live that way, even practical things like pensions, wills, and insurance take on deeper significance. They become tools for continuity, ways to protect the life and love you've built, so they keep working long after you're gone.

Rethinking Legacy

When most people hear "legacy planning," they think of trusts, inheritance tax, and complex legal structures.

But legacy has less to do with the size of your bank account and everything to do with the depth of your values and how you live them out.

I think of it as the difference between riches and richness.

Riches are the numbers on the spreadsheet. Richness is what those numbers allow: the laughter, the lessons, the love. It's what people carry forward about you.

I see this through three interconnected pillars: Values and Wisdom (who you are), Wealth and Stewardship (what you build), and Impact and Contribution (how you give).

The Three Pillars of Legacy

Pillar 1: Values and Wisdom - Who You Are

This is the heart of your legacy: the stories, lessons, and truths you carry and share. It's about authenticity, living a life that's true to who you are, not who the world thinks you should be.

You've already done this work in Part One through Energetic Alpha and the Authenticity Wheel. You know your values and where you're living authentically, and where you're not.

This first pillar is continuing that work. When you live in alignment and act with courage, you create a legacy of wisdom, not through what you say, but through how you live.

Now that you understand the three pillars, let's get practical about Pillar 2: Wealth and Stewardship. This is where philosophy meets paperwork, and both matter.

Pillar 2: Wealth and Stewardship - What You Build

Financial wealth matters. It gives you choices, safety, and opportunity. However, wealth without stewardship is fragile.

Legacy stewardship has three parts: protect what you build, structure it intentionally, and educate the next generation so it continues with wisdom and purpose.

Protect What You Build

Let me share a story that completely changed how I think about protection.

A close friend of mine is living through a heartbreaking situation. Her father has dementia, her mother has health issues, and for years, they avoided serious conversations about their finances. They didn't create Lasting Power of Attorney (LPA) documents. They didn't update their wills.

Now it's too late. The state has stepped in, and the family has no legal authority to act.

That was my wake-up call.

Last year, I finally sorted out my own estate planning:

- Created both Health and Wealth LPAs through the government website (£85 each)
- Made a simple will using an online service
- Wrote clear instructions so my children know exactly where to find everything

It wasn't glamorous, but it brought deep calm knowing my affairs are in order.

Protection is love in action. LPAs and wills are non-negotiable; everyone needs them. They take an afternoon to complete in basic form.

Structure: Building for Generations

Once your foundations are in place, the next step is structure; how you hold and grow what you've built. As your wealth grows, intentional structuring becomes essential, including inheritance tax planning, trusts, and estate planning.

Many people assume trusts are only for the ultra-wealthy, but that's changing. The structure I'm currently exploring with a wealth manager is a beneficial trust, which can offer probate avoidance, creditor and divorce protection, and multi-generational benefits.

It's flexible, can start with a nominal sum, and costs around £2,500–£5,000. It's not for everyone, but it's worth knowing these options exist. The key point: as your wealth grows, understand your options. Seek professional advice and ensure the structures serve your intentions, not the other way around.

Education: The Lost Conversation

This is what most people miss. They focus on structures and protection but forget to educate the next generation.

Research shows that family wealth is often lost within three generations, not through bad investments, but through lack of education and shared values.

Stewardship means conversation. Teach your children about money, responsibility, and purpose. Create those dinner-table conversations, what security means, how wealth is built, what it's for.

I'm having them now with my own children: with Thomas, building knowledge so he'll always have options; with Charlotte, helping her understand investing so she can pursue her passion in the world of rugby without fear of financial dependence.

This is legacy in motion, not just building wealth, but ensuring those who come after us have the wisdom to steward it well.

Pillar 3: Impact and Contribution - How You Give

This pillar can be activated at any wealth level. It's about using whatever resources you have to create positive change.

That might mean volunteering, mentoring, impact investing, or supporting causes that align with your values.

For me, it's about creating an ecosystem where women build wealth and reinvest in other women.

You don't have to wait until you have "enough." Legacy isn't built at the end; it's built every day, through the choices you make and the impact you create.

Your Living Legacy Reflection

Now that you know the three pillars, take a moment to reflect.

What do you want to be remembered for? What impact do you want to create?

You'll find the *Living Legacy Reflection* in the *Fearless Wealth Playbook*. It guides you through questions like:

- What values do you want to be known for?
- What protections would give you peace of mind?
- What money conversations need to happen in your family?
- What cause or community will you support?

The goal is clarity, to turn intentions into action.

The Continuity We Create

Legacy isn't something you leave; it's something you live. It's the continuity of care, courage, and consciousness moment by moment.

When women claim their financial voice, align wealth with values, and act boldly, we shift what's possible for those who come after us.

That's the power of feminine wealth. It connects money and meaning, and multiplies both.

This book is for my daughter, so she can follow her heart without apology.

It's for my son, so he grows up seeing financially independent women are the norm.

It's for you, so you know that building wealth isn't selfish. It's important. It matters.

Every time you invest consciously, protect what matters, and act in alignment with your truth, you're creating a legacy that says:

This story doesn't end with me. It continues.

That's the real inheritance, not just money, but meaning, love, and the spirit carried forward.

It's the spoke on the *Wheel of Wealth*: where awareness, alignment, and action come full circle into continuity.

What Comes Next

You've now explored the different Wealth Builders: the spokes of your Wheel of Wealth: investment strategies, pensions, emotional mastery, and the living legacy you're creating right now. You have awareness, knowledge and tools. This is a powerful foundation.

What I know from my own journey, though, is that the gap between knowing what to do and actually doing it is where most wealth-building plans fail. Knowledge without action changes nothing.

In the next chapter, I'm going to share a framework I've been using for years, personally and with my clients, to deliver the results they want in their lives. It's simple but extremely effective.

This moves you from good intentions to actual wealth-building. From inspiration to implementation.

If you are ready, let's structure the next 90 days to build your wealth.

Key Takeaways

- **Legacy is how you live now** - Your legacy isn't what you leave behind; it's already happening through every conscious choice you make today
- **Richness matters more than riches** - depth of values over size of bank account
- **Three pillars build legacy** - Values & Wisdom, Wealth & Stewardship, Impact & Contribution
- **Legacy stewardship requires structure** - LPAs and wills are essential, trusts become relevant as wealth grows, and professional guidance ensures proper protection
- **Wealth is lost within three generations** - without financial education and intentional stewardship
- **Impact can be activated at any level** - you don't need to be wealthy to make a difference

Practical Actions

1. Complete your Living Legacy Reflection in the Fearless Wealth Playbook.
2. Create or update LPAs for health and wealth - £85 each via gov.uk.
3. Make or update your will.
4. Write clear instructions for your family about where to find documents.
5. Have one honest conversation about money and values with your family.
6. If building significant wealth, consult a wealth manager/IFA/lawyer about trust structures.
7. Make one contribution this month - time, mentorship, or values-aligned investment.

Chapter 26

THE AAA FRAMEWORK

Your Operating System for Turning Knowledge into Wealth

I hope you're inspired by what you've accomplished so far. The work you've completed, the knowledge you've built, the legacy you're already living.

Inspiration is powerful. But inspiration without consistent action changes nothing.

If you've been taking action as you read, getting clear on your numbers, calculating your Freedom Number, and completing the Wheel of Wealth, you have a solid foundation. If you've been reading and making mental notes, that's learning too, and now we'll turn it into action.

What you need now is a system that keeps you moving consistently. Knowledge alone won't close your Freedom Gap. What changes everything is having a framework that turns inspiration into implementation, day after day, decision after decision.

This is what this final part of the journey is about.

Let me tell you why this matters so much to me.

From Inspiration to Implementation

I know what it's like to feel fired up by an idea and then… do nothing.

Years ago, I was a serial course junkie. I attended every workshop going: "How to Sell from the Stage," "How to Build an Online

Business," "How to Create Wealth While You Sleep." I spent thousands, took pages of notes, and came home buzzing with ideas.

And then life resumed, the kids, the school runs, the broken boilers. All that information and inspiration turned into expensive entertainment because I didn't yet have a system for turning learning into action.

That's what this chapter is about: closing that gap.

Over the years, through my own financial experiments, missteps, and breakthroughs, and through the work I've done alongside others, I've found one framework that consistently transforms good intentions into real results.

I call it the **AAA Framework.** It's the framework I return to again and again because it reliably turns good intentions into real results. Not through complexity, but because it reflects how people actually create change and sustain growth.

Authority is giving yourself permission and responsibility to act.

It's the decision point, where intention becomes commitment. In practical terms, Authority means deciding what you want and translating that decision into a clear 90-day plan, so your intention has direction and momentum.

Accountability is doing what you said you would do.

It's about creating simple structures that keep you in motion when motivation fades. Applying consistent action, regular check-ins, and staying engaged rather than slipping back into avoidance.

Acknowledgement is how progress compounds.

It's the practice of noticing what's working, what isn't, and refining your approach. Reflection here isn't indulgent; it's strategic. This is how learning integrates and self-trust deepens over time.

Together, Authority, Accountability, and Acknowledgement form a continuous cycle, one that keeps you moving forward with clarity, consistency, and self-leadership.

Sidebar -The AAA Framework in Practice

- **Authority** = Decide what you want → Create your 90-Day Plan
- **Accountability** = Do what you said → Show up consistently
- **Acknowledgement** = Discover what works → Reflect and refine

Part 1. Authority - Claiming Permission to Lead Your Wealth

This is where everything begins. Authority is about stepping into leadership of your own financial life; deciding what you want, claiming responsibility for it, and giving yourself permission to act decisively.

It doesn't mean knowing all the answers. It means trusting that you'll find them.

For many women, the hardest part isn't learning about investing, it's giving ourselves permission to want wealth in the first place.

We've been conditioned to believe that focusing on money is selfish, that caring about wealth makes us materialistic or "not spiritual." We worry about being judged. We tell ourselves we should be grateful for what we have and not want more.

Authority isn't arrogance. It's responsibility.

When you step into financial authority, you're not being greedy, you're claiming your right to economic sovereignty. You're saying, "I deserve security. I deserve choice. I deserve to build something that outlasts me."

This isn't about apologising for wanting wealth. It's about recognising that your financial freedom creates ripples far beyond yourself; it changes what's possible for your children, your community, the causes you care about.

When you calculated your Freedom Number earlier in the book, you did something powerful: you gave yourself permission to want financial sovereignty. Not what you think you should want, what you genuinely want. That permission wasn't just for dreaming. It was for building wealth and closing your Freedom Gap. Now let's turn that permission into action.

Deciding What You Want

Stepping into your authority starts with a decision, not a perfect plan. It's the moment you stop waiting for certainty and start leading yourself. When you take responsibility for your financial life, you stop waiting for someone else to do it for you and start managing your wealth.

I call it becoming the CEO of your own wealth. CEOs don't wait for someone else to make the decisions. They look at the available information, choose a direction, and take the next step, even when they don't have all the data. That's self-leadership: the mindset that moves you from "I wish" to "I will."

For me, that shift came when I decided to write this book. I'd mapped out the chapters months earlier, but then froze. Every time I thought about it, I felt overwhelmed.

Then one day I thought, Right, Isabel, just start somewhere. I made a plan (on a spreadsheet, of course!) and suddenly could see the next step: one action a day. A sentence. A paragraph. A tweak to an outline.

That single act of planning broke the inertia.

That's the magic of authority: the moment you decide, you create momentum.

Planning as Permission

You've probably heard the saying, "Fail to plan, plan to fail." It's true, not because the absence of a plan means failure, but because without a plan, you're operating without a blueprint. A plan gives your ideas direction and your energy a home.

I love creating my MAP annual plan each December, and this is a very powerful tool for moving life forward in all areas. The plan I want to share here is a simpler version of the annual plan, called the 90-Day Wealth Activation Plan.

Use both your Wheel of Wealth and your Wheel of Authenticity to create your plan. When I did this myself, I realised that most of my life mapped onto these two wheels. My coaching income, investment strategies, and property decisions sat on the Wheel of Wealth. My purpose (writing this book), relationships with my children and friends, building my network, energy and vitality - all of that sat on the Wheel of Authenticity.

Start by asking yourself:

- What matters most to me over the next 90 days?
- Which areas of my Wheel of Wealth need attention?
- Which areas of my Wheel of Authenticity would support or accelerate my inner wealth-building?
- What are the smallest actions that would move the dial?

Give yourself permission to act. Every plan, however simple, gives you the framework to do it.

Now you have permission and a plan. Next, you need momentum.

Part 2. Accountability - Turning Plans into Progress

Small steps, done consistently, change everything.

If Authority is about deciding what you want, Accountability is about doing what you said you would. It's the bridge between a plan on paper and results in real life.

The Shift from Victim to Ownership

There was a point in my own life, during the Landmark Forum years ago, when I realised something that changed everything for me: I am 100% responsible for my life; not partly, not when it's convenient, but completely.

That realisation wasn't heavy; it was liberating. It taught me that self-accountability isn't optional if you want to create change. It can be the same for you.

Once you claim ownership, you stop waiting for perfect conditions and start shaping them. You stop being a passenger in your own story. But even when you know you're responsible, life gets busy. Things get hard. That's when accountability keeps you moving, starting with yourself.

Self-Accountability in Practice

Some areas of life seem easy to show up for. During lockdown, I became religious about Heather Robertson's 30-minute home workouts on YouTube. No trainer. No gym. Just me, my laptop, and showing up every morning.

In other areas… total procrastination. Like this book. I told myself I was researching. I wasn't. I was avoiding it because I was scared it wouldn't be good enough.

That's the truth about discipline: it's contextual. You can be incredibly consistent in one area and struggle in another. It doesn't mean you're lazy. It means you're human.

Why Self-Accountability Matters

Self-accountability is where real change begins. It's the bridge between intention and integrity, the quiet moment when you say, "I'm doing this because I said I would."

When you keep even the smallest promises to yourself, you rebuild trust in your own word. That's when confidence compounds. When you can rely on yourself, everything else gets easier.

Self-accountability is the foundation of personal freedom. It's how you learn to trust yourself, to back yourself. It's how you steer your own ship, even when the sea is rough.

Just like any skill, it gets stronger with practice and the right tools.

When Self-Accountability Isn't Enough

You might be thinking: 'I'll need more than my own willpower.' You're right. Sometimes we all need external accountability, not because self-accountability failed, but because some goals are bigger, scarier, or newer. Even the most successful people deliberately use external accountability. Human willpower is fallible.

Years ago, I signed up for the *Étape du Tour,* which is a brutal 140km/3500m mountain stage of the Tour de France. Living in Chamonix, I'd been skiing all winter (which involved, in truth, more vin chaud than cardio), and suddenly I only had six weeks to become a cyclist.

So I called my friend Kristen. We trained together, checked in every week, and on race day, we both finished. Admittedly, I had six punctures, three meltdowns, and one unforgettable medal later, but I did it because *we* did it.

More recently, it was Dorothy and options trading. I knew the Options Wheel Strategy inside out, but hadn't implemented it. I had been dragging my heels, having been stuck with the trading software. Dorothy and I agreed to become accountability buddies. We now have weekly calls, set small targets, and have honest conversations. This is what is turning theory into progress.

This is the power of external accountability, the momentum you get from doing something with someone else.

I used to think accountability buddies worked because you didn't want to look bad. Turns out there's neuroscience behind it. Psychologists call it social commitment theory: when we make promises to others, our brains rewire to stay consistent. Sharing progress triggers dopamine and oxytocin - motivation and connection combined. Accountability isn't a weakness. It's how we're wired

Finding Your Accountability Edge

Think of accountability as a spectrum:

Form	Description	Example
Self	Showing up because you said you would	Habit trackers, time blocks, journalling
Buddy	Mutual encouragement	Check-ins with a friend, like Dorothy
Coach / Mentor	Structured reflection	Someone holding space and asking better questions
Community	Shared goals and group energy	Join a group walking the same path as you

Choose what fits your personality and what you are trying to achieve. What matters isn't the format, it's the consistency.

Accountability transforms "someday" into steady progress. It's what turns the plan you wrote into a life you live.

You're moving. Now you need to make sure you're learning.

Part 3. Acknowledgement - The Secret Accelerator

Even with a plan and accountability in place, sustainable progress depends on one final piece: reflection. I call it Acknowledgement, it's more than thinking about what happened; it's recognising, learning, and adjusting.

The Learning Curve No One Talks About

Imagine being six years old, gripping a steering wheel bigger than you are, pretending to drive. You're blissfully unaware that you have no idea what you're doing. This is unconscious incompetence.

Fast forward to your first real driving lesson: the clutch, the mirrors, the constant corrections. Overwhelm hits. That's conscious incompetence, the valley of frustration every learner must cross.

Investing is no different. Everyone starts in that messy middle, unsure, awkward, second-guessing. The difference between those who grow and those who give up isn't talent. It's whether they acknowledge what's actually happening.

The Cycles That Create Mastery

There are two repeating loops in any transformation: *The Cycle of Mastery* and *The Cycle of Productivity*. Acknowledgement connects them.

Picture two interconnected wheels. Your *internal learning* wheel rotates through four stages as you develop any new skill: from not knowing what you don't know, to the awkward awareness of learning, to conscious practice, and finally to automatic mastery.

Your *external action wheel* spins through four repeating phases: starting something new, doing the work, completing it, and acknowledging what happened.

Here's the magic: every time you complete one full rotation of the action wheel—start, do, complete, acknowledge—you advance through your internal learning wheel. Acknowledge after one options trade, and your next trade starts from a more competent place. Skip the acknowledgement, and you repeat the same cycle without growth. The wheels keep spinning, but only acknowledgement makes them work *together*.

Your Learning Journey (Internal):

Unconscious incompetence → Conscious incompetence → Conscious competence → Unconscious competence

Your Action Cycle (External):

Start → Do → Complete → Acknowledge

Most people skip that fourth step. They rush from completion straight into the next start. But acknowledgement connects your external actions to your internal learning, and that's where growth accelerates.

Why This Matters

When you extract the lesson from one action, you apply it to the next ten. Without reflection, you repeat mistakes. With it, every completion makes every future start smarter, faster, and more confident.

So how do you actually do it? Here's a simple framework I use:

The "What / So What / Now What" Reflection

When you review your month, your week, or even your day, use these three simple prompts:

- **What?** — What actually happened? What did I achieve?
- **So what?** — Why does it matter? What patterns do I notice?
- **Now what?** — What will I adjust or continue next time?

This keeps reflection practical and forward-focused. It's not nostalgia; it's navigation.

Highlights and Disappointments

When I do my own monthly reviews, I start with highlights, every win, big or small. This isn't natural. Our brains are wired to focus on threats, a hangover from when missing danger meant becoming lunch for a predator. So we have to deliberately rewire ourselves toward confidence instead of fear by listing wins.

Then I look at my disappointments: the things that didn't go to plan. Not to self-criticise, but to see what's stealing energy from growth.

Highlights show you what to repeat. Disappointments show you what to improve or replace.

Reflection Rhythms

A rhythm of reflection keeps momentum alive:

- **Weekly (10–15 mins):** Quick check-in, key highlights, any disappointments, one next step.
- **Monthly (60 mins):** Review your 90-Day Plan. What did you complete? What did you learn? Notice whether you're making progress in both external wealth-building and inner development, or whether you're overweighting one dimension.
- **Quarterly (90 mins):** Full reset. Re-score both your Wheel of Wealth and Wheel of Authenticity - measure your increase in Energetic Alpha. Score each goal (green/amber/red). Refresh your plan for the next 90 days.

Progress vs. Pivot

Acknowledgement also tells you when to hold steady and when to adapt. You're progressing if you're learning, acting consistently, and asking better questions, even if results aren't immediate. You need to pivot if you're repeating the same frustrations without movement, or if your approach conflicts with your values or lifestyle.

Pivoting isn't quitting. Pivoting is powerful. It's wisdom in motion.

Why Acknowledgement Matters

Reflection builds self-awareness. Self-awareness builds mastery. And mastery, not perfection, is what creates fearless investors.

You stop waiting until you "know everything" before you act.

You stop judging yourself for the messy middle.

You start trusting your ability to learn and improve.

Acknowledgement turns experience into expertise. It keeps you authentic as you evolve.

Acknowledgement is one of the simplest but most powerful tools I know if we actually use it to learn and grow. When I look back now, I can see exactly what keeps me stuck, which means I can change it. My procrastination about this book was classic perfectionism. Half the time, all we need to do is laugh at ourselves, simplify, and begin again.

Part 4. Bringing It All Together - Your Wealth Operating System

Here's how it all fits:

- **Authority** — Decide what you want and give yourself permission to act.
- **Accountability** — Do what you said you would; keep moving even when it's hard.
- **Acknowledgement** — Discover what works, refine what doesn't, and accelerate your progress.

Or more simply: **Decide. Do. Discover.**

This isn't just a framework for wealth. It's your personal operating system for growth in investing, business, health, relationships, and life.

It's not complicated. It's cyclical. Each round builds confidence. Each cycle compounds momentum.

You don't need to get everything right. You just need to keep showing up for yourself, your plan, and your future.

This is how transformation really happens:

One decision.

One action.

One reflection at a time.

Closing Thought

You've reached the point in the book where thinking turns into doing. Everything before this prepared you. This chapter is your activation.

Awareness gave you clarity. Alignment gave you purpose. Activation gives you results.

Trust yourself. Use the framework. Take the next small, deliberate step. Momentum is built through consistent action, not perfection.

You don't have to do this all at once, and you don't have to do it alone. The structures you've discovered here are designed to support you as you move from intention into execution.

Key Takeaways

- **The AAA Framework is your operating system** - Authority (decide), Accountability (do), Acknowledgement (discover) turns knowledge into wealth
- **Authority starts with permission** - you don't need all the answers; you need to trust you'll find them
- **Self-accountability builds confidence** - keeping small promises to yourself consistently teaches you to trust your own word
- **Discipline is contextual** - you can be consistent in one area and struggle in another; this is normal
- **External accountability is strategy** - not weakness; use buddies, coaches, or community for bigger goals
- **Acknowledgement accelerates everything** - reflection using "What / How / Now What" extracts lessons and applies them forward
- **Reflection creates fearless investors** - when you learn from one action, you improve the next ten

Practical Actions

1. **Download and complete your 90-Day Wealth Activation Plan** - Use your Wheel of Wealth to choose 2-3 priority areas and translate them into small, achievable goals.
2. **Choose your accountability approach** - Self-tracking (habit trackers), an accountability buddy, a coach, or a community like the Fearless Female Investor Collective.
3. **Schedule your check-ins now** - If using external accountability, commit to weekly or bi-weekly calls. If self-tracking, block weekly reflection time (10-15 mins) in your calendar now.
4. **Start your "What / So What / Now What" journal** - Review your week using these three questions. Track 3 highlights (what to repeat) and 1 weed (what to replace).
5. **At 90 days, do a full reset** - Score each goal (green/amber/red), celebrate what worked, pivot what didn't, and refresh your plan for the next quarter.

Chapter 27

THE FEARLESS FUTURE

Invest Boldly. Live Authentically.

You've made it here. And so have I.

We're standing at the summit together, you with this book in your hands, me having just written the final words. Climbing this mountain is an achievement, not for writing or reading a book, but because we have stayed in a conversation about money, power, and freedom. And for many women, this is an act of courage.

Every mountain brings its own kind of clarity. The doubt, the wobbles, the moments you wanted to turn back, they're all worth it for this: the perspective from altitude.

The view from here is clearer, not because we've arrived at some perfect destination, but because we can finally see where we've come from and where we're going next.

Old paradigms, where women were taught to shrink around money, to outsource decisions, to feel shame for wanting more or guilt for having it, to believe that wealth and soul live on opposite sides of a divide, are being broken.

What feels important to name, standing here, is that this isn't happening in a vacuum.

This conversation about money, power, and freedom is arriving at a very particular moment in history. We are in the middle of a profound paradigm shift.

Old systems, financial, institutional, cultural, are straining under their own weight. Structures that once felt immovable are being questioned, decentralised, reimagined. Technology is accelerating faster than our social norms can keep up. AI is transforming how we work, create, and make decisions. Decentralised finance is challenging who gets access, who gets to own, and who gets to participate.

This is unsettling for many people. But it is also full of possibility.

Moments like this don't come with instruction manuals. They come with choice.

You can cling to what's familiar, even as it erodes, or you can learn, adapt, and consciously take your place in what's being built next.

This is why now matters. Not because you need to chase every new thing, but because this is a once-in-a-generation opportunity to engage with money, power, and ownership differently, with more awareness, more alignment, and more agency than ever before.

Women do not need to be protected from this moment. We need to be equipped for it.

Because when women build wealth, we allocate it differently. We invest in what matters to us: our communities, our values, the things that create lasting impact. We circulate rather than hoard. We create returns that extend beyond ourselves.

In this moment of profound change, as old economic structures crumble and new ones are being built, we have an unprecedented opportunity. We get to be capital allocators. We get to shape the economic landscape that's emerging. This isn't just about personal wealth, it's about who gets to influence what comes next.

The opportunity before us is to build sovereign wealth and live sovereign lives.

This book exists to say we can design wealth reimagined.

The F Word Was Never Just About Money

Finance is not cold or clinical. It is a tool, neutral until intention gives it meaning.

Freedom is not escape or excess. It is choice, agency, and the ability to live in alignment with what matters to you.

Female power is not dominance or comparison. It is sovereignty, the capacity to stand fully in who you are, without apology, and to direct resources accordingly.

Material wealth without soul is empty. Soulful purpose without structure is fragile. Real wealth lives where the two meet.

That is what we have been building here.

The Frameworks Are Now Yours

The Wheel of Wealth was never about perfection, only balance and awareness. The Wheel of Authenticity was never about self-improvement, only truth and alignment.

Together, they form a living system: inner and outer wealth, evolving as you do. You don't need to "complete" them. You return to them, season by season, decision by decision.

They are not instructions. They are mirrors.

They are here to help you navigate uncertainty with clarity; to make grounded decisions when the noise is loud; to stay anchored in who you are whilst the external landscape shifts.

The Wheel of Wealth gives you structure without rigidity. The Wheel of Authenticity keeps you honest with yourself as you grow.

One helps you build strength in the world, what markets might call alpha. The other helps you build strength within yourself, the energetic alpha that compounds over a lifetime.

Together, they create fearless wealth.

Fearless doesn't mean unafraid; it means moving forward anyway, taking the leap even when you're trembling. True wealth is the integration of inner and outer wealth, soul and strategy working together: financial security that doesn't cost you your authenticity, spiritual grounding that doesn't require you to reject material abundance.

This is integrated wealth. Fearless wealth. Wealth you build on your terms, that you can allocate to what matters to you.

That is the real work now.

Time to Launch

Do you remember Charlotte, my six-year-old daughter standing at the top of that ski jump, terrified but choosing to launch anyway?

I'm there right now. You're there too.

And you know what? If we land in a heap, if things don't go perfectly, if we make mistakes, we'll just pick ourselves up and do it again. Because that's what we do. That's what fearless women do.

Your Invitation Forward

This isn't an ending. It's a beginning.

Reading changes perspective. Action changes lives.

The **Fearless Wealth Playbook** is where reflection becomes reality. It's designed to help you clarify your numbers, define your values, and begin building wealth in a way that feels aligned, grounded, and sustainable.

When you're ready, scan the QR code below and step into activation.

https://fearlessfemaleinvestor.com/playbook

And when you want community, the **Fearless Female Investor Collective** offers a space where empowerment compounds fastest: in company.

This journey was never meant to be taken alone. It isn't just about reading a book; it's about connection. Connecting with women who are finished choosing between soul and strategy, finished accepting money as taboo, and finished playing small with their financial power. When we build wealth together, we create something far more powerful than any of us could alone.

One Last Truth

The first word of this book was "brave." And here we are at the end, completing the circle. You've been brave enough to read this far, to question old conditioning, to imagine something different.

I'm about to release this book into the world, my leap off the ski jump. You're about to close these pages and take action. Your leap. We're both launching.

You've always been an investor, in time, love, courage, and energy. What's different now is that you're ready to invest consciously in your financial future too. Not by choosing between soul and strategy, but by integrating both.

You don't need to have everything figured out to begin. You don't need permission to engage with money, to build wealth, or to claim your power. You are living in a moment that is asking something of you. So take what resonates. Leave what doesn't.

Invest boldly, not just financially, but in yourself and in the future you want to help shape. Live authentically, because alignment, not perfection, is what sustains you over time. And when you feel the fear, remember the six-year-old at the top of the jump, skis pointed forward, heart open, already in motion.

This is your wealth. This is your freedom. This is your power.

The world needs what only you can build.

Build wealth that matters.

Epilogue

A WHISPER TO THE UNIVERSE

This was never just my book. It found me, nudged me, and poured through me. I resisted it for a long time, and then one night, I stopped arguing with destiny and started listening.

Every word that followed has been a collaboration between my pen and something much greater, infused with all who came before me, all who walk beside me, and all who are still to come.

This book was never meant to end on its final page. It is a living energy, a spark that moves from one heart to another, awakening courage, clarity, and creation. Its purpose is not to tell you what to think, but to remind you of what you already know. That you are the author of your own destiny, and the architect of both your financial and spiritual worlds.

It calls you to step beyond well-worn paths and trust your inner compass. To balance the forces within you: intellect and intuition, structure and surrender, strategy and soul. It will shake loose what no longer serves and ignite what has been waiting patiently to rise.

In its wake, may it leave a generation of fearless creators. Women and men who lead with wisdom, act with will, and align their minds with love. May you remember your inner authority, the quiet knowing that you are both student and teacher, dreamer and doer, creator and creation.

May these words spark courage in you, and may that courage move through the world as light. May you always give yourself permission to create.

For those who find themselves here, at the very end, thank you. You are part of the continuation.

This is our collective whisper to the universe. We were never here to play small. We were here to build worlds together.

ACKNOWLEDGEMENTS

This book is my story, and like all stories, it has been shaped by many people: those who have loved me, supported me, challenged me, and taught me. Some did so gently, others less so. All played a part, and for that, I am grateful.

To my mum, thank you for modelling what it means to be a strong, sovereign, independent woman. Long before I had language for it, you showed me what courage, self-respect, and quiet determination look like in practice.

To my children, Thomas and Charlotte, you were an unexpected gift from the universe, and you changed everything. You are my why. You continue to teach me more about love, presence, and truth than any book or teacher ever could. If this work becomes part of the legacy you carry forward, then it has already served its purpose. This is for you.

To Ella, thank you for your friendship, your truth, and for planting the original seed of this book. You offered the spark, the title, the permission, and the belief long before I could see where it might lead.

To Michelle, thank you for walking this path alongside me, and for your steady confidence, encouragement, and soul-led support in helping bring this work over the line.

To my closest circle of friends, who have held me through thick and thin, thank you. For the laughter, the honesty, the steadiness, and the willingness to listen when things were uncertain. You know who you are. And to my wider circle of friends, who enrich my life in so many different ways, thank you for the joy, perspective, and connection you bring. Friendship has been one of my greatest sources of strength, and I do not take it for granted.

Thank you also to Anna for helping bring this book into its final published form.

Finally, thank you to you, the reader. If you are here, you have given your time, attention, and openness, no small thing in a busy world. I hope this book has met you where you are and encouraged you to take your next step, however that looks for you. If each person who reads this chooses to engage more consciously with money, wealth, and their own life, then together we begin to shape a different future.

If our paths cross again, online, in community, or in person, I look forward to continuing the conversation.

With love,
Isabel x

ABOUT THE AUTHOR

I've spent much of my life around money and just as much time unlearning what I thought it meant.

After managing the equivalent of £1 billion in emerging markets at blue-chip institutions, I stepped away from the trading floor for fifteen years in the French Alps to learn to ski powder, develop property, and redefine what success meant to me. I trained as a coach, started my coaching practice, and began asking deeper questions about wealth, purpose, and what it means to live authentically.

Along the way, I've made sound decisions and costly mistakes; I've built, lost, rebuilt, and kept going. If there's one thing experience has taught me, it's that confidence doesn't come from getting everything right; it comes from staying present, curious, and willing to learn when things don't go to plan.

This book isn't written from the certainty of having "arrived", but from the lived reality of walking the path. I've been brave, I've been cautious, I've trusted my instincts, and sometimes ignored them. Like many of us, my wealth has been built over time through resilience more than brilliance, and through courage more than control.

Today, I work with values-aligned women and men: founders, professionals, and people ready to be inspired by themselves, who want more than just financial success. They want financial sovereignty paired with authentic living. Through the Fearless Female Investor Collective and my coaching practice, I support clients to become confident capital allocators while designing businesses and lives that genuinely reflect who they are.

If this book has stirred questions, courage, or a quiet sense of possibility, you're warmly invited to explore further. You can find the Fearless Female Investor Collective, the accompanying Fearless Wealth Playbook, and my wider work at:

www.fearlessfemaleinvestor.com

However you continue your journey, know this: you don't need to know everything to begin; you just need to begin, and be willing to keep walking.

FRAMEWORKS: QUICK REFERENCE

This section brings together the key frameworks from the book in one place for easy reference. Think of it as your navigation toolkit, the essential models that turn awareness into aligned action.

Wheel of Authenticity

Your inner wealth framework – the energetic portfolio that powers everything

1. **Values-Driven** – Living by what truly matters to you; your internal compass keeps decisions clear even under pressure.
2. **Self-Awareness** – The reflective capacity to see yourself clearly: your thoughts, emotions, motives, and impact.
3. **Clarity of Purpose** – Knowing your why; purpose gives money and action meaning, turning movement into momentum.
4. **Brave Action** – Courage in motion: taking values-aligned risks, setting boundaries, speaking truth.
5. **Self-Congruence** – Walking your talk; integrity in action, where your choices match your words and you feel whole, not divided.
6. **Real Relationships** – Depth over performance; connections built on honesty, empathy, and mutual respect that see and support the real you.
7. **Energy & Vitality** – The physical and emotional aliveness that arises when you stop leaking energy through misalignment.

8. **Inner Peace** – Calm acceptance of what is; the shift from blame to responsibility where consciousness replaces the need for control.

Energetic Alpha – Your personal outperformance; living an authentic life measured using the Wheel of Authenticity. It compounds as it grows and represents the measurable uplift in freedom, flow, finance, and fulfilment.

Wheel of Wealth

Your financial wealth framework – the practical spokes for building material wealth

1. **Cash Flow Power** – Your income engine: the money flowing in each month from all sources that funds your investments and builds your freedom.
2. **Wealth Shield** – Your financial protection system: emergency cash, tax efficiency, and insurance that lets you take smart risks without derailing your long-term plans.
3. **Property Portfolio** – Real estate investments generating income or growth, whether buy-to-let, commercial property, or REITs.
4. **Investment Strategies** – Your long-term growth engine: the asset classes (ETFs, Bitcoin, Private Equity, Options) and approaches you use to build wealth over time.
5. **Financial Knowledge** – What you understand about how finance works: from fundamentals like compound interest to sophisticated strategies around tax efficiency and asset allocation.
6. **Emotional Money Mastery** – Your relationship with money: behavioural patterns, discipline, and the resilience to stick to your strategy through volatility.
7. **Pension Planning** – One of your largest assets: workplace pensions, SIPPs, and SSAS structures that build tax-advantaged wealth for your Freedom Number.

8. **Legacy & Impact** – How you protect what you're building and use wealth as a force for meaning: estate planning, values-aligned giving, and living your legacy now.

AAA Framework

Your operating system for using your plan to turn knowledge into wealth

Authority – Give yourself permission and responsibility to act; decide what you want and create your plan.

Accountability – Do what you said you would; show up consistently through structures that keep you in motion.

Acknowledgement – Reflect, refine, and compound your progress; discover what works and accelerate your learning.

Two Ladders of Freedom

Where inner wealth meets outer wealth

True wealth requires climbing two ladders simultaneously:

The Financial Freedom Ladder (Outer Wealth) – From Scarcity → Survival → Security → Growth → Flexibility → Freedom → Legacy. This is your material wealth: income, savings, assets, and structures that create choice.

The Energetic Freedom Ladder (Inner Wealth) – From Fear/Scarcity → Awareness → Inner Stability → Resilience → Flow → Inner Freedom → Abundant Spirit. This is your energetic wealth: self-awareness, authenticity, purpose, and peace of mind.

Climb only one ladder and you'll always feel unbalanced. Climb both together and you discover genuine freedom: where material security meets energetic alignment.

Values Words

Values shape every decision you make about money, work, and life. The list below isn't a checklist. It's a starting point for discovering your core drivers.

Circle words that resonate

A–C	**D–H**	**I–R**	**S-Z**
Abundance	Diligence	Impact	Security
Achievement	Discernment	Independence	Self Expression
Adventure	Diversity	Inner harmony	Serenity
Alignment	Effectiveness	Innovation	Service
Authenticity	Empathy	Integrity	Sharing
Autonomy	Empowerment	Intelligence	Simplicity
Balance	Equality	Leadership	Stability
Beauty	Excellence	Learning	Stewardship
Belonging	Fairness	Love	Strength
Boldness	Faith/Spirituality	Loyalty	Support
Calm	Family	Maverick	Sustainability
Caring	Flexibility	Open-mindedness	Synergy
Challenge	Freedom	Optimism	Teamwork
Charity	Friendship	Passion	Tenacity
Clarity	Fun	Patience	Transparency
Communication	Generosity	Personal development	Trust
Community	Giving	Professional growth	Truth
Compassion	Growth	Prosperity	Uniqueness
Competence	Harmony	Purpose	Variety
Confidence	Health	Quality	Vision
Connection	Helpfulness	Recognition	Vitality
Contribution	Honesty	Relationships	Wealth
Courage	Hope	Resilience	Wholeness
Creativity	Humility	Responsibility	Wisdom
Curiosity	Humour	Risk-taking	Zest for Life

GLOSSARY

Financial terminology can feel like a foreign language. This glossary translates the key terms used throughout the book into plain English – grouped by theme and alphabetised for quick reference.

Core investing concepts

Asset – Something you own that has value and can generate income, appreciate over time, or protect what you've built.

Asset Allocation – How you divide your money across different types of investments (equities, bonds, property, cash, alternatives) based on your goals and risk tolerance.

Bear Market – A period when investment prices are falling, typically 20% or more from recent highs; fear and pessimism dominate.

Bull Market – A period when investment prices are rising; optimism dominates and investors are confident.

Capital Gains – The profit you make when you sell an investment for more than you paid for it.

Cash Flow – The movement of money in and out of your life each month; positive cash flow means more coming in than going out.

Compound Interest / Compounding – Earning returns on your returns; the process where your money grows exponentially over time as gains generate their own gains.

Diversification – Spreading your money across different investments so that one setback doesn't destroy you, but you hold few enough to actually monitor.

Dividend – Regular payments some companies make to shareholders from their profits; passive income from owning shares.

Liability – Money you owe or financial obligations that take money out of your pocket (mortgages, loans, debts).

Liquidity – How quickly you can convert an investment into cash without losing value; shares are liquid, property is illiquid.

Market Capitalisation (Market Cap) – The total value of a company calculated by multiplying share price by number of shares; indicates company size.

Net Worth – Your total assets minus your total liabilities; the true measure of your financial position.

Portfolio – The collection of all your investments held together; your financial ecosystem.

Portfolio Rebalancing – Systematically selling some of what's grown and buying more of what's lagged to return to your target allocation.

Risk Tolerance – Your capacity to handle investment fluctuations without panicking; it's not fixed and can expand with knowledge and experience.

Volatility – How much and how quickly investment prices move up and down; it's movement, not risk.

Investment funds

Active Investing – Attempting to beat the market through research, stock picking, and timing; requires expertise and typically incurs higher fees.

Benchmark – A standard (like the FTSE 100 or S&P 500) used to measure investment performance.

Brokerage Account – The account you open with a platform like Trading 212, AJ Bell, or Interactive Brokers to buy and sell investments.

Dollar-Cost Averaging / Pound-Cost Averaging – Investing fixed amounts regularly regardless of price; smooths out market volatility and removes emotion from timing.

ETF (Exchange-Traded Fund) / Index Fund – A basket of investments (usually hundreds of companies) that tracks a market index; trades like a share and offers instant diversification at low cost.

Fund Manager – Professional responsible for making investment decisions on behalf of others; managing portfolios to deliver returns.

ISA (Individual Savings Account) – UK tax-advantaged wrapper where your investments grow tax-free and you pay no capital gains tax on profits.

Market Alpha – Excess return above a benchmark; the holy grail of fund management but scarce and temporary in markets.

Mutual Fund / Unit Trust – A professionally managed fund pooling money from many investors; in the UK often called a unit trust, typically higher fees than ETFs.

OCF (Ongoing Charge Figure) – Annual fee for holding a fund, automatically deducted; keep below 0.75% for most investments.

Passive Investing – Tracking market indexes rather than trying to beat them; lower cost, less effort, and historically outperforms most active managers over time.

REIT (Real Estate Investment Trust) – A company that owns or finances property portfolios, traded on the stock market so your money stays liquid; offers property exposure without the hassle.

Stocks & shares

Blue-Chip Stocks – Shares in large, established, financially sound companies with a history of reliable performance.

FTSE 100 – The index of the 100 largest companies listed on the London Stock Exchange; a benchmark for UK equities.

Market Order – Buying or selling an investment immediately at the current market price.

NASDAQ – U.S. stock exchange focused on technology companies; home to Apple, Microsoft, Amazon, and other tech giants.

S&P 500 – The index of 500 largest U.S. companies; widely considered the best benchmark for the American stock market.

Stocks / Shares / Equities – Ownership stakes in companies; when you buy shares, you own a piece of that business and benefit from its growth.

Bonds

Bonds / Fixed Income – Loans you make to governments or companies in exchange for regular interest payments; typically lower risk than equities.

Yield Curve – Graph showing interest rates across different time periods; when short-term rates exceed long-term rates, often signals economic trouble ahead.

Economic indicators

GDP (Gross Domestic Product) – The total value a country produces; measures the economy's heartbeat and overall health.

Inflation – The rate at which prices rise over time, slowly eroding the purchasing power of your money.

Interest Rates – The cost of borrowing money; set by central banks to control economic growth and inflation.

Property & real estate

Leverage – Using borrowed money to increase your investment capacity; amplifies both gains and losses.

Net Yield – Annual rental income minus all costs (mortgage interest, maintenance, void periods) divided by purchase price; the real return on buy-to-let.

ROE (Return on Equity) – Measures how hard your equity tied up in property is working; shows whether capital could earn more elsewhere.

ROIC (Return on Invested Capital) – Measures return on the cash you still have left in a property after refinancing.

Bitcoin & cryptocurrency

Bitcoin – A decentralised digital asset with a fixed supply of 21 million coins; designed as a store of value outside traditional financial systems.

Blockchain – The underlying technology behind Bitcoin; a secure, transparent way to record transactions without middlemen.

Cold Wallet – Hardware wallet storing Bitcoin offline (Ledger, Trezor); more secure for significant holdings.

Cryptocurrency / Crypto – Digital currencies beyond Bitcoin (Ethereum, Solana, etc.); most are owned by companies or foundations and serve specific platform purposes.

DeFi (Decentralised Finance) – Financial services (lending, borrowing, trading) operating without traditional banks or intermediaries.

HODL – Originally a typo meaning "hold"; the philosophy of holding Bitcoin long-term through volatility rather than trading.

Hot Wallet – Digital wallet connected to the internet (exchange accounts); convenient but less secure for large amounts.

Stablecoin – Cryptocurrencies pegged to stable assets like the dollar (e.g., USDC); designed to avoid Bitcoin's volatility.

Tokenisation – Converting real-world assets (property, art, businesses) into digital tokens that can be fractionally owned and traded.

Private equity

Due Diligence – The research and verification process before investing; examining financials, market, team, and risks.

EIS (Enterprise Investment Scheme) – UK tax relief offering 30% income tax relief on investments in qualifying early-stage companies, plus tax-free growth after 3 years.

IPO (Initial Public Offering) – When a private company first sells shares to the public on a stock exchange.

Private Equity – Investing directly in private companies before they go public; typically requires longer time horizons and higher capital.

SEIS (Seed Enterprise Investment Scheme) – UK tax relief offering 50% income tax relief on investments in very early-stage companies; up to £200,000 per year.

Valuation – The estimated worth of a company based on revenue, growth potential, comparable companies, and investor appetite.

Options trading

Assignment – When your option is exercised and you're required to buy (put) or sell (call) the underlying shares.

Call Option – The right to buy shares at a specific price; buyers bet prices will rise, sellers collect premium for offering that right.

Covered Call – Selling call options on shares you already own; generates income while you hold the shares.

Options – Financial contracts giving you the right, but not the obligation, to buy or sell an asset at a set price within a set timeframe.

Premium – The payment collected by the option seller; your income for taking on the obligation.

Put Option – The right to sell shares at a specific price; buyers bet prices will fall, sellers collect premium for offering that right.

Strike Price – The predetermined price at which an option can be exercised (bought or sold).

The Greeks – Mathematical measures (delta, theta, gamma) showing how options prices respond to various factors; not essential for basic strategies.

Wheel Strategy – A systematic options approach: selling puts to acquire shares at your chosen price, then selling calls on those shares to generate income.

Pensions

Defined Benefit Pension – Pension guaranteeing a specific income in retirement based on salary and years of service; typical for public sector.

Defined Contribution Pension – Pension where your retirement pot depends on contributions and investment performance; typical for private sector.

LPA (Lasting Power of Attorney) – Legal document allowing someone you trust to make financial or health decisions if you can't; essential estate planning.

Pension Tracing Service – Free UK government service helping you locate old workplace pensions from previous employers.

SIPP (Self-Invested Personal Pension) – UK pension giving you control over investment choices; you can consolidate old pensions and choose exactly what to invest in.

SSAS (Small Self-Administered Scheme) – UK pension for business owners offering maximum investment flexibility including commercial property and lending to your business.

Made in the USA
Monee, IL
04 November 2026

67387150R00203